50 PERCENT OF THE PROCEEDS FROM

MY BOOSTER!

GO TO BERGIN UNIVERSITY OF CANINE STUDIES TO FUND THE ESTABLISHMENT OF SCHOLARSHIPS FOR STUDENTS SEEKING TO BETTER THE WORLD UTILYZING THE CANINE-HUMAN BOND

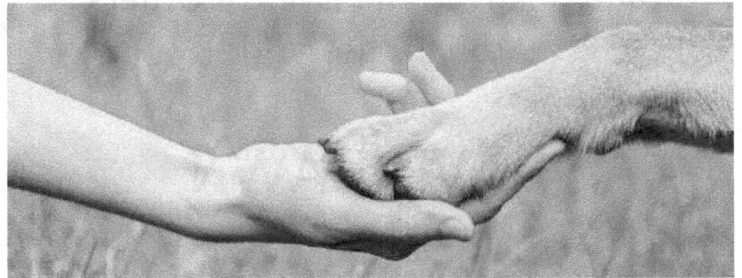

BOOSTER WOULD WANT THIS!

MY BOOSTER!

HE SAVED MY LIFE . . .

and Changed the Lives of Others
Around the World!

DAVIS HAWN

DAVIS HAWN EDITOR
P.O. BOX 273
Pyatt, Ar. 72672

www.boostertheservicedog.com

Copyright © 2024 by Davis Hawn First Edition — 2024

All rights reserved.

No part of this publication may be reproduced in any form, or by any means, electronic or mechanical, including photocopying, recording, or any information browsing, storage, or retrieval system, without permission in writing from Davis Hawn.

www.boostertheservicedog.com

ISBN
978-1-965462-19-5 (Paperback)
978-1-965462-17-1 (eBook)

1. BI0CRAPHF & AUT0BI0CRAPHF, PERS0NAl MEM0IRS

Distributed to the trade by Davis Hawn

ACKNOWLEDGMENTS

I express my unrelenting appreciation for the Al-Anon program, the lamplight for self-focus that brought clarity and direction into my life. I was taught to believe in a Higher Power greater than ourselves, and for me, it is my dog, Booster.

I want to lovingly thank Dr. Bonita (Bonnie) Bergin, who nurtured my canine-enriched education, empowering my relationship with Booster. Her selfless dedication to canines and classrooms profoundly changed lives, making the world a better place in which to live.

Dr. Elizabeth Pluhar, you heralded hope for a miracle in my darkest moments of misery-inspired desperation. You simultaneously cured Booster's cancer and morphed my depression into optimism. Booster accomplished so much as a direct result of your medical intervention that cheated his certain death.

Dr. Aubrey Beacham, your dedication to veterinary medicine saved my Booster's life upon myriad occasions. When others gave up, you never did.

Professors Hwang-Woo-suk and Taeyoung Shin, you granted me the lifesustaining ability to go forth in life when my Booster trotted across the Rainbow Bridge. With his progeny, Boosted and Busted, by my side, I had a newfound responsibility to further Booster's legacy, my canine studies, and my love of life. I am profoundly and eternally grateful.

Dr. Pamela Tuli, as my oncologist, life began anew when you rescued me within forty-eight hours of impending death, affording me precious time to complete my book.

To my lifelong friend, Robert Bodenheimer, when the chips were down, you gathered them up, giving me the will to live before your passing. I miss you dearly, my friend.

PREFACE

As society becomes more complicated, we more often turn to dogs for a solution. When my life became unmanageable, a puppy insidiously sauntered in, and untangled two decades of emotional devastation. As the puppy grew, so did I. Quite simply, I owe my very life to a dog. My quest for codependent self-destruction morphed into a passion for self-betterment and a desire to help other similarly downtrodden individuals. Whereas I once dated death and suicide, a dog taught me how to live life on life's terms. This book is an attempt to explain the metamorphosis that transpired once I learned to communicate with a dog and accept his proffered teachings. In a Helen Keller-like moment, having almost committed suicide the night before, I got it!

Simply changing my life wasn't enough for this special dog. He traveled the world, bettering the lives of others, helping to get laws passed for the disabled. Many might think it isn't possible for a dog to have such an impact on the world stage. Since he passed away years ago, I've struggled through turbulent emotional montages of memories that immortalize his accomplishments. For the skeptics, the internet provides proof of his larger-than-life, benevolent acts of unconditional love. Unwittingly named Booster as pup, he lived up to his name. He *boosted* my life and the lives of others around the world.

It's incredibly difficult to open up, share one's shattered life, and subject it to the scrutiny of your fellow man. I only do so to pay tribute to my Booster so others will have a chance to know the enormity of his canine accomplishments. It's the least I can do to pay tribute to the dog that saved my life, changed it, and changed the lives of so many others. I tearfully welcome you into our hearts.

Davis Hawn
Pass Christian, Ms, August 1, 2023

"I have found that when you are deeply troubled, there are things you get from the silent devoted companionship of a dog that you can get from no other source."
— DORIS DAY

Table of Contentes

Acknowledgments iv
Preface v
Foreword viii
Introduction 1
Chapter 1: In The Beginning 2
Chapter 2: Surrender And Exodus 25
Chapter 3: My Epiphany 32
Chapter 4: We Were Tested 46
Chapter 5: Hell's Infernal Condo 52
Chapter 6: The Dawn Of Education 61
Chapter 7: Thailand Bound 85
Chapter 8: Family Life Mine Theirs Ours 92
Chapter 9: Self-Investment Bucks For Bucs 108
Chapter 10: Life On An Even Keel, Bahamas Bound 117
Chapter 11: Project Fidelity 132
Chapter 12: Testing The Waters 172
Chapter 13: My Dear Peggy 179
Chapter 14: The Enemy Within 188
Chapter 15: Peru For Us Two 204
Chapter 16: Ticked Off 209
Chapter 17: The Heart And Seoul Of Cloning 221
Chapter 18: Cloning: Trials And Tribulations 259
Chapter 19: Love Thy Neighbor: Mexico 286
Chapter 20: The Love Returned 323
Conclusion 331
Afterword 339
About The Author 343

FOREWORD

Please don't be fooled by this book. Davis Hawn is one of those exceptional individuals who credits others for all his exploits, undertakings, successful — in life. His generosity (and gifting of credit to others) is who he is, what he's done, and where he's gone, to help make life a little better for others.

Booster was his sidekick in these endeavors, and the two of them, through thick and thin, life and death, goodness and graciousness, brought a legion of hope and help to others worldwide.

I insisted he write this book about these remarkable memories and moments, and true to his benevolent nature, he credited others for providing him these opportunities. Generosity eeks from his being and when the time comes, as it will for all of us, his legacy will be that of living for and loving others.

In this foreword I am the voice of the thousands who would have wanted to say these very things about him, maybe phrased differently, in different languages, accompanied by different experiences, but the end result would have touched the same reality — through and with Booster, he touched us all.

INTRODUCTION

"What are you going to do with that dog?" I was asked. It took me over a decade to answer that question. If I'd immediately answered, "The dog's going to save my life (twice), motivate me to return to college to earn a master's degree, promote international relations, participate in finding a cure for cancer, introduce me to world-famous scientists, and hug children with HIV, while letting children with cancer know that they can *live* with cancer . . . all the while overcoming his impending death over and over . . ." I would have been deemed insane. Truth be known, my beloved dog, my Booster, accomplished all this and a lot more. He *boosted* the spirits of all those he met. He lives on in a most unusual way, fitting for a dog brought into this world for a divine purpose. We welcome you into our hearts as we share our amazing journey guided and protected by a power greater than ourselves . . . a Higher Power.

How *my Booster* rescued me from the bowels of depression and impending death is unfathomable. He saved my life and changed the lives of others worldwide. He was unequivocally the greatest teacher I've ever known. His life lessons included addiction, codependency, spirituality, unconditional love, and how to live life itself. He instilled within me an unrelenting passion to share what he taught me to better the lives of others. I call upon that passion to share the most intimate details of my life so others can comprehend the enormity of the miracle of *my Booster*. Enter the twenty-year, stagnated cesspool of my life as it was, when my *Booster* pump kicked in, and the tides of emotional effluent slowly changed, making me the man I am today.

CHAPTER 1
IN THE BEGINNING

"What are you going to do with the dog? You know you can't take care of a dog," admonished my brother.

My life had fallen into an abyss of fear, and my brother was worried about a damn puppy! Really? I'd lived a life of walking on eggshells for so long that life became a cruel hoax years before. I breathed in fear and exhaled the accomplishment of having lived another second. Living had become a curse . . . a burden. Struggling to survive the moment transcended any thought about tomorrow. *What am I going to do with a dog? Really . . . REALLY?*

What remained of my life was in shambles. A dirty bomb of addiction had permeated my otherwise simple life. My addiction was to a needy person, not a drug. I'd become addicted to the addicted. I suffered from what is clinically called *codependency*.

> Codependency is a learned behavior that can be passed down from one generation to another. It is an emotional and behavioral condition that affects an individual's ability to have a healthy, mutually satisfying relationship. It is also known as "relationship addiction" because people with codependency often form or maintain relationships that are one-sided, emotionally destructive and/or abusive.[1]

When not looking over my shoulder or "word-checking" every comment I half-heartedly uttered to the addict in my life, I wondered where I had gone wrong. I'd sought love, given my all and suffered

---

[1] "Co-Dependency," Mental Health America (Alexandria, VA: 2023). https://www. mhanational.org/co-dependency

because of it. I'd unwittingly become involved in two relationships with Guinness World Records addicts, the first addicted to alcohol, the second addicted to crack cocaine. I didn't know they were addicts when I met them, but I guess I was attracted to that personality type. I dedicated a decade of my life to each.

Once I was vested in the relationships, I was bound and determined to fix the addicts in my life. Love conquers all, or so I thought! The pain and suffering, physical confrontation, and emotional devastation would be righted by the knight in shining armor. After all, I'd taken care of two alcoholic parents. I'd fought doctors writing valium prescriptions for my alcoholic father by writing a letter to the American Medical Association and threatening to mail it. Since the age of eight, I'd poured booze down the drain. I had a master's degree in addiction long before puberty ever set in.

Recently, I found a book with scribbling on the cover that I'd written on February 7, 1969: "Daddy fell." I'd witnessed my father fall down the stairs full throttle in a drunken stupor while blood poured from his head. In my forties, my life became unmanageable, unlivable, and undesirable due to my codependency with my addicts. I was trapped, so hypervigilant I couldn't take time out to concentrate on an escape path. I couldn't drive to the store to buy razor blades to end it all without succumbing to my addict's edict, "Where are you going? . . . You better not talk about me . . . I'll know if you do!"

One night, my alcohol addict raged and demanded money I didn't have. I ran out into the darkness of night with my addict in full pursuit. Suddenly, I felt a thud as a solid projectile hit my back, instantly causing horrific pain. I later learned I'd been hit by a tire iron. If it had rotated another 90 degrees, it would have stabbed me, releasing me from my misery. In retrospect, I know I'd have welcomed the ill-fated freedom. That night, I slept in the mud under my raised log cabin, wallowing in puddles of tears, sobbing silently. Any vocalization would surely have revealed my whereabouts.

The mosquitoes reveled as they feasted on my welt-laden body. As they completed their blood drives, I swatted the offending lances. Immediately, I felt remorse. I was a killer. The external pain succumbed to internal pain, and I cried. The welts of a broken me were dividing, multiplying, and metastasizing in a cancerous way. I was terminal, a warrior, wounded on the battlefield of life. I prayed for a ride on God's stretcher. There was no coming back . . . no pill . . . no therapy . . . no answer . . . and certainly no hope.

The night erupted into a mental montage of flashbacks from years gone by. Once again, I found myself in a codependent labyrinth with no apparent way out. No one would ever comprehend the totality of hopelessness my life had become. I'd fallen into a deep, dark hole of despair and had long since given up scratching to escape. *Why me?* I pondered. Tumultuous memories bombarded my consciousness as I found myself still trapped in the perilous minefield of my codependency fraught with others' addiction.

I remembered taking my alcohol addict out west to go camping years ago. I figured Mother Nature's splendor might cure a battered soul bolstered by fourteen 40-ounce bottles of malt liquor a day. Along with a tent came bottled-up emotions and beer. One snowy night in a dry county in Utah, I'd struggled to get a few hours of sleep. I was abruptly awakened by an earthquake, or so it seemed. It was the alcoholic hand rocking the codependent's cradle. "I'm out of beer. We gotta go!"

Completely drained, emotionally and physically, I was in a tent atop a 2-footdeep bed of snow in a sleeping bag, freezing. I explained that there's no beer to be had at 3 a.m. in a dry county, but my logic fell on deaf, inebriated ears. When I refused to answer the bugler's call, it was "Taps" for me. Within seconds, the tent was pulled down, and I was stuck in a straitjacket of a sleeping bag inside a collapsed tent. I eventually emerged in boxer shorts in zero-degree temperature, my face sandblasted by wind-driven snowflakes. I was going to freeze to death.

Suddenly, I bolted to the campground shower building. Once inside, I latched the metal door and jumped into a hot shower. I trembled uncontrollably, cold and consumed by fear. I planned to sleep on the floor and let the steam of the shower keep me warm. Just as my adrenaline subsided, I heard a loud *BANG*, followed by another and another. My addict was kicking in the grate in the door's bottom.

MY BOOSTER!

"I'm going to kill you!" came the scream over and over in a Halloweenesque, haunted house, looped recording fashion. The end was near once again. I crawled up off the cement floor, naked, pitifully resigned to awaiting my fate. The raging, puffing bull on steroids bounded through the chute. With Godgranted resolve, I pathetically looked up. "I'm almost ready to go. If you were knocking, I couldn't hear you cuz I was in the shower." The bewildered bull released steam like a pressure cooker blowing its lid. It was fast and furious, but effective. Soon, we were in the car, bound for booze. My addict thought a hidden can of beer remained in the glove compartment. When the "safe" was opened, there was no ace in the hole. The angry bull threw the car registration papers out of the window, over the cliff's edge.

If I said that night was an exception, I'd be lying. Twelve-step programs, like Alcoholics Anonymous (AA) and Narcotics Anonymous (NA), define insanity as doing the same things over and over and expecting different results. I was unequivocally insane, to say the least. *What is sane? I pondered. What does it look like? Does it exist? Is it ever free of pain of devastating import?* Such was life on a daily, hourly, minute by minute basis. I was locked in a perpetual state of hypervigilance and violence cushioned by booby-traps of intermittent, perceived vestiges of counterfeit love. This was my life for almost two decades . . . one second at a time . . . every day, for 24-hour eternities. I hurt so badly that I felt love like an amputee's phantom limb.

*What are you going to do with the dog? What are you going to do with the **dog**?* My brother felt more love for a dog than his own brother! I guessed he'd summed it up to my stupidity for have an addict in my life. In deference to my brother . . . and I pray most others . . . he couldn't know what I'd been going through all those cataclysmic years. He'd run away from the family catacomb of addiction years ago and had almost lost his life navigating the underground railroad to freedom. I thought he, of all people, would understand. There are none so blind as those who refuse to see. Perhaps the lack of understanding was denial and self-preservation.

I attended countless AA and NA meetings with my addicts. It's often said that self-medication with alcohol and drugs preserves the addict's life until they are prepared to seek help and process the pain. I eventually learned about the Al-Anon program, where you learn to put the focus on yourself rather than the addict in your life.

> Al-Anon Family Groups, founded in 1951, is an international mutual aid organization for people who have been impacted by another person's alcoholism.[2] Local and virtual Al-Anon family groups provide support to people affected by someone else's drinking. In addition to weekly meetings and literature written specifically for their dilemma, members find new ways to deal with the problems they face. Al-Anon's Three Cs – I didn't cause it, I can't control it, and I can't cure it – are one of the things many members find helpful early in the program.[3]

When I attended my first Al-Anon meeting in New Orleans and tried to relate my story as a newcomer, I uttered a fractured sentence and was suddenly wracked with an uncontrollable tsunami of limb-fletching emotions and torrents of tears. I was molten flesh in a pool of life's effluent and never regained my composure. Two angels walked me to my car and offered to drive me home, over a hundred miles away.

After that meeting, I reunited with my alcohol addict, paid the price, and rode all the rides once again. It was *years* before I exited the turnstile of Disneylike drama. Mother Nature couldn't free the lock of addiction for my alcohol addict, who eventually latched onto another unknowing soul, abandoning me. The reprieve was temporary, as I later found myself in a relationship with my crack addict.

One hot night in Florida, I gave my crack addict a ride to a friend's house. The "friend" turned out to be an accomplished purveyor of drugs for the needy. He descended upon my truck and demanded payment for goods delivered. I punched the gas pedal as my crack addict punched me and

---

[2] "Alateen," *Wikipedia,* https://en.wikipedia.org/wiki/Al-Anon/Alateen

[3] "Al-Anon's Three Cs," *Alcoholics Anonymous,* https://al-anon.org/blog/al-anons-three-cs/

grabbed the keys from the ignition. The physical confrontation expressed itself as condensation on the truck's windshield. (Years later, when driving and the windshield fogged up, I would involuntarily start to shake. I'd have to pull over and relax before continuing down life's highway). My crack addict found a butter knife in the truck's door pocket and lunged. I know not how I magically avoided the sharp reality of what life had become, a momentary reprieve from destined death.

I often awakened at night in a sweat-drenched pool of fright, dodging the knife destined for my soul. The recurring nightmares made me fearful to seek sleep. I became tired of almost dying night after night. I survived the daily realities of codependency to succumb to the terrors of the night. Once again, I felt hopelessness and the inability to go on.

What am I going to do with a damn dog? Really? I subsequently reserved two letters of the alphabet for my "beloved" brother. One letter precedes the letter G and the other codependently follows the letter T.

I'd died internally long ago and experienced a slow, methodical, charring, emotional cremation. *What are you going to do with the dog?* "F you and the damn dog, OK? OK? OK? OMG, please . . . somebody help me . . . please . . . pleease!"

"What are you going to do with the dog? You can't take care of a dog."

Truth be known, my brother was right. I subsequently made yet another wrong decision, or so it seemed and kept the damn dog.

The dog my brother referred to was a puppy I'd gifted to my crack addict. In yet another moment of desperation, I somehow figured it might become a catalyst for change, a curative agent. Surely Mother Nature couldn't fail me twice! The love and dependence of an animal would surely right the spoiled fruits of my emotional apple cart. *What a brilliant idea*, I thought. I started searching the New Orleans newspaper for puppies. My crack addict insisted on getting a Labrador. I suggested a female puppy, thinking it would be clingier and more effective. After being reprimanded by my addict, I obediently sought a male pup, thinking it wouldn't be as effective, but anything was better than nothing!

Much to my chagrin, there were only two Labrador-puppies-for-sale ads in the paper. I called the first number and was told, "Sorry, we sold all the pups this weekend." With greater anticipation than watching ketchup flow from a bottle, I called the second number, fearing a similar response. The phone was answered by a guy who explained he had one puppy left. He'd saved the pup for a family member who had changed their mind at the last minute.

"Would you please keep the pup for me until I can drive from Mississippi to Louisiana to pick it up in a few hours?" I frantically requested. There was no doubt about it; I was on a mission! I was going to cure my addict with the kiss of the canine tongue!

In Sherlock Holmes fashion, I stepped outside to make a call. The second I hung up, my addict walked outside and asked, "What were you talking about?"

I replied, "Family stuff." Within minutes, we were on our way to an NA meeting. We soon entered the building, ran for the coffee pots of substitution, and took our seats among the downtrodden. I listened to countless stories of how their lives had become unmanageable. I looked upon them as sirens in the modern world, luring the innocent in order to wreak devastation far greater than they had ever endured. After all, they had the alcohol and drugs to numb their pain. I had no such benefit. They were all Mendelas, recklessly experimenting with the otherwise normal lives of others. Listening to all the depressing stories made me want to get drunk ASAP. But that wasn't an option. I was on a mission to get a puppy and fix my crack addict.

After the ritual's conclusion, I suggested to my crack addict it was a nice day to take a ride. Having nothing better to do because *work* wasn't part of the crack addict's vocabulary, we bounded aimlessly down the potholed highway of life. I prayed it was to become, as Robert Frost's poem alludes, "The Road Less Traveled." Surely, the canine cure-all morphed into my addict's soul. I later learned that NA/AA has a saying: "Keep a plant alive for six months and then maybe you can have a pet. Keep the pet alive for six months and maybe you can have a relationship with a human."

"Do you really want a Labrador puppy?" I asked. "Yeah, why?" came the response.

"Well, we're on our way to look at one an hour's drive away. Are you *sure* you'll take care of a puppy if we get one?" I asked. In my day-to-day survival mode, it hadn't dawned on me that a Labrador puppy becomes a hundred-pound burden of responsibility. Giving a puppy to an addict whose life had become unmanageable was insane. *I* was insane. My life was far more unmanageable; at least my crack addict managed to get drugs. In that regard, my crack addict excelled.

"Really? Cool," came the response. Like an addict looking for that missing rock of crack that had somehow gotten away, enthusiasm blossomed. "I really want a male dog, OK?"

It was well known that what the addict wanted, the addict got! If I'd dared to suggest getting a female puppy, I risked not only the *cure* but my vehicle's windshield. "Well, there isn't much choice to be had. There's only one puppy, and it's a male."

"Why only one?" came the rapid-fire response. It was a glorious example of divine intervention. I'd searched the entire New Orleans newspaper classified pets section, and there was only one Labrador puppy for sale, **coincidentally** a male.

"Let's just go check it out. It's a nice day for a drive and we can have lunch somewhere," I said.

My explanation was received with addict-like suspicion. Crack-heads often bend the slats of Venetian blinds, peering outside into the abyss of the outside world. Like the Elvis Presley song title, they have "Suspicious Minds." I had to endure the endless commentary. "I bet there's something wrong with that puppy. We should look at more before deciding on one. Why are we going to look at just one?"

Always agreeing with my crack addict, I replied, "Hey, you're right, but we're halfway there. It's a nice day, and something to do." My retort seemed to appease my crack addict almost as much as the first hit on that glass pipe of perfection.

Eventually, we pulled into the driveway of a modest suburban home. We were greeted by the smile of an affable graduate student. He and his friend had bred their Labradors. It was a hookup of the highest magnitude and good intent. They both adored their dogs and wanted others to experience the satisfaction of Labrador love. Some pups had been spoken for once the very thought of breeding them was conceived. Surely the puppies had been cradled and loved from the day they graced the human world. If only my crack addict had similarly been born into a world of innocence and trust! Perhaps the puppy could somehow morph those long-lost, life-requisite qualities into my addict's tattered yet redeemable soul.

"Miracles are always happening," I often read in NA/AA-related literature. In adherence to that ambitious ideology, my crack addict was soon walking around the plush green lawn with a beautiful bundle of yellow fur in fast pursuit. The NA/AA programs also advocate living "one day at a time." My crack addict's lust for destruction reduced it to one moment at a time. In this God-granted moment of serenity, my crack addict rolled in the pasture of freedom, clutching canine-inspired love, acceptance, and need.

"I've got to go to the car," I told the now canine-connected group. Somehow, I made it to the car, fell inside, and the dam of damnation burst. I was shaking and cried until I thought I'd become dehydrated. I could no longer accept the good in life without emotionally overreacting. *What is wrong with me?* I asked myself. *I should be happy now, not crying, and men aren't supposed to cry!* When the plethora of tears subsided, I struggled to regain my composure. I took an old shirt from the floorboard of my truck, poured water on it, and sponged up the aftermath of emotional wreckage.

I nonchalantly returned to the scene further unfolding in the front yard. "When was he born? How many were in the litter? How many boys and

how many girls? What are you feeding him?" The questions were fired in rapid succession. *Remember the Alamo!* A battle of equal import was being fought on a suburban battlefield. The puppy was winning by the grace of God. I had never been a religious man, and spirituality had long ago evaporated from my world. This was as close to something spiritual as I'd *felt* in a very long time. I took the proceeds of my unemployment check and unwittingly bit off more than I could chew, or than the puppy could chew!

"What should we name the puppy?" my crack addict asked.

Before I could respond, the crack addict answered the self-posed question. "Mom had a dog called Brewster, so I'm going to call him

MY BOOSTER!

Boostie. Wait," extolled my crack addict, as if struck with an epiphany of untold proportion, "I want to call him Booster!"

With reckless abandon, we zoomed off to the nearest pet store to peruse the aisles of collars and leashes. Debate subsequently raged as to which was the best dog food fit for a king . . . King Booster! The puppy basked in the womb of affection as my crack addict proudly focused his attention on the relentless manifestations of innocent, unconditional love. In accordance with the NA/AA ideology "just for today," my crack addict found happiness, acceptance, and love. I could let my guard down and relax for the first time in a great while.

Oblivious to the world, the puppy snoozed on my crack addict's feet for the duration of the ride home.

Once home, little Booster romped in the tall grass, bounding with great zeal. He found a carrot in the grass and ran around, celebrating his new find. The carrot was the first of many things he would discover in life, as the doors of reality soon opened. Was this innocent vessel of virtue capable of withstanding the ravages of the human world into which he had precipitously fallen? *Just for today,* my crack addict possessed a new-found addiction. There was a developing bond between the helpless, unfolding before my eyes. Cuddle after curative cuddle, they took turns relishing mutual affection and intimacy. The puppy babysat my crack addict as I watched the scene unfold on the great stage of life.

Suddenly, the phone rang. "Hey, it's Mom," said the voice at the end of the line.

"Mom, I got a puppy, Mom. This puppy's special. You don't understand, Mom. It's different."

Baby Booster's first television appearance.

I was suddenly worried that Mom, no stranger to addiction, would go off on a tangent and not listen as intently to my crack addict as need be. The penalty would be my crack addict's frustration expressed in rage. Just the night before, I'd dodged a ballistic phone thrown at me out of frustration in response to Mom's comments concerning the addict's stepfather. The webbing of the mahogany rocker I'd given to my mother years ago received the phone like a basketball thrown at the goal. The phone missile missed my head but easily sailed through the rocker's webbing. Even a rocking chair had fallen prey to my crack addict's rage. It suddenly dawned on me that I'd put a puppy in the middle of the firing range to come.

Inevitably, my crack addict became frustrated, as Mom preferred to rant instead of listen. The conversation went nowhere, as usual. Surprisingly, however, my crack addict terminated the conversation and said, "She's mad again. Drinking, as usual."

Rather than act out and throw something, my crack addict picked up the puppy and walked inside. Soon, the puppy was lapping up water as though

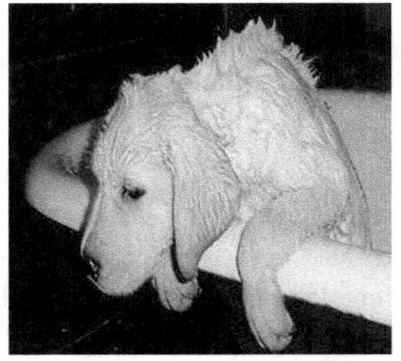

He hadn't learned to appreciate water yet.

he'd been stranded in the desert for an eternity. Within minutes, the young puppy was peeing on the floor with reckless abandon. Someone was going to have to train the puppy to eliminate outside. I counted on my crack addict to take responsibility for his newfound soul mate. After all, the puppy was *special*. Before long, the dynamic duo was fast asleep on the couch, oblivious to the outside world. The curative seeds were growing.

In the morning, I awoke to piles of used dog food in the living room. My crack addict snored somberly as the puppy chewed on the furniture. Now I had two destructive forces in my life. I suddenly realized that the

MY BOOSTER!

cure might be worse than the illness. Quickly, I took the puppy outside and introduced him to the concept of watering the lawn. I hoped he'd also poop while he was at it, but no such luck. Once back inside, I fed the puppy and started to mop the floor. Before I finished mopping up the ponds of urine, the puppy squatted. "NO!" I screamed as the puppy built his pyramid of poop.

My crack addict awakened, jumped up, and screamed, "Don't yell at my puppy!"

"I'm sorry," I said apologetically, later wondering who was more submissive: me or the young puppy. Long ago, I realized that it was easier and safer to submit rather than fight back. You *never* question. You learn to choose every word to avoid the seemingly inevitable confrontation to come. Life becomes a circus act of walking on eggshells.

"Want some breakfast" I hurriedly asked to change the subject. "OK, after I feed Booster," replied my crack addict.

At the risk of further confrontation, I explained that I'd fed the puppy earlier. I overlooked sharing that I'd mopped up the floor and successfully relocated the pyramid of poop. Sure enough, the addict doled admonishment, "It's my puppy, and that's my job."

"Sorry," I said, "I was just trying to help." I soon served breakfast while my crack addict played with the puppy and sipped coffee. Soon, the puppy was eating scrambled eggs, and I accused my crack addict of "egging" him on!

"That's so stupid," came the reply. It was indeed stupid, yet safe.

I'd learned to choose my words carefully, trying to inject humor wherever possible. The humor, corny or not, was a smoke screen that soon encompassed my life. I'd become the king of unpunny puns.

Without much ado, the duo decided to go for a walk. I lived in the country on 20 acres of what had been useless land. It was a collection of gullies I'd purchased from a classified ad. I later bought a plethora of damaged building supplies and built a log cabin. I had no septic system for five years, and the weeds grew to love me. The snakes loved the weeds, and I had a bona fide ecosystem in my own little world before long. I managed to borrow a bulldozer, built a dam across the gullies, and created a pond. I ended up with waterfront property on the redneck Riviera. My property was my ark. I had goats, pigs, sheep, and critters.

Life was bliss until I introduced a human species . . . *Homo sapiens addicta.* The predatory nature of the species made it difficult for other life forms to survive. Before long, it was just me and my addicts. There's no time for others when you have an addict in your life. I often failed to visit my father in the nursing home in favor of codependently fixing my addicts. Like water lilies languishing in a choked pond, my life stagnated.

"Hurry," beckoned a call.

I ran to the front yard to see the puppy running to my crack addict.

"He already knows his name. I'm going to teach him to shake hands. I can't wait for Mom to see him," boomed the voice. In the days to come, my crack addict's face turned crimson from days spent frolicking in the sun with the curative bundle of joy. "Shake . . . Shake . . . Shake," beckoned my crack addict. The puppy obliged before the day was out. Either my crack addict had a hidden talent, or the puppy, with the patience of Job, learned that he, too, needed to be subservient. Either way, both my crack addict and the puppy were learning.

I suddenly reflected on the duality of the puppy. He was simultaneously student and teacher. Just ten weeks into his life's journey, the puppy was already teaching a human how to live. I postulated that the unconditional love of a helpless puppy transcended the suspicious, non-trusting personality of the helpless addict. Superman was vulnerable to kryptonite; perhaps my crack addict was vulnerable to unconditional canine love. Rather than judge, the puppy simply accepted and adored.

How was it possible that my crack addict, who'd eaten out of dumpsters, slept in the woods, and sold shoes off tired feet for rocks of crack, suddenly radiated pride? Crack addict and puppy were inseparable day and night. The puppy attracted nice people in pet stores, parks, and playgrounds. "Want to pet him?" my crack addict often queried.

Once the bystanders petted the puppy, he was placed on the ground for the grand finale. "Shake," dictated my crack addict and the puppy's paw triumphantly met the stranger's hand without malice aforethought. The puppy knew what was expected and seemed to relish the opportunity to please not only his master, but all those who aspired to meet him. I later learned that people who love animals are special people. Those who don't are defective merchandise that should be returned to vendors for reprogramming.

The puppy gave his all for the first several weeks, encapsulated in a symbiotic relationship of the highest magnitude. It was quite a spectacle to behold as my crack addict felt pride and took responsibility for a helpless canine soul. Such was the miracle unfolding before my bloodshot eyes. Within weeks, however, the novelty waned, and I found myself supplementing the puppy's caretaking. The puppy was growing, and so was the amount of time I devoted to its wellbeing. The pyramids of puppy poop soon became urban sprawl.

A few weeks into the cure, things changed. The novelty of unconditional love and acceptance was not enough to justify the effort of taking care of a puppy. One day, my crack addict screamed, "He tore up another toy, and I've gotta clean it up . . . and he chewed the laces off of my shoes, damn it . . . the ones I just got!" Those were the shoes pilfered from a store, the shoes that almost got me arrested. My crack addict had walked into a store and swapped old shoes for the new ones. Once inside the car, I was directed to hurry because the police had been called. I was an accomplice to addiction once again. I was proud of the puppy that destroyed the illegal contraband, easily obtained, and easily destroyed. Both my crack addict and the puppy were destructive. I called it puppy parity!

Suddenly, the puppy cried out in pain as he was harshly hit by the hand he'd learned to love and trust.

"Why'd you hit the puppy?" I beseeched. "Because he bit me, and it hurt!"

"That's what puppies do," I explained, "as they chew and cut their teeth." "Well, he's not going to bite *me!* He's gonna learn!"

Unfortunately, the puppy learned, and it saddened me. The human he'd placed on such a high pedestal of admiration started to pay less attention to him, resented him, and physically hurt him. The process was insidious, yet undeniable. The dynamics were in place for the inevitable. It wasn't a question of *if,* but rather *when* the puppy would be hit too hard or thrown across the room like the phone that had pierced the rocker's webbing.

I hate myself, I thought. It was my fault this was happening. I'd relied on another soul to help me with my codependency problem. An innocent was suffering and likely to be killed. I had to find a way out. There had to be a way other than the repetitive prayers that went unanswered. Even God had left me to my demise. How cruel is a godless world filled with codependency and addiction, a world in which a beautiful, innocent, trusting, unconditionally loving, cuddly puppy pays the price? I hated the world, I hated myself, and most of all, I hated life.

The next night, I awakened, and my crack addict and puppy were nowhere to be found. No doubt my addict was on another crack run in the neighborhoods of damnation . . . this damn nation! From crack to meth, to heroin, to God knows what . . . people were suffering endlessly. I watched the television show *Intervention* and witnessed grandparents crying in the arms of children, weeping in solidarity with their loved ones fallen on the battlefields of addiction. The family members were dutifully enabling in their own world of codependency. I wanted no part in the continuing madness of reality. Why would I? For *what*? I started crying and shaking, then vomited the little food I'd eaten hours before. I'd lost weight, sleep, and any vestige of self-respect I *might* have once had. As my life spiraled down, I watched the sun rise. The only thing about to turn around was the doorknob. My crack addict entered the cabin, peered through the blinds, making sure the KGB was no longer following.

"Where's the puppy?" I asked.

"Puppy? Oh, it's in the truck, but I'm not going out there."

I went out and brought the damn puppy inside and went to bed. I didn't give it water or food. When I awoke hours later, I rushed to feed the puppy, who wagged his tail in gratitude like a windshield wiper, washing away the resentment he might have rightfully harbored. Things got progressively worse, as surely expected. Nights and days, like magnets attracting each other, were soon as one. Light became darkness, and darkness became light. I learned to seek sleep when my crack addict blessed me with disappearance. Yet, I also worried about my crack addict, the drugs, the guns, the police, and death. I didn't worry about the puppy that also came and went. Somehow, the puppy was lost to my consciousness. There simply wasn't any more room in the inn for worry. I was mentally and emotionally bankrupt.

My life soon became a blur. I couldn't remember what had transpired yesterday, much less any other day. Events merged, faded, and even disappeared.

I struggled to conceptualize what had transpired and worried I was in the early stages of Alzheimer's, or perhaps the later stages. I was frightened by the thought. To this day, I cannot formulate a timeline of events that occurred. Life had become a cesspool of murkiness beyond clarification. I wallowed in the sediment of life's excrement. "God grant me the ability to accept the things I cannot change, change the things I can, and the wisdom to know the difference," proclaim the twelve-step programs. Now *that's* a concept I identified with in total clarity! I could not change the things happening in rapid-fire succession in my life. After almost two decades of domination, I seriously considered ending my life. I was looking forward to the all-enabling freedom. I was a master at enabling others. For once, I deserved to enable myself!

One day, in absolute desperation, I called one of the few friends I had left in the world. Oddly enough, he was a guy my crack addict and I had once befriended at an NA meeting. We often attended meetings together, went out to eat, or see a movie. It was like the three misfit Musketeers, fighting together to salvage sanity *one day at a time*. Seeking sanity in the world of addiction was maddening. It was truly a classic oxymoron. The best that could be said was that there was strength in numbers. That day I called upon that strength and friend to please come help me escape from my Alcatraz. Within an hour, my crack addict friend's chariot arrived, smoking like a diesel freight train. The body of the car resembled my friend's body; both were scarred and damaged.

"Hey, man, how are you?" asked my friend.

"A little bored," I replied. "Let's go to the casino and hang out, maybe score a few free drinks. We can pretend to be gambling!"

My crack addict listened intently but opted out of joining us. He obviously had a plan in motion. I was grateful that I could get away and had no plan except to escape. Worn out once again, I jumped into the smoky car, and off we went. My friend knew I was suffering, as he'd faced exhaustion on the streets on myriad occasions. I looked into his eyes and said, "Thanks, man." In the AA/NA programs. I learned that you "only get to keep it by giving it away," referring to serenity. By doing service work to help others, addicts supplant the feeling of worthlessness with self-esteem. My friend valued helping me as much as I valued his help and friendship.

We spent the afternoon walking around the casino, watching those with money give it away. It was yet another perilous minefield of pending addiction waiting to explode. Like the long-forgotten landmines in Cambodia, eventually some would fall prey to the perils of the past. Today's exhilarating fix would need to be met again and again at some future time. For many, it wasn't a question of *if* but rather *when*. Everywhere I looked in my world I saw addiction. It took the wonders of the Al-Anon program to bring my myopic world into focus and put the focus on *me*.

At the end of the day, I couldn't face going home. I couldn't stay with my friend, as he was living in a downtrodden halfway house for recovering addicts. I called a lady friend who was in the Al-Anon program. She and another lady lived together in a nice home on the outskirts of town. She invited me to stay at their home. We talked for hours upon hours about the ravages of codependency. I listened to "codependency kills" repeatedly.

"Can I invite my crack addict over sometime?" I asked.

She replied, "You must never tell your crack addict where we live. We want you to always have a safe haven to go to, and we don't want your drama invading our home."

Wow, I thought, *what a double-edged sword comment.* My crack addict wasn't welcome, and I had a hard time understanding why.

I stayed in their guest bedroom that night. In the middle of my sleep, I had nightmares that made Freddy Kruger seem like a philanthropist. I suddenly catapulted up and projectile vomited the contents of my stomach across the white wall. I struggled to breathe, suffocating as the liquid clogged my breathing passages. Finally, I found a way out. It was awful. It was really awful. I couldn't breathe for what seemed like an eternity before I could wheeze in and breathe slowly. It wasn't enough air to do any good, and I had to pull it in with force.

MY BOOSTER!

Eventually, I started coughing and cleared my airways. Suddenly, the light was turned on, and I looked up at my two lady friends. I started sobbing. One sat on the bed and held me, squeezing me, forcing love into my veins. I looked over at the vomit now dripping down their wall. I trembled with embarrassment. How pathetic I'd become. Like my father used to say, "Useless as tits on a bull." I was one great big bull tit! The ladies scrubbed the wall as I sat shaking in the bed. They turned off the light and left the room after I reassured them I'd be OK.

I awakened around noon with a knock at my door. "Coffee's on," was the bugle call of the day. I got dressed and joined the ladies for coffee. I was later instructed to go out into the backyard and lay in the hammock. It was a warm and sunny day, so I stripped down to my boxers, and into the hammock I went. These gals had never had a man walk in, strip down, and lay out in their backyard. Rather than think of it oddly, they were happy they could help me, and that I was willing to try to help myself.

I couldn't live with the ladies forever. I had to return to the dungeon of depression.

"Hey guys, as much as I wish I could stay with you forever, I have to go home." "We understand and just know if there is anything we can do to help reach out to us."

"Well, to be honest, I am afraid my crack addict is going to be angry that I stayed away. Would you be willing to go with me to help smooth things over?"

When we got to my home, my truck was nowhere to be found. I was relieved yet worried. I didn't have to confront my crack addict, but it meant I'd have to do it alone in the future. The ladies gave me a hug and bid me farewell. I turned on the TV and half-heartedly watched sitcoms. Hours later, I discovered a day-old puppy pyramid. It suddenly dawned on me that the puppy wasn't in the house, either. Both the puppy and my crack addict had vanished for the time being. It was a waiting game as to when, or if, they might return and what condition each would be in.

Eventually, I was lulled to sleep by a symphony of crickets cavorting in the moonlit weeds surrounding what had once been my Walden's Pond. My mind was like a NASCAR racetrack, with thoughts competing with one another for dominance. Finally, the thoughts collided, and the checkered flags of sleep waived precariously. I somehow pulled in for a pit stop of sleep, knowing that the perilous pathway of my life might resume at any moment. *Just for today*, I slept.

I awoke in the morning to a phone call. "Say, man, where's the puppy at?" I recognized the voice as my crack addict's main drug dealer. Weeks before, the dude and his ole lady had been invited to sleep in my cabin at my crack addict's insistence. This was a guy who took my crack addict to shopping malls to do "returns" to get gift cards for returned merchandise without receipts. Of course, there were no receipts, as my crack addict brazenly took items from store shelves and sauntered over to refund counters, returning one *birthday present* after another. "There's a puppy I'm supposed to get."

Fuck . . . fuck . . . fuck . . . fuck . . . fuck . . . I thought. The puppy was going to be "trafficked" into a life on the end of a rope, staked to the ground by a threefoot piece of enslavement. Assholes that do that should themselves be tethered to the ground with a rope the length of equal justice.

I was worried about my crack addict and, to a much lesser extent, the puppy. I couldn't allow myself to worry about a damn puppy. The world was full of abused puppies. I needed to concentrate on one thing at a time. I needed to fix my crack addict. The puppy would have to wait. *Where's my crack addict?* I wondered. *Where's my truck?* Luckily, I had a secondary vehicle. I tried to go about my life, but it soon became apparent I had no life without my crack addict. I'd grown so accustomed to the roller coaster of my crack addict's lifestyle that a normal lifestyle, whatever in the hell that might be, felt abnormal. Days went by with no word from my crack addict. I was Hansel without Gretel and no stones to guide me, totally lost on the path of self-destruction. I had lost all purpose and direction. I couldn't focus. The main ingredient of my life's gumbo, primordial soup, was missing. Simultaneously awash with worry and relief, I was totally fucked up. In other words, I was a ship without a rudder, a canoe without a paddle. Days turned into weeks, and I eventually had to file a police report on my missing truck. This wasn't the first time my crack addict had forced me to file an unauthorized use report concerning a vehicle.

MY BOOSTER!

The local sheriff's office was reluctant to take the report. "We'll take a report one last time. After this, we aren't going to waste our time!" bellowed the officer. I got it. I couldn't blame the sheriff's office. After all, it was *my* crack addict, not theirs. The report was subsequently filed, and the insurance company was notified.

A month passed and no crack addict, no truck, and no puppy. I'd returned to work on the trailer park I was building. Luckily, I'd hired a retired couple to work for me to manage it. They knew what was going on. The duo managed my trailer park business without getting into my personal business. They were the gemstones in my garbage pit of life; they cared yet never critiqued. They had the wisdom of age and knew the scenario had to play itself out, however it might be. Jules Verne himself couldn't have envisioned the days to come.

One afternoon, the phone rang incessantly. I just knew it was my crack addict, tired of living in the hood, eating out of dumpsters once again. I ran to the phone.

"Hello, it's your auto insurance company calling. We'd like to know if you ever recovered your vehicle?" queried the insurance company's representative.

"No," I replied, "and I sure miss it."

"Well, it's been over thirty days and we're prepared to make you an offer," bellowed the man's deep voice. He made an offer, and I accepted without reluctance. After all, I was only worried about my crack addict, not the truck, or money.

The very next day, I heard the phone ringing. I once again ran like the track and field athlete Jesse Owen to answer the beckoning call.

"Hello, is Mr. Dave Hawn there?"

"Who wants him?" I asked curtly.

"This is Auto Wreckers. The Louisiana State Police had us tow in a truck when the person driving it was arrested. We wouldn't be calling you except that there was a puppy inside," explained the man. "You need to name that puppy 'Saved You Money.' Usually, we contact our state police headquarters, and they contact your state police headquarters, and someone in your state eventually calls you. We earn storage charges all the while."

A police officer in a neighboring state had pulled the truck over in the wee hours of the morning. The wrecker driver who worked the night shift (6 p.m. to 6 a.m.) just happened to wake up in the middle of his sleep the following day. He remembered there was a puppy in the truck he'd hauled in the previous night.

*What a remarkable **coincidence**, I thought.*

He called his boss, who subsequently ran out to the truck in search of a likely dead puppy. It was approaching 100 degrees on a sizzling summer day in Louisiana. The junkyard boss broke a vent window to access the locked truck. Within moments, he found the desperately panting puppy on the front seat, patiently awaiting his master's return. The puppy was oblivious to its impending death, having trusted that his human would surely return. We'd both waited for our human to return so we could get on with our respective lives. Ironically, reality dictated that we both faced death by association. As it turned out, the wrecking yard owner was a dog lover and ***coincidentally*** his nephew worked at the jail. He had his nephew locate the driver of the truck to ascertain a contact number for someone to come get the puppy.

I called my trailer park manager, my Rock of Gibraltar, and shared the news. The prince of a man insisted on driving me to get my truck and the abandoned puppy that'd narrowly escaped death by abandonment, death by human. When we finally arrived at the junkyard, the owner told an employee to fetch the puppy from the house. Shortly thereafter, the puppy emerged, carried in the man's grease-covered arms. Though he barely knew me, the puppy responded as if he'd overdosed on happy pills. I took possession of the beast of burden, not impressed that he was looking into my eyes in route to the quick of my soul.

When I got home, I let the puppy run around in the front yard while I immediately went to the phone to ascertain the visiting hours of my crack addict's jailhouse abode. The next day, I went to visit my crack addict. The conversation rapidly escalated into a verbal confrontation. Apparently, it was my fault my crack addict was in jail because I'd filed an unauthorized use report, as required by the insurance company. It wasn't my crack addict's fault for absconding with the truck and running a red light!

MY BOOSTER!

I knew it wouldn't be long before my crack addict would be released early for good behavior. Addicts are the finest actors in the world, having honed their skills to weave their webs of deception. My crack addict could charm a rabiesinfected rattlesnake and, with Houdini's talent, escape his confinement, legally or otherwise. I was caught in a web and wanted out. Once the treacherous tentacles of codependency got a hold of me again, I knew it might be for the last time. I was twenty years into my self-destructive lifestyle, and there wasn't much left of my former self. *What had I been like pre-codependency?* I asked myself in self-interrogation and introspection. I couldn't live in my home any longer. The fear of my crack addict returning, and the accompanying repercussions, was too great for me to handle.

I called my friend Charles and begged for help. He'd changed his life after years of abuse by learning to take care of himself and shun negative influences in his life. He became so good at self-protection that he often dismissed friendships before they ever took root. If Charles smelled a rat, he acted before reflecting and thus potential friendships often died on the vine. He insisted I go live with him in the spare bedroom of his modest mobile home. He had an above-ground pool in the backyard and often held pool parties. He was a master at enjoying a simple lifestyle. I envied him. He immediately drove to my cabin to protect me should my crack addict show up unannounced, as was always the case. I grabbed clothes, threw them in a Samsonite garbage bag, and tossed them into my truck.

Oh yeah, I tossed the puppy in, too. Charles loved animals and had a rottweiler on a lead in the backyard. I wondered if the rottie might somehow devour the puppy. I hoped not, but preventive precautions weren't on my priority list. Solely self-preservation. I felt like a burden to my friend. After all, he'd raised his kids. He didn't need to raise another! I felt helpless, useless, and hopeless, as usual. I was another bull tit.

I once read that when American Indians became aged and unproductive, they went with dignity into a cave to die. Ready to enter my cave, long ago stripped of what dignity I might once have possessed decades before, I felt naked and vulnerable wherever I went. *Wow*, I thought, *just like a puppy!* Speaking of puppy, I looked over at the great pyramid architect yet again constructing a new testimonial to his talent.

Shit, I thought, all pun intended, as the puppy released his bowels once again inside the cabin. I was pissed, but I knew in my heart that the puppy hadn't had a chance in life to learn to adapt to the human world. My alcohol and crack addicts had shit on me day in and day out, so why not the puppy? Life was a proverbial bucket of shit with the handle on the inside! I walked out of the cabin, puppy in hand, and went to my savior Charles's home. The next day, I ran out of pyramid construction material, aka dog food. I grabbed the puppy, all but threw him into the truck, and headed out to the store. While driving, I noticed a little eggshell of a camper being pulled by a worn-out, white Ford pick-em-up truck. **Coincidentally**, it was an exact clone of the truck I was driving! At that very moment, I had an epiphany. Perhaps I could get a small camper and pull it behind *my* truck. Later that night, as was the custom, I watched the news with Charles, with whom I'd been living for longer than I could remember. I felt as though I was becoming a burden, but Charles was too fine a friend to acknowledge it. I shared my idea with Charles, and the following day we started looking for a camper that I could pull with my truck. It was to be my escape pod. If NASA astronauts could have one, then so could I!

Within days, we found a suitable camper that was quite nice. **Coincidentally**, I'd gotten a credit card in the mail a few weeks earlier, so I took a cash advance on the card and bought the camper. I called my park managers and informed them of my plans to escape. They never knew the true depth of the depravity that had encapsulated my life. They knew I needed to get away, but they didn't know it was literally life or death. I was incapable of explaining my loss of self-identity. I later read about the concept of "betrayal bonding," in which a person becomes enmeshed, co-dependently bonded, with another for a prolonged period. The codependent refuses to break the sick bond as it would render the entire relationship meaningless. It was an ultimate betrayal to know that all you'd invested in the relationship could be summed up as being taken advantage of. Rather than a partner, you were simply an enabler.

CHAPTER 2
SURRENDER AND EXODUS

The next day, I struck out, towing my new home, without a clue where I was heading. I'd debated whether to bring the damn dog and reasoned that he'd already suffered at the hands of the crack addict, just as I had. I couldn't bring him to the dog pound or leave him for my crack addict to finish him off by way of neglect. Odds were my crack addict would trade him to his crack dealer for another rock of crack. I didn't want the puppy, but I didn't want him to become an integral part of a sacrificial ritual. At last, I was free! I rolled down the truck's window and took a deep breath of 70 miles per hour air. I panned to my right and noticed the puppy's nose sticking out of his window as he rode shotgun by my side. Canines have a keen sense of smell, far greater than humans. The puppy smelled freedom at an early age.

I gave up on myself . . . but my Booster never did. Little did I know that traveling with a dog would complicate my life. When I stopped to get gas, I had to walk the damn dog. Every time I ate in a roadside eatery, I had to leave the truck running with the AC turned on. On rare occasions when I elected to get a hotel room, they often denied me access because I had the damn dog. Some RV parks across the country wouldn't allow pets on the premises. I often fed the puppy wonderful human treats of scraps and he, in turn, rewarded me with lava-like flows of diarrhea. Such fine thanks, right?

My ultimate resentment was the fact that every time I walked the damn dog, from RV parks to fields behind gas stations, people *always* came up to me, asking to pet the damn dog. "I miss my dog; can I pet yours?"

I thought, "It's *may* I pet the dog, you ignorant SOB." "What a cute puppy," they would often say.

I'd be thinking, "What's cute about diarrhea, you dork?" "Walking a dog is such great exercise," said others.

My desired response was, "I wish you'd exercise your right to walk away, asshole."

The list of nice comments elicited by the accompaniment of a dog, especially a puppy, was uncanny. *Damn dog*, I thought, *how can he do this to me?* I didn't want to talk to any damn body. The puppy was lucky I talked to *him*! Usually, my canine comments were harsh. "Get your head out of my lap. You drooled on my leg when you saw the potato chip, damn it. I can't believe you farted again." The endless list was growing! I grew resentful of the damn dog. But he hung in there, exuding unconditional love, nonetheless.

One day, while barreling down the highway of escape, I got a call. It was from my lady friends, who were out west and were living in a motor home. They'd sold their house, divested themselves of most earthly possessions, and sought the spiritual enlightenment of the open road of uncertainty. They knew their "Higher Power" would take care of them . . . they "let go and let God," yet another twelve-step concept. I'd decided long ago there was no such thing as God, as my life wouldn't be hell on earth, before earning placement on the ultimate inferno's hot seat.

"Hey, man, we're in Oregon. Come on out and join us," they prompted.

I didn't want to talk to anyone, much less join anybody. I wanted to be left the hell alone. The ladies had once spun a cocoon around my vulnerability. I'd never felt more secure as I had when they'd opened their home and hearts' doors to me, a perfect stranger. I should say, an *imperfect*

MY BOOSTER!

stranger. My heart still functioned while my brain backfired. I couldn't "not see" my soul's saviors and unwittingly plotted a survival course.

"I've got the damn dog I'd given to my crack addict," I explained.

"Cool, man, your dog can visit our dog, Sunny," came the enthusiastic response.

"The dog's a real pain in the ass," I explained. I really fucked up when I bought the puppy. "What was I thinking?" I asked them. My bitching fell on deaf ears.

"Just get your ass out here. Can't wait to see you and the puppy. We'll tell our dog Sunny to expect company."

Dizzy broads! I thought. I wondered what their game was. Life was *not* that easy. Life was a bucket of shit with the handle on the inside. What was in it for them to portray my skewered life in such a skewed manner? *I'll head out west, but I'm not going to join in the dizziness!* I thought quite assuredly.

The puppy sat shotgun in the truck, taking in the scenery, oblivious to drama. He'd sit up and look out at the vistas and in turn crash out and relax. He was practicing the twelve-step concept of "everything in moderation." There'd been no moderation in *my* life. I had endured two decades of extremism. How dare the damn puppy proclaim a concept like moderation existed or was even possible? I was jealous of a puppy. I wished it were possible to live life on life's terms and be as happy as the puppy, once abandoned in a truck on a hot summer's day. He was fucking happy. How dare he!

Life soon became a blender of obscurity. I found myself extinguishing the flames of depression with firewater—the obvious irony being that I medicated my depression while simultaneously fueling a dependence on the cure-all of alcohol. I once offered the puppy a sip of the remedy, only to be rebuked by a "No thanks" and a wag of the tail. The puppy rejected the potion I had learned to value. Yet, he was happy. He was really happy, resigned to sitting by my side, drooling and farting. I postulated the puppy was into sadomasochism, deriving pleasure from inflicting pain on others. Damn the damn puppy!

Eventually, I ended up somewhere out west with my lady friends. They were Al-Anon freaks, and I was becoming a slave to that which they rightfully considered poison. Some days, I'd walk the damn dog and order him around. He soon learned not to provoke my ire. I said, "Sit," and by God, he fucking sat! I dictated, "Wait," and the SOB waited. All the while, my lady friends witnessed me controlling the puppy. I'd lived a life out of control, and soon became enthralled with the ability to successfully control a living entity. I wanted to rescue the wounded bird by introducing control into the lives of others when, in reality, *I* needed to learn self-control.

My lady friends called me out on it. "Why can't you just simply let him be a *dog*?"

What the hell? I thought. *The puppy needs structure in his life, and I am damn well going to provide it for him.* In retrospect, what the hell did I know about structure in one's life? I had left my family, friends, and business behind. My home was a cocoon on wheels from which I reluctantly, periodically emerged.

When I was a child, my mother raised parsley in the yard. Seemingly from nowhere, caterpillars would miraculously appear on the leafy parsley and attach themselves to the stalk. My mother would place the caterpillar-laden stalk inside a jar and make us watch the caterpillar spin its cocoon. Once encapsulated inside, all signs of life ceased. I used to wonder what the caterpillar was doing inside! Magically, one day, the cocoon would open, and a beautiful butterfly would emerge.

I, too, was living in a cocoon. Unfortunately, I *had* to emerge periodically, and the damn puppy was usually the causative agent. I was content—no, grateful—to live my reclusive existence in my cocoon. I was safe, like a baby protected in the embryonic sac surrounded by protective fluids, and never wanted to emerge. In my case, the fluid was alcohol, yet equally protective. I never envisioned emerging from my cocoon or traveling down the fallopian jet stream of life. The puppy was the causative agent for my far-too-frequent emergence as a butterfly. Allowing me to isolate just wasn't an option. The puppy caused me to become a butterfly.

I perceived the puppy to be a chronic irritant, the greatest impediment to whatever was going on. One morning, I awoke to a sack of dog food torn open all over the floor of the camper. I reluctantly played 52 pickup and summarily cursed the damn puppy once again. I resorted to putting the puppy's food in a plastic tote box outside on the camper's tongue . . .

MY BOOSTER!

to keep it away from the damn puppy's tongue! The damn puppy just complicated everything.

The following night, I *coincidentally* and inexplicably awakened from my usual drunken stupor to hear an uncanny sound of rustling outside of the camper. I looked out and saw a potbellied pig trying to scratch its way into the dog food box. I ran to the camper door, opened it, turned to the damn puppy, and said, "Go get 'em, damn it." The puppy jumped up and bounded for the door. Suddenly, I experienced an involuntary, inexplicable contraction. Something deep within forced me to slam the door quickly, almost on the puppy's neck. I'd won the race to the door with a millisecond to spare. I was on remote control. How I responded in such a fashion, having awakened from a dead sleep, I will never, ever know.

I then heard *more* profound scratching and looked out the window and witnessed another supposed potbellied pig jumping on the dog food box. Within seconds, more arrived to feast on the fodder of Chef Purina's shredded lamb and rice. What I had originally thought was a pet potbellied pig that'd escaped from a neighboring motorhome was something called a javelina. I was in Ajo, Arizona, and a pack of hungry javelina hogs, bearing tusks of the finest culinary capability, had descended upon my camper in the middle of the night. Had I let the puppy out, the javelinas would have feasted on shredded Labrador puppy that night. *Damn lucky puppy . . . why couldn't I ever be that lucky?* I asked myself. The night before, I'd awakened to find the camper door left open and the puppy nowhere to be found. I stumbled out of the camper and started looking for the damn puppy. I briefly thought about leaving him to his own demise, like I was experiencing. He would be better off on his own than saddled with a dysfunctional human, I postulated. I walked throughout the RV park in darkness with a flashlight in hand, to no avail. Problem solved, no more damn puppy, and there wasn't anything I could do about it. I stumbled and fell on my way back to the camper. It was just happenstance that I glimpsed a moving object far away in the distance. It was the puppy, trotting down the highway of life in the middle of the road. He was as lost and oblivious as I was. I screamed, "COME!" and he did exactly that. He remembered the command I'd taught him the week before when my lady friends had chastised me for not just letting him be a dog. He did indeed come running back into my life.

My daily ritual continued . . . drink, eat a little, drink, not eat, drink some more, all the while shooing away the puppy who always sneaked back to my side. I grew to resent the puppy, who was as codependent as I was! I often watched the puppy stealthily crawl across the floor so he could be with me. At night, I'd awaken to take a piss and find the puppy sleeping in the bed once again. I'd toss the puppy out of bed, do my business, and go back to sleep. Every time I awoke, the puppy was back in the bed, sleeping by my side. The damn puppy cleverly found ways to intentionally piss me off, or so I thought.

Plans were being made for a sojourn to Mexico. I had to make sure my truck and camper were roadworthy and all systems were GO! Turned out, the taillights weren't working, so I begrudgingly jacked up the camper and set in on concrete blocks. One block shifted, and the camper fell onto my leg. It pinned me to the ground, and I struggled to get free. Suddenly, I suffered physical pain in addition to my mental madness. I hobbled back inside my cocoon, drank a few swigs, and crashed.

When I awoke, my left calf was painful and swollen. I soon realized that I couldn't bend my left leg. Hell, I couldn't reach my left sock. I kicked my shoes off but showered wearing my left sock. When I emerged from the shower, the puppy came running to greet me in his usual blissful manner. I ritualistically kicked him away with great fervor. This time he didn't take no for an answer, and the little bastard started playing tug-of-war with my sock. You can't win 'em all and I subsequently lost my sock to the dog. In retaliation, I tossed a shoe at the damn dog to show him who's boss, and the SOB got it and brought it back to me! He was accustomed to bringing things back into my life . . . things I needed . . . like love.

MY BOOSTER!

I didn't give a damn about seeing a doctor as long as I could drink and numb my pain. My travel plans were on hold until my leg functioned better . . . or so I thought. After a week, the swelling hadn't subsided, and I had to learn to deal with a fucked-up leg. Funny thing. The dog started carrying my shoes and tugging my socks off for me. Before long, the dog I disliked was helping me in ways that I didn't even realize. It just didn't register.

CHAPTER 3
MY EPIPHANY

One night, I drank myself to oblivion once again. I was alone. The puppy was sleeping, and there was no noise. I was in a vacuum of worthlessness. My head was pressed in a vice grip of depression. I downed vodka from the bottle and grabbed a knife. The final curtain of resolution was drawn. It was indeed the final act. Peace was at hand . . . or should I say, my wrist? I was a victim of an emotional Ponzi scheme; the more I invested, the less was returned. I wanted out! Suddenly, everything went dark.

The following afternoon, I experienced a rhythmic stereo pounding in my head. Painful pulses of a horrible hangover besieged my brain, yet it didn't account for all the noise. Somebody, or some*thing*, was beating mercilessly upon my camper door. I struggled to my feet, knowing I'd likely pave the way with a pathway of vomit. It took three attempts to open the door, but it eventually sprung open to reveal two humanoids . . . cursed children! The rug rats were holding the end of a rope attached to a dog. Then came the screechy voice from hell. "Mister, can our dog play with yours?"

I bumbled out, "Yeah, take the darn dog. Take him. Go!"

The invaders got what they wanted (the puppy), and I got what I wanted . . . their ouster from my cocoon. Not fast enough, I might add.

I fell back onto the bed and snoozed. Then it happened! Thirty minutes later, I heard the most pitiful shriek of unmistakable pain. A soul was dying. It was a piercing cry of

MY BOOSTER!

anguish, unmistakable even to my pickled brain. It was the puppy crying out. I just knew he'd been hit by a car and lay shredded in the street. Everything in life at the time was bleak, dark, and foreboding. I'd almost taken my life the night before. Why would I think any differently? I walked to the camper's door of doom and swung it open. I'd been ready to bury myself the night before, so I was surely up to the task of burying a puppy. What happened next changed my life forever. The puppy was sitting up, screaming at the top of his lungs, holding his paw up in the air. He was in such pain, I thought. The children were crying and hugging him, consoling him like I'd never cared to do.

I started crying torrents of tears.

"He's OK, mister. He's OK. He hit his paw on a car when he was playing with our dog," they dutifully explained. "He's OK, mister. He's OK! He'll be OK!" When the children saw me sobbing, they got even more emotional. They too began to cry!

What happened next is a blur. I started sobbing uncontrollably. I was shaking as the puppy excitedly responded to my emotion. The puppy had stalked his prey and relished the conclusion of the hunt. It was as though the puppy had witnessed his first rainbow. He put my needs above his own. Somehow, he knew that day was special. Dogs have emotions; they are sentient beings. He was happy. His tail wagged fast and furious, his tongue darted rapidly in and out, lapping up my tears, and his paws were slapping my face.

As for me, I started crying even harder! I later wondered if he could differentiate between tears of happiness and those of sorrow. He was no longer "the damn dog." He was now officially "My Booster." I'd broken through life's obscurity due to the divine intervention of a dog. I slept with my Booster in my arms for three days. When I awakened, I looked into Booster's eyes and ended up in his soul, just as he'd looked into my eyes and ended up in my soul the day he almost died in the junkyard. I awakened every morning hence to a joyous tongue lashing from the puppy doing what he'd always done . . . expressing unconditional canine love . . . tugging at the threads of my cocoon . . . hoping to find the butterfly within. No matter how I'd treated him, he never gave up. I had given up long ago. He never did.

I turned to Booster with tears in my eyes and hugged him like there was no tomorrow. I knew in my heart there might not be a tomorrow without Booster by my side. I made him a promise.

"Hey, my friend, I will never take life for granted or end my life leaving you alone in the world like I once was. I'm going to share you with the world so you can help others like you helped me."

I suddenly realized that he'd stuck by me through thick and thin. He'd received abuse and returned love. It dawned on me that he'd been pulling me back to people . . . happy people . . . quality people . . . who love animals and are pure of heart. He'd kept me hanging on to the precipice of life while trying his darndest to reintegrate me into society. I'd resented his ability to take abuse and return love. I'd resented his happiness. The epiphany occurred when he was miserable and hurting, just like me. I suddenly got it in Helen-Keller-like fashion.

As I lay in my bed with Booster by my side, I thought I heard him purr! I jumped up and thought, I've gained a dog but lost my mind! The startled pup went running, only to stop, turn, and look back. When he saw me laugh, he gleefully returned to my side, marking his path with a puddle of piddle. So many times, I'd run away when consumed by fear, never stopping long enough to look back and reassess the situation, trusting change was possible. I, too, had pissed on myself with submissive self-pity. The seeds of emotional devastation sewn long ago had grown into a labyrinth of tangled webs, wreaking mass destruction upon my soul. I'd masterfully crafted my protective cocoon to later find an unwanted puppy nipping at its threads, clueless as to the import of what had transpired days before. I was in the eye of my life's hurricane. Having suffered category five, life-threatening devastation, I'd somehow survived. Was I lulled into a sense of false security by a momentary lapse in destruction, in the storm's eye, while waiting for the second half of the storm to present itself? Would I be buried under the rubble of despair to come?

I marveled at how Booster was solemnly sleeping by my side, inhaling and exhaling without a care in the world. I matched my breathing pattern to his. In and out, I mimicked Booster's breathing until I no longer could. At some point, I fell into a deep slumber, the depth of which I'd never previously achieved without my friend "Jack" (Daniels) by my side.

MY BOOSTER!

Unbeknownst to either of us at the time, Booster's nipping away at my cocoon's threads resulted in the hemorrhaging of the *spirited*, protective, embryonic fluid that had surrounded me and permeated my life. My dependence on alcohol waned. After two decades of emotional destruction, I'd never found betterment until that moment. My Booster taught me how to sleep, a burdensome endeavor that had proven elusive. "Take a deep breath, hold it, exhale, relax, and sigh with satisfaction. Repeat as necessary."

On a rainy morning, while surfing the web out of boredom, I searched for "dogs that help people." I soon found myself staring at a web page describing service dogs. *What the heck is a service dog?* I pondered. I read they helped disabled people. Some service dogs picked up things and brought them to their human partner. Some helped people get dressed or undressed. Suddenly, I realized Booster had done many of these very things for *me*. I then searched "service dog training," and it pulled up a web page describing Dr. Bonita Bergin and the Assistance Dog Institute (ADI). *How interesting*, I thought.

Over time, my relationship with my friend Jack dissipated, and I kicked him out of bed in favor of sleeping with my Booster. It was quite the rivalry. It was an Olympic jousting event of epic proportions. Winner takes all; they were fighting for my soul. The transference of codependency exploded, immeasurable on the standard Richter scale of life. The scenario that unfolded was just too much for a lost soul living in a cocoon to handle. I had to escape once again, and go somewhere else; the farther, the better. I convinced my lady friends to go with me to Mexico. I was unknowingly crafting a *geographical cure* . . . all my troubles wouldn't exist if I just lived anywhere else.

Rather than self-destruct in newly discovered self-reflection, I occupied my time constructively socializing with Booster's help. Things were different now. I was no longer alone. I had a partner—a genuine, loving partner. Suddenly, I'd gained a need to protect and nurture a deserving soul that exuded unconditional love and expected little in return. It was years later that I learned, through the enlightenment of the Al-Anon program, that I needed to do the same for my soul. Even with the help of the Al-Anon program, I doubted I'd ever be able to love myself like I did Booster.

One day, my lady friends walked over to my camper and asked, "So, dude, when we gonna head out to Mexico?"

Spontaneity being my Holy Grail, I responded, "How about now?"

"We need a little time before breaking everything down and leaving," they replied.

Women, I thought, *gotta powder their noses before doing any damn thing!* Suddenly, Sunny came bounding out of their motor home to greet Booster. They were so joyous together. Every day was Christmas for the two dogs that had just recently met. One had been loved, the other resented, yet they frolicked together harmoniously. *Could it be that dogs have the ability to cope with emotional baggage whereas humans do not?* I suddenly wondered. *Dogs live in the here and now. Perhaps that explains it? They don't obsess about the past and are incapable of plotting for tomorrow. They follow the twelve-step philosophy of KISS . . . Keep It Simple, Stupid!*

The dogs played as the humans shared a lunch of bean sprouts and hummus prepared by the gals. I was tempted to grab some of Booster's lamb and rice!

"Where's the diet Coca-Cola?" I asked.

"Those chemicals are really bad for you. They'll kill you," came the rapid-fire response.

No, I thought, *relationships are far more deadly.* If there'd been a Coke, Booster would have gladly fetched it for me. He wasn't interested in controlling, just helping, and loving unconditionally. *Too bad*, I mused, *that you can't have a relationship with a dog . . . or so I thought!*

The ladies were hardcore Al-Anoners, I didn't drink around them. I did, however, make up for it when I returned to my cocoon, self-medicating with the embryonic fluid while feeding and watering Booster. *Damn*, I thought, *Booster sure drinks a lot!* The floor was always covered with splashed water after he quenched his ever-present thirst. I suddenly thought, *Hmm, Booster and I have more in common than I thought!*

MY BOOSTER!

Eventually, I jumped into bed and snuggled with Booster by my side. He always fell asleep faster than I. That meant that I had to listen to his snoring, which caused me to drink more to be able to sleep. I always acquiesced during such troubled times. It was the least I could do for the puppy that had endured so much for so long. I downed the extra drinks, never complaining. Perhaps I, too, was capable of unconditional love. Therein lay the proof . . . 86 proof, at that! I drank out of my love for Booster . . . really?

The morning came quickly, and the ladies were ready to go. I cleared the clouds in my head and broke down my campsite. An hour later, we played leapfrog on the highway to Mexico.

We crossed the border within hours and found a beautiful campsite on the beach in Puerto Penasco, Mexico. It was a fascinating small town near the border. It's the closest beach to Arizona. I paid five dollars for my first night's rent and was told that high-rise timeshare developments would replace our campsite the following year. *How sad*, I thought. Reality dictated that gangs would take over the area in the years to come. Drugs, damn drugs, would prevent others from sharing utopia. *Will it ever change?* I wondered.

I let Booster out to play with Sunny on the beach, grateful he had a companion to play with. I was ready for a drink, and the ladies obliged, handing me a bottle of water! We sat on our five-dollar Riviera and watched the sun set while its rays morphed into panoramic pastels. I later looked down, and Booster and Sunny were lying together at my feet, coated in sand. We had no steady water supply—only 50 gallons in a holding tank—as we were dry camping. We took the dogs out into the waves, washed off the sand, and then toweled them dry. Then we retired to our respective abodes with our hounds in hand.

In the morning, I arose to Booster greeting the day as he always did.

He was excited and hungry. I fed him and let him out for a walk. He ran out onto the beach and ceremoniously threw the sand between his legs—he'd do that all day long if I let him. Then, he ran to the water and chased the waves as they receded into the ocean, only to run from them when they miraculously reappeared moments later. It was a fight until the end that never came. I had to drag him away from the water he loved.

Later that day, we walked down the beach, and I ended up talking to a cool Mexican guy who liked my T-shirt. I liked his weed. A compromise was drawn in the sand; he got my shirt, and I picked weeds! I was no longer a virgin to the wonders of Mexico. I took a siesta, and when the cloud of distraction cleared, Booster was nowhere to be found. My heart skipped an emotional, loving beat for the first time in a long while. I frantically looked down the beach and saw paw prints in the sand. In the far distance, I saw Booster rolling around on something like he was getting a Thai massage! Turned out he'd found a dead seal swelled in the sun, covered with maggots. He was bonding!

MY BOOSTER!

It took hours to unbind the seal stench from Booster's thick coat. *Why couldn't he have been one of those tight-haired Labradors?* I asked myself. I only had 50 gallons of fresh water with which to bathe myself. If I used it on Booster, I was surely going to smell like I, too, had rolled around with a dead seal! With laundry detergent and perseverance, I washed Booster like there was no tomorrow. The reality of the day was that, for the first time in decades, I looked forward to a *tomorrow*. I couldn't wait to witness the sunrise on the beautiful beach. I envisioned golden rays of sunlight illuminating Booster's golden fur while he trotted down the beach, chasing the relentless waves.

That night, I walked with the ladies and the canine duo down the beach. The moonlight illuminated our path as we sauntered aimlessly en route to

39

nowhere. "Why do you keep looking over your shoulder?" they asked me suddenly.

"I didn't realize I was," I said.

"You know you do that a lot. It's like you're never relaxed."

I almost laughed aloud as the word *relaxed* was never a part of my vocabulary. "See, you did it again, dude," they blurted out moments later.

Sullenly, I walked away from the pack and sat on a log, looking out into the vast ocean. I started crying, slowly at first, and then the floodgates opened. I was oblivious to my surroundings until an intruder broke my concentration. Booster came running full throttle into my lap, damn near knocked me over, and broke my hypnotic trance! His tongue frantically mopped up my tears just like it had that fateful day in the camper when I'd had my breakthrough moment. As time went on, Booster became quite adept at responding to my exaggerated emotions. Amazingly, he was equally adept at responding to a lack of emotion by breaking me out of trances. The ladies walked over and sat by my side as Sunny lay by Booster, and we talked.

"Dude, you're a mess, man . . . you're really messed up. You know, codependency kills. You can't keep running from yourself. It's not the addicts doing it to you . . . it's *you* doing it to you! *Just for today*, you're safe and with friends; four, to be exact."

I looked around to see who the other two mystery friends were. Then I realized she was talking about our canine family members. It took years to realize the importance of those words. Friends? I had no friends. Over the years, I'd concentrated on fixing the addicts in my life, and my friends had wisely opted out. My family became estranged as I became enmeshed in madness. I didn't even realize that my speech was impacted, as I checked my words before I spoke and surveyed the terrain as I walked. My AWAK (whack job) defense system was in force 24/7. I was on a beach with my four friends, living safely in a mobile cocoon, and yet I was hypervigilant. To this day, I have body twitches from an overactive nervous system. Years later, on a cruise, my brother was embarrassed when he thought I was coming on to someone on a cruise ship when I twitched my eye. At first, I got pissed, then thought . . . *God, I wish it were that simple!*

MY BOOSTER!

The ladies were wonderful that night. They said what they said bluntly. Eloquence was never a requisite for Batgirl and Robin. They were becoming the superheroes I turned to when life became unbearable, as it inevitably did. We talked for hours that night. The whole while, Booster's head was in my lap, and never a whimper or complaint sounded. He was at peace, content that he could be with me. Occasionally, he would dream and twitch, just like me, but that's where the similarity ended. My Booster was a confident, non-aggressive social being. He wasn't afraid to *let his fur down* in public and just be himself. He solicited attention, whereas I shunned it. He was sensitive, a quality I'd lost long ago. The more I thought about it, the more I realized why I'd resented him so. We were personality opposites . . . like the North and South Poles.

Many dogs end up in a shelter because their human chose a dog with a personality contrary to the needs of the human family. Statistics show that when a family chooses their next dog, it rarely ends up in a shelter because the family learned that the personality match . . . canine–human . . . is critical for the success of the adoption of a dog into the family unit. Booster's personality type was not a match, and he was a likely candidate to be surrendered for adoption had my life scenario been typical. Miraculously, my personality changed to match Booster's, resulting in a life-changing partnership that developed over time. Eventually, I became an extravert just like Booster, and evidenced confidence just like him.

We walked back to our campers, and I told the ladies and Sunny goodnight. I had a few drinks, and off to bed I went to join Booster, who'd claimed my pillow. I slept without the pillow that night; he deserved it. He'd unconditionally listened to all my crap for hours. Really, he earned far more than a pillow; he'd earned his wings! He was an angel sent from above.

Booster had an uncanny ability to sense human emotions. He was totally in touch with my emotional mood swing on the beach. He instinctively lay calmly by my side yet engaged me when I needed motivation. The first time I realized this was when I took him to a nursing home in Truth or Consequences, New Mexico, to visit Alzheimer's patients. I asked the ladies to go with me, but they adamantly refused, even though I was fearful and needed their reassurance. Instead, they reassured me that I still had balls and was fully intact, though I might have thought otherwise! The nursing home director insinuated the folks would enjoy a doggy visit, but sadly, they wouldn't remember it. I walked into a room with seniors sitting in chairs in a circle. I wasn't sure what I was going to do, but Booster sure did. Once I was certain no one was afraid of Booster, I gave him a stuffed bunny rabbit. He walked up to an elderly man, who reached out, tugged on the toy, and robustly petted him on the head. Without ado, Booster then strutted, rabbit in mouth, to an elderly lady with flowing gray hair.

Booster never missed visiting a single person in the room that day, including the administrator. Before leaving, I walked into the hall and thanked the staff for the opportunity to visit. The gentleman who had tugged on Booster's bunny wheeled himself out into the hallway.

The administrator asked the man, "What'd you think of the dog?"

I know the administrator was expecting to hear, *What dog?*

In a booming voice, the man proclaimed, "Amazing dog, amazing dog . . . did you see what he did? *I* had a dog!"

With Booster in tow, I abruptly rushed outside. I was crying again, shaking and twitching. Buried emotions erupted from deep within. I felt like such a freak. Only a freak would react in such a manner. I was an emotionally dead man walking. Later that night, I told the ladies about what had transpired. They smiled. They fuckin' smiled! I was pissed. "It's not funny," I said.

"Sounds like Booster enjoyed himself, dude," they said.

I was angry. *They missed the boat on this one*, I thought.

With clarity of time comes reflection. Booster absolutely enjoyed himself that day, along with the patients, staff, and administrator. He taught us all the depth of the canine–human connection. Just as he brought an Alzheimer's patient's memories to the surface, he did the same for me. He exposed my vulnerability and the accompanying need for change. I wanted what *he* had!

I was so shocked by what I'd seen and learned that I summoned enough courage to call a newspaper to share it with the world. Booster had done his best. Now it was up to me to keep my end of the bargain. I'd promised him I'd share him with the world . . . the world I didn't like. I called the local newspaper and explained what'd happened the day before in the nursing home. I'm sure my sniffles and lapses of speech tipped off the reporter that it was very emotional . . . very real for me. When the story appeared in the paper, I held it up before Booster. "You see, I'm trying to keep my promise to share you with the world." I told him.

When Thanksgiving finally arrived, we were all ready to celebrate. Fore to now, celebrations were nonexistent in my life. On this sunny day on the beach, the humans and their canine counterparts simply relished the sun, water, and stress-free environment. We all sang, barked, ate, slept, and farted together. We were one. It was a harmonious time. The ladies prepared a wonderfully bland and healthy meal. We feasted on foods that would be fodder for the gods. I devoured roasted corn on the cob and gave the cob to Booster. I wanted him to enjoy the vegetarian bone of delight. He chewed on the cob for what seemed like an eternity before an afternoon slumber on the sun-soaked beach. We listened to music and watched the waves meander in and out on the beach. It was a Thanksgiving unlike any I'd experienced in the previous twenty years. I was happy in the moment, as was Booster. In fact, we were *all* happy! I had to pinch myself to ensure that I wasn't dreaming. Eventually, my vodka-laden mead kicked in, and I had to snooze. I lay back in my bed, Booster joined me, and I fell into the previously elusive comfort zone of sleep.

As time marched forward, Booster pulled me to more and more people, and I was forced to talk to complete strangers. I would *never* have walked up to people with tattoo-covered bodies or Rastafarian hairdos . . . much less homeless Mexican guys sprawled out drunk on a sidewalk from tequila and tacos. Booster never discriminated; he was an equal opportunity lover. Gandhi had nothing on Booster. My cocoon eventually imploded, overwhelmed by the positivity proffered by a dog. It was soon apparent that Booster had a master's degree in social work. He did what I could never do. He greeted people, collaborated with them, and appreciated them for who they were, unconditionally. His philosophy was innocent until proven guilty; mine was guilty before being given the ability to prove innocence!

As a canine–human entourage, we went walking through the town. It was so cool seeing metal sculpting and bright-colored souvenirs of all varieties. The smell of ocean salt permeated the balmy air. It was so profound. Mexicans were hawking their wares ... "Señor . . . Señor!" I suddenly became agitated by the constant prodding of the street peddlers. They should have taken lessons from Booster, who had an uncanny ability to beckon people to his side with adoration as opposed to resentment.

A cute Mexican boy approached Booster and reached out to pet him. Booster raised a paw to shake his hand. *Language isn't necessary to communicate*, I thought. Upon reflection, I realized that Booster constantly communicated through body language. Even the least-educated human could relate to him. When he offered a paw, the human offered a hand. When he was excited, he shared his exuberance by jumping up and down. He became a master at motivational speaking through body language. He would walk between people's legs and stop. Soon he'd get a butt scratch of indeterminate length. When he knew he had you on the hook, he would slowly roll onto his back, and the humans instinctively knew to give him a belly rub. Those from Britain would say . . . it was all quite brilliant!

The Mexican boy instantly fell in love with Booster. With highest regards, the little boy suddenly gave Booster his popsicle stick to lick. In one fell swoop, the stick vanished! Booster had swallowed the gift in its entirety. Grabbing Booster's head and prying his mouth open, I saw about an inch of the wooden popsicle stick. I frantically shoved my hand down his throat, fingers like tweezers, and extracted the 3-inch piece of wood. I will never know what might have happened had Booster swallowed the offending stick. That Thanksgiving Day, I gave thanks.

We walked on throughout the town of Puerto Penasco, taking in the wonderment of a foreign city. Later in the day, I let my guard down and relaxed as I was tired, having walked long distances in the hot sun. Suddenly, the leash ripped from my hand. I thought someone was stealing Booster. I looked up to see Booster running across a dock and jumping up into the air. He grabbed a shrimp from a Mexican man's

MY BOOSTER!

fingers, held high to show off the shrimp he was selling. Amazingly, Booster got the shrimp, leaving the man's fingers wholly intact. The man swung around in a fit of fury to witness Booster feasting on his shrimp. A volcano of fury morphed into a celebratory smile. The toothy Mexican man grinned and said, "No problema." Perhaps he was happy that someone put forth such an effort to appreciate his shrimp. Frankly, I was not so impressed.

CHAPTER 4
WE WERE TESTED

Life on the run gets old. I'd been running from reality for two decades, and it finally dawned on me that such a lifestyle wasn't sustainable. Emotionally and economically, it just wasn't feasible. It was now do or die. With Booster by my side, I chose to *do*. I thought about the folks who had maintained my business in my absence. Sure, they kept their paychecks rolling in, but they really cared about me. They knew a bit about what I was going through, yet never interfered; they were supportive, not invasive. I had shirked my responsibilities for far too long. Christmas was approaching, and I decided to go home and face my evil(s). One crisp morning, Booster and I jumped into the camper and set the compass for home. We crossed the Mexican border, and my knees started to shake. My body betrayed me. I was suddenly wracked by fear. I was going back home, spelled *H a d e s*. Subconsciously, my emotions quelled while walking him, so I stopped more often than necessary to walk Booster. Somehow, his confidence and calmness became mine. We were growing in symbiotic ways. All good ways, I might add.

While walking Booster, I noticed he was eating grass more than he normally would. Days later, he was still eating grass, and then he started throwing it up. He tried to poop but couldn't. The following day, I awoke to a pile of poop in the shower. *Well, at least he's hygienic*, I thought. As the days progressed, I realized Booster's process of elimination wasn't quite right. He would throw up and try to poop, but nothing came out. *Weird*, I thought. By the time I was within a day's drive of home, I became concerned.

Oddly enough, I was in a town where my alcohol addict's mother lived. She was one of the greatest souls on the planet. I called her and explained that I was on my way back home and I was worried about my dog, Booster. She invited us to stay in her home while I sorted it all out. As it was Christmas Eve in Lafayette, Louisiana, I wondered if my alcohol addict would show

MY BOOSTER!

up to visit. More importantly, I wondered if Booster would be OK. When we arrived, I was shown to my room, and Booster was shown to his yard. He dutifully went outside and tried to eliminate, unsuccessfully. He then threw up. I looked across the fence and saw a cute boxer. Booster didn't notice her, so I knew he must truly be sick. The boxer's name was Maggie, and her human soon approached me.

"Hi, what a cute boxer" I mumbled half-heartedly.

"Her name is Maggie and she's such a sweetheart" came the reply from Maggie's human.

My boy's name is Booster and we just returned from Mexico. Something's wrong, I think he's sick."

"There's a veterinary clinic not too far away" she replied. "But it's Christmas Eve" I responded.

"I'm sure it's open and if he were my dog, I would get him checked out."

Back inside the house, Mom said, "That's what dogs do . . . they eat grass and throw up."

I said, "That's not what Booster does."

"Well, be prepared to spend a bundle," she said.

I didn't have a bundle, but I did have a credit card with a partially devoured credit limit. I beckoned Booster, and we were off to the Lafayette Animal Emergency Clinic.

When I walked in, I met Dr. Moreau. "My Booster's sick," I explained, "I'm worried about him. People think I'm crazy, but something isn't right." Tears flowed down my embarrassed cheeks.

Dr. Moreau reassured me, "Let's take a look."

Booster was given something to make him poop, but he didn't. Dr. Moreau said he would run some tests to determine if there was a blockage. Booster was boosted up on a table for an X-ray. Upon reviewing the film, there was no trace of anything tangible that would account for a digestive issue. Just as I began to think it was just a dietary problem, Dr. Moreau suggested we run a barium test. A barium X-ray illuminates the pathway through the digestive system. Sure enough, it abruptly stopped at one point along the way. Booster was turning septic and had at most forty-eight hours to live unless the blockage was eradicated. A costly operation was needed.

Even though I was a poor man at the time, psychologically and economically, I gave the go-ahead and paid a deposit using my one credit card. I wasn't sure of the balance owed, as I'd been traveling, but it worked to get Booster into the operating room later that day.

Back at the house, I spun a new cocoon. I didn't want to talk or eat. Drunker than ever before, I hadn't consumed a drop of drink. I felt cold and alone and worried about how Booster felt. He was also alone in a cold, foreign room of concrete and cages. *This world surely sucks. Why had Booster prolonged my agony only to be taken away when I needed him the most?* I hurt so badly from the inside out. Even though I'd eaten no grass, I, too, vomited. Listless, I sat for hours, going from a life of hypervigilance to a hypnotic trance. I was no longer in a cocoon; I was in a tomb.

BOOM came a knock at the door. "Hey, you've got a phone call," Mom blurted.

Who in the hell wants to talk to me? I wondered. I listened to the voice on the phone. "Hello, this is Dr. Moreau. Can you please come into the clinic?" implored the veterinarian I'd met hours before.

I shrieked in pain, cried, sobbed, and dropped the phone. Mom rushed to my side and held me.

"It hurts!" I screamed. "Even Booster's betrayed me. He's died, damn it."

With the strength that only a mom has during trying times, she picked up the phone and said, "Hello." She then turned to me and said, "He's going to be OK."

I sat down and waited for the aftershock tremors to subside. I was in no shape to drive. Mom drove me to the clinic. I walked into the waiting room, and minutes morphed into hours, or so it seemed. Dr. Moreau came in with a smile and invited me into the examining room. "It took two attempts to find it, but here's the problem," he said resolutely. He showed me a piece of a corn cob. "Corn cobs can be deadly for a dog. Veterinarians cut them out of dogs' stomachs year-round. It isn't always a corn cob, however. A month ago, a lady brought in a dog that had swallowed a metal shoe buckle. I cut it out, but she returned two weeks later when the dog developed the same symptoms. I operated again and removed the buckle from the other shoe!" "That was an expensive pair of shoes," I half-heartedly joked. As always, I used humor to shield my overwhelming, painful emotions in the moment. *Just for today,* life would be good again because I had my Booster. I paid my bill with the credit card that had just enough limit to cover the cost of the operation. WOW, another **coincidence**, I thought.

I took Booster home to Mom's house. His belly was full of stitches, but he never complained. I brought him into my room and rubbed his stitch-filled belly. Suddenly he rose, whimpered in pain, and licked my face. Again, I sobbed. Soon Booster's tongue was lapping up tears faster than he could grab them. He was more worried about *me* than his own pain. I soon got up to leave, thinking he would chill out on the bed. I walked two steps, and he jumped onto the floor. *Oh my God, he's going to bust his stitches open*, I thought. He didn't care about anything except being with me. Again, I started to cry.

Hours turned into days as Booster healed in the safety of Mom's home. He followed me from room to room and refused to allow me out of his sight. Often, when I went to take a dump, I dropped my pants to find they'd landed on Booster's head! A symbiotic relationship of the highest import was developing at lightning speed. I wouldn't go anywhere without Booster, and he wouldn't go anywhere without me. There was nothing I wouldn't do for him, and he knew it. In turn, he stood by my side as I perilously navigated the minefields of life with a skewed navigational system.

One day before I left Mom's house, she looked at me and said, "Dave, that dog's special . . . he loves you . . . in fact, he adores you." I didn't know what to say, but I certainly wasn't worthy of being loved. An emotionally bankrupt, hollow shell of a human being, I didn't know what love was, much less how to recognize it.

On the drive home, I kicked myself in the ass for having given Booster a corn cob to chew on, which I'd thought was a great vegetarian bone. *I didn't know,* I kept telling myself as I cradled Booster in my arms as he sat in my lap. I felt so guilty. It'd been a long time since I had felt emotions, and now they were kicking my ass. Funny thing was, Booster didn't seem to mind the experience. He was happy to simply be in my arms. I was more than happy because he was alive. The ability to feel that way simply wasn't human, or was it? I didn't know what it was, but it felt new.

Luckily, I'd taken out a pet health insurance policy for Booster. The company offered a policy with a rigid payout schedule with a limited reimbursement rate. They justified it by saying that it was an economical policy. "Then why not charge a dollar and pay out fifty cents, assholes?" I asked them, totally convinced that most people didn't have the ability to pay the remaining portion of the bill and pets summarily lost their lives. I submitted a claim for the foreign body removal (corn cob), and the agent shook me down and demanded all my Booster-related veterinary records since Jesus was born.

"Why are you shaking me down?" I asked.

"Sir, if your dog's ever swallowed anything before, then that's a psychiatric condition, and we don't cover psychiatric conditions," the prick replied.

I lost it and politely told the agent, "Fuck you, asshole. You're all the same . . . you take money, fight claims, and try to prove pre-existing as a way out."

Though I have reservations about politicians, I applaud President Obama's fight to remove the word pre-existing from the human health insurance companies' executives' bowels. FACT: A dog would never treat a dog the way many insurers treat their insured. I once read about an insurance company that gave bonuses to employees that denied legitimate claims and got away with it. Booster ended up having more lives than a cat, and his lifetime veterinary expenses exceeded $40,000, of which the insurance company paid out roughly half. I relished the fact that I beat the insurance company at its game. Ironically, Booster saved my life, elevated it, and consequently, I was later able to afford the exorbitant copays.

After what seemed like an eternity, we arrived home to a weed farm. I turned off the truck's engine and sat there with the doors locked. After looking north, south, east, and west, I gingerly lowered the truck window to half-staff and smelled the air. I didn't smell food cooking nor crack pipe vapor trails wafting in the breeze. It took a while, but eventually, I opened the truck door and stepped out. It was one small step for me, one giant leap

MY BOOSTER!

for my life. It took a while, but eventually, I opened the truck door and stepped out. Oblivious to all, Booster ran to a tree, lifted his leg, peed pools of urine, and claimed his stake. This was *his* home now. *We* were home. The eagle had landed, and I was on life support, fueled by unconditional canine love. I walked to the door of the cabin and opened the unlocked door. I sent Booster in to survey the surroundings, but wasn't prepared, but for what happened next. *Nothing,* absolutely nothing! Nothing! Nothing! Nothing!

How beautiful nothing was. Surrounded by a sea of tranquility, my mind went completely blank for the first time in decades. I sat in the middle of the floor in a hypnotic trance. Suddenly, Booster ran and jumped into my lap. I squeezed him so hard I thought he'd pop, but he never complained. I looked into his eyes, ventured into his very soul once again, and cried, knowing that whatever happened, I wasn't alone. Waiting for one of my addicts to appear, I subconsciously surveyed my surroundings on autopilot. It simply never happened.

I slowly glued the pieces of my life back together. What had once been shattered was reassembled, held together by a mist of canine glue. *It can't last*, I thought. The only constant in my life was Booster. He celebrated every moment of his existence. I marveled at how he smelled deer dung and loved it. Simply peeing graffiti turned him on to no end! He wasn't affiliated with any gang, yet his graffiti sprayed everywhere, proclaiming something. He'd often just run out into the yard, throw himself on the ground, and roll around in the sunshine. Booster knew how to live life on life's terms and get the most out of it. *How is that possible?* I wondered.

Turns out, my addicts had moved on. I had no way of knowing for how long or if and when they might return. They'd likely latched on to other codependent innocents lacking self-esteem and equally needy as I was. My hypervigilance grew rather than waned. It simply wasn't possible to be so safe. There was something terribly wrong with this picture. Somehow, with Booster's talents, I persevered, and life became doable. I wasn't alone. I had Booster and Al-Anon. Often, I searched the internet, seeking information about my addicts. I kept my shields up, in Star Trek fashion. Sadly, I recently learned that my alcohol addict died alone on the streets of San Diego, California.

CHAPTER 5
HELL'S INFERNAL CONDO

Life calmed down with no addict to fuel the roller coaster. Just as things seemed to level out, I received a phone call one morning. My crack addict's father-inlaw called me to let me know that one of his employees had run into my crack addict, who was living in a condo in Destin, Florida. Years before, I'd purchased a vacation condo in the resort beach community. My crack addict wanted to be close to family, so I'd purchased a condo there. There was nothing I would not do for my addicts. Time revealed that my crack addict was living in *my* condo, which I hadn't visited in a long time.

I called the condo security office. They later informed me that the individual living in my condo claimed to be a resident, proffered a key, and showed clothing in a closet to prove it. The key was my hidden key. My crack addict had climbed up the outside balcony of my second-story condo and had broken the lock on the sliding patio doors. Security refused to get involved, so I called the sheriff's department. They wouldn't have got involved either, except my crack addict had outstanding arrest warrants.

After being given repeated reassurances that my crack addict was incarcerated, I drove to my condo. The security guards told me they'd seen my crack addict hiding something under the couch. When I moved the couch, I found a crack pipe. Later, I found other crack pipes strewn about my precious vacation home, which had always made me high with pride of ownership. The condo was the one beautiful thing in my otherwise polluted life. I looked out the windows at the waves pounding the beach. It reminded me of when Booster chased the waves in Mexico. How I wished Booster and I could enjoy Destin like we'd enjoyed Mexico. We rarely entered the sacred condo grounds, due to the selfish, self-centered condo association board that relished its no-pets policy.

When I returned to my cabin, I was once again consumed with fear. My crack addict's abode was once again a jail cell. I would get the blame and suffer the consequences. It wasn't a matter of if, but when. I petted Booster until I thought his fur would fall off. He sensed my trepidation and was clingier than ever. I suddenly wondered why the condo association didn't allow dogs on the premises. Turned out, while it had originally been a dog-friendly condo development, a new junta had gained control prior to my purchase. Pets were suddenly forbidden, and townhouses were built upon grounds that had once been pet walking trails. *How clever!* I thought.

It's been postulated that as our society grew, we moved away from Mother Nature and created urban environments of cold concrete and steel. Children have suffered immeasurable harm as a direct result. A young British girl named Florence Nightingale rescued a dying dog and nursed it back to health in the 1800s. It was a life-changing event that started with the canine–human bond. She later became known as the mother of nursing. The advent of no-pets housing created a disconnect from nature, and children no longer learned empathy, caring, and the responsibility of caring for another soul. It was the *me* generation. The consequence manifested itself in juveniles who had no problem snatching a purse or pulling out a gun and killing someone. *When one of these blue bloods becomes a victim of a crime,* I thought, *they help perpetuate their own demise through self-centered selfishness.*

I suddenly thought I should be able to enjoy the nice things in life like sand, sun, and beach. If anyone needed such serenity, it was I. My condo was the nicest thing I owned in my life. I wanted to enjoy my condo, on which I was paying a king's ransom mortgage. I'd really stretched to buy it and struggled monthly to pay for it, so I figured I might as well try to use it. When I'd purchased my condo, I hadn't cared about the no-pets policy because I didn't own a pet. I only had my crack addict to take care of! Hell, I hadn't thought about anything when I'd bought it except that it brought my crack addict closer to family.

One day, I penned a letter to all the condo owners, beseeching them as to why pets were not allowed. I coupled pictures with humor and mailed out hundreds of letters. After all, Booster had saved my life. I'm sure not all pets possess such accolades, but most deserve credit for the unconditional love they bestow upon their humans. It set off a firestorm of consequences. I unwittingly ignited a policy bloodbath.

The condo blue bloods' cauldrons boiled over and the ruling junta balked profusely at the thought of dogs walking on the hallowed, sacred grounds of the gods. Ablaze with indignation, the aristocratic board members stopped making martinis long enough to bitch about the guy who wanted to allow canine family members on the grounds. One individual on the board was so hateful that he made Lucifer seem like a pacifist! His blood was so self-described blue that it was in fact purple!

I received letters of all descriptions. Many were grateful for my efforts. Some were pitiful, like the man who'd lived in his condo for over twenty years and had had to leave because the association wouldn't allow him to have his prescribed service dog. One fellow condo owner sent me a lovely email stating said that her dying husband arranged to buy her a dog while on his death bed in a hospital. She explained that she never went anywhere without that dog because it was her last connection with her now-deceased husband. The condo board never allowed her to bring her bastion of humanity, her *raison d'être*. I shed tears then, as I am now. I will never forget her, and I will always remember how kind she was to have taken time out to share such intimate details of her life. Condo country was a bold dichotomy of selfish versus selfless!

1/26/2005

Dear Mr. Hawn,

I am the owner of a unit and in receipt of your letter dated January 5, 2005 . . . Pets were allowed at that time . . . In 1999 I was diagnosed with Hep "C" due to a blood transfusion . . . The treatment was like nails being driven into every joint in my body the beaten with a baseball bat

MY BOOSTER!

> *... my husband was diagnosed with cancer ... He had chemo, radiation, and surgery ... Christmas of 2003, he gave me another border collie (Dakota) ... While I would like very much to spend time at the Towers, I will not leave either of my dogs ... I lost my husband November 2004 and he loved the two members of our family as much as I do . . . You have my total support, hopefully, someday everyone will know and experience the love of a pet, Good Luck.*

After a while, the steam of the cauldrons subsided. I never formally asked for permission to have Booster in my condo. At that time, I avoided confrontation at all costs and just wasn't up for the battle. Things settled long enough for the next catastrophe to enter my life roughly a year later. Her name was Katrina! Category 5 Hurricane Katrina barreled down on my life and business. I clutched Booster in my arms and headed for the only refuge I had. I went to the hallowed condo grounds, out of harm's way. When I arrived, I was greeted by a puppet. She was the property manager who served at the beckoning call of the ruling junta. It was her job, and I had nothing against her. I just hate how some humans are forced to be more submissive than a chained dog. She approached me and said, "Mr. Hawn, you know you can't have a dog on the property."

"I had to evacuate my home and my dog Booster is my canine kid. Booster means everything to me. These chunks of concrete blocks pale in comparison. The board can move to evict me, but it will be after the storm passed when we are safe and out of harm's way.

She replied, "So we agree to disagree."

I politely retorted, "Yes, ma'am, we do indeed." Like a Davidian from Waco, I held my ground.

Other condo owners, similarly seeking refuge for their canine and feline family members, approached the board and said, "Well, if Mr. Hawn can have his dog, we can have our pets too!"

The board eventually acquiesced and let owners know that they could have their pets for the time being. One step for my Booster, a giant leap for man*KIND*! That evening, the sunset was beautiful, a panoramic vista of the most vivid purple one could ever imagine. Livid merged with vivid. *Humans could find a way to complicate a bowel movement; the junta was so far up everyone's ass!* I thought.

What Booster and I experienced at Condo Hell was a result of blue blood, self-centered, myopic ignorance, at the very least. In the days and years that followed, I learned how ignorant and insensitive public officials were in the same regard. These *pubic*  officials, in positions of trust, failed to understand the depth of the animal/pet–human bond. It is during such times that humans acutely need the unique, therapeutic, loving attributes that animals unconditionally provide. They failed to comprehend that people would not abandon their canine family members, canine kids, especially during catastrophic events such as hurricanes. As a direct result, countless people lost their lives.

A supervisor for the Federal Emergency Management Agency (FEMA), was asked by a reporter attending a press conference, "What about the dogs and cats that have been stranded?" His response began, "They are not our concern."

There were many tragic animal-related stories documented in the aftermath of Hurricane Katrina. One rescuer stated, "FEMA has told us we cannot take the pets. They told us that we could not take one cat or dog in our boats . . . It's a stupid rule. More people are going to die because of that." I remember reading about a young boy who was sheltered in the New Orleans Superdome. When he tried to board a bus to Houston with his small white dog, a police officer had to take the dog away from the boy. When I read the pet-related Katrina stories, I still shed tears. I helped shape a temporary, transformative policy at hellacious condo grounds. I just wish that others acting in an official capacity would've had the benefit of a *Booster* in *their* lives. Somehow, they *missed the boat*. This is yet another glaring example of what happens when you sever the tie between Mother Nature and human beings. No-pets housing leads to insensitivity, ignorant humans, and no pet-sense. It resolutely made me even more grateful I had Booster in *my* life.

In the years since Katrina, many state and federal laws have been passed to ensure we no longer treat the animal-pet-human bond in the same callous regard. In 2006, Congress passed the *Pets Evacuation and Transportation Standards Act* (PETS, H.R. 3858). President Bush signed the Act, and it became the law. It incorporated animal welfare in disaster plans, including transportation, rescue, recovery, tracking, etc. Kudos to Congress and the president for espousing sensitivity, leadership, and what I refer to as "common sense."

After the hurricane passed, I started going to the condo, but abided by the rules and housed Booster at my crack addict's father-in-law's house in Destin. He had a nice fenced-in yard, but it simply killed me to abandon Booster. At night, I reached out for him in a bed of emptiness. Without Booster by my side, I just could not enjoy anything life had to offer. Hercules had his hair, and I had Booster. What is . . . is! I could no longer justify going to my condo home without Booster. It was unhealthy for me, and it hurt Booster, who couldn't possibly comprehend why I would abandon him.

The junta had signs planted on the property that prominently displayed their arrogance. It had a chilling effect and boarded on intimidation. To think that any human would do such a thing regarding access for the disabled left me absolutely dumbfounded. I question the legality of the verbiage, as supportive documentation proving the dog has training or the individual is qualified to have a service dog is not required for access. Proof of vaccination records might be reasonable, in certain cases. NO PETS ALLOWED EXCEPT SERVICE ANIMALS WITH APPROPRIATE DOCUMENTATION, ADVANCE NOTICE IS STRONGLY

RECOMMENDED TO ENSURE ALL PAPERWORK IS IN ORDER. Advance notice? What paperwork? Was a presidential seal required to enter the hallowed grounds with a service dog?

At that juncture, I decided I would never return to my condo without Booster. I went to my crack addict's father-in-law's home to pick up Booster for the ride home. He greeted me with leaps and bounds, as usual. Before long, we were on our way home to the cabin. We were both quiet except for a few of Booster's intermittent coughs along the way. Once home, Booster's coughing got worse. I took him to a country vet, who said it was likely kennel cough. He prescribed an antibiotic, and that was that. Booster continued to cough for a week, and he suddenly started walking in the shadows. He refused to walk in direct sunlight. He pulled me to the shade. It was strange. I took him back to the vet, and he prescribed a different antibiotic.

That night I suddenly awoke at 4 a.m. for no apparent reason. Booster wasn't on my bed, so I knew something was wrong. We were Siamese twins . . . we never separated; it just wasn't possible. I walked into the kitchen, and he was on the floor. He struggled to raise his head. Drool fell to the floor like liquid plastic. He looked at me with eyes I will never, ever forget. It was as though he was saying, "I'm dying. Help me if you can, but if not, I understand."

I panicked. My heart beat so hard I didn't think my chest could withstand the attack. Taking Booster by the paws, I dragged him to my truck and drove a hundred miles an hour down the highway to the 24-hour emergency clinic. I went in and proffered my canine soul to the strangers within. Once again, I was reduced to rubble. The receptionist was more worried about me than Booster! The veterinarian later informed me that Booster had a 107-degree fever, and his lungs were full of blood. I couldn't handle the sadistic teeter-totter of life. *Why is my soul being tortured?* I asked myself.

"Go home. We'll call you," the receptionist said.

At the cabin, I could hear the cockroaches fart. I sat all alone and cried, shook, and cried some more. I thought about the times I'd kicked Booster away. I thought about the toothy grin on the Mexican man's face when Booster *boosted* his shrimp from his hands. I thought about the time he'd reared up, despite his stitches, to kiss my face after the operation to remove the corn cob from his stomach. I remembered the gut-wrenching yelp when he'd hurt himself in Ajo playing with another dog.

Booster was dying. If he died, I would also die within. I wasn't capable of living life on life's terms without Booster by my side. Later that day, the phone rang. I shook. My alcohol addict's mom wasn't around to field the call this time. I had to do this myself. An invisible hand took mine and helped me answer the phone. "Hello, it's Dr. Sutton. Booster's going to be OK, but it was close. Seems he ingested rat poison, which prevents blood from clotting. Luckily, he got a hold of rat poison we can counteract with Vitamin K. He's weak but stable. We're going to keep him and suggest you take him to your veterinarian when we release him, hopefully tomorrow."

I dropped the phone and took a deep breath. If I'd slept through the night and awakened like most other mornings, Booster would have been dead on the kitchen floor. *Why had I awakened? Who woke me up?* It was one hell of a **coincidence** ... one more in a string of **coincidences**. I cried myself to sleep in disbelief. When I awoke, I wondered where in the hell Booster had gotten ahold of the rat poison. It dawned on me that it must have been in my crack addict's father-in-law's home. I called to share the story and learned that he had indeed put rat poison in the yard the year before, but not where Booster had been . . . or so he thought. I then cringed and remembered my crack addict's words, "If I find out you care about that dog more than me . . ." After all, Booster was the one thing preventing my crack addict from being able to live full-time in a beautiful beach home near family. I will never know the reality of what happened. Did Booster happen to find the rat poison, or did my crack addict give it to him? Had we stayed in the condo I was so proud of, this never would have happened. Booster didn't like walking in direct sunlight for the rest of his life. He exhibited learned behavior. He'd walked in the shade when affected by the rat poison. The heat had exacerbated his ability to breathe due to his fluid-filled lungs. The sun was the enemy! I sold my boat because Booster didn't want to be out in the sun. For the love of Booster, I traded a beautiful tan and black Z4 convertible beamer for a lime green Honda Element. A sweet, elderly lady at the Honda dealership asked me, when I was trading in the beamer, if I'd purchased the tan dog to match the tan top of my former car. I rapidly responded, "No, ma'am, I bought that car to match my dog!" The Honda salespeople were shocked that I was trading a BMW Roadster for a Honda Element. There simply wasn't anything I would not do for Booster's betterment!

CHAPTER 6
THE DAWN OF EDUCATION

One day I thought about my unfulfilled promise to my Booster to share him with the world. I realized I needed an education and some form of credentials to do it, so I started reading everything I could about dog training. I'd taught Booster sit, down, stay, and settle. He'd learned to open the refrigerator and bring water. He'd been super socialized in RV parks around the US and Mexico. It was time for a more advanced education for me *and* my Booster. I read about Camp Gone to the Dogs, where owners accompany their dogs to summer camp. Instead of sending your human kid to camp, you brought your canine kid!

I called the business owner, who explained that she'd retired from corporate America and started the business years before. She sublet a portion of the Marlboro College campus located in Marlboro, Vermont. Attendees could stay in the dorms or rent a hotel  room. I ended up taking Booster and my camper to Vermont. Most of the human participants were female, but a few males were scattered about. Dog trainers from across the country came to camp to train owners and their dogs. There was a plethora of activities to choose from. You could take your dog to retrieve rubber ducks from a pond, teach him to do cute tricks, learn obedience commands and more.

There were lectures at night concerning veterinary topics, dog food nutrition, etc. Many people enjoyed making *pawtraits.* You chose colors of paint and applied it to poster board. You then encouraged your dog to walk across the board and voila, an artist is born. A Booster Van Gogh soon appeared! Booster had a habit of pulling me around. One instructor noticed my being taken for a walk by Booster and subsequently introduced me to a

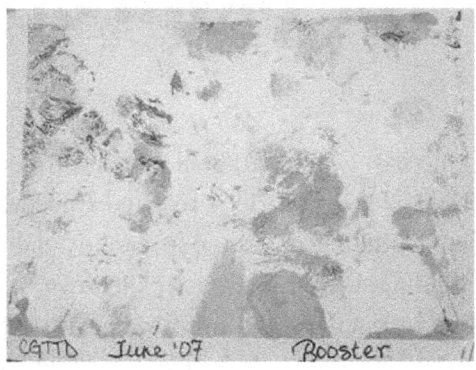

dog headcollar called a Gentle Leader. It wasn't a muzzle, but it looked like one. The Gentle Leader was useful in keeping a dog from pulling. My Booster was stronger than me, so it instantly changed our walking relationship for the better. At camp, I learned the proper way to give a command to a dog, and the importance of positive reinforcement. I learned how to effectively use food to lure a dog and shape its behavior. I also paid an instructor for one-on-one lessons.

The American Kennel Club (AKC) had representatives at camp. They administered a test called the Canine Good Citizen Test (CGC) which judged how well your dog responded to commands, acted in public, and around other dogs. It was a tough test, but Booster passed and received a CGC patch, which he later wore on his vest for years to come. Rather than just let him be a dog, I'd worked with him every day when I'd gone out west. Booster had learned from a symbiotic relation with a human he cared for and wanted to help. It absolutely helped him pass the CGC test. Dogs have a work ethic and Booster had more than most. We taught each other, neither having any formal teaching credentials. I was so proud when Booster passed the CGC test based upon our street smarts learned together. If Booster could have spoken, I'm sure he would have expressed his delight with *my* social progress as well.

I paid an instructor to go with us to a supermarket and evaluate Booster in public and write an evaluation because I wanted to do things correctly. Booster excelled in all ways possible. He was a natural and always behaved well in public. I, on the other hand, often lost it in public when confronted, going from zero to a hundred at a moment's notice. While I sometimes used unbecoming language when confronted, Booster never barked a word in public. When my outbursts occurred, I often looked at Booster and started to breathe slowly and methodically. I would exit the situation and go for a walk with Booster to calm down. Soon, I became reluctant to go places without Booster by my side. I needed him to accompany me wherever I went.

After ten days at camp, we headed home in our cocoon. Having been totally motivated by attending the canine camp, I researched stories about how dogs help people. I read a story on the internet about an organization called the International Association of Assistance Dog Partners (IAADP). I learned that it was founded in 1993 by Dr. Ed Eames, a professor who went blind due to retinitis pigmentosa at forty years of age. He subsequently chose to be partnered with a guide dog to help him navigate life's challenges in Manhattan, New York. I called the IAADP, and Ed answered the phone. He fielded my questions with the patience and understanding of Job. He explained that one of the greatest impediments to maintaining his independence wasn't his lack of vision but, rather, the inability of fellow human beings to *see* the importance of his guide dog benefactor, Perrier. The magnificent black Labrador guided Ed through thick and thin and resolutely remained by his side. The long white cane is a great tool for the blind; however, it doesn't have a heart that beats like your own as it comforts you reassuringly, letting you know life's going to be OK.

The empathetic man explained that taxis often passed him by because he was partnered with a guide dog. If the taxi driver was afraid of dogs, or a member of a faith that taught dogs were somehow unholy and unclean, the problem was exacerbated. The *Americans With Disabilities Act* (ADA) requires that all taxis grant access to guide dogs, but it doesn't prevent taxis from speeding off.

Ed further explained that, upon occasion, he pretended to be shopping and looking through a storefront window. He would ask a stranger to hail a taxi. Once the door was opened, he'd jump in with Perrier. Often, the taxi driver would scream, tell him to get out, and threaten him. On one occasion, a taxi driver physically grabbed him and tried to pull him out of the taxi! Often, the police would have to intervene to help Ed get a taxi.

The IAADP was founded to help people partnered with assistance dogs. For generations, the association functioned as a mediator of sorts when disputes arose between businesses and the disabled partnered with assistance dogs. Ed was impartial. He called 'em as he saw 'em, blind with respect to partiality. He informed me that there was going to be an IAADP Conference in Baltimore in a few weeks. I was welcome to bring my home-schooled service dog, but if my dog caused a problem, I would immediately be asked to leave the conference. "Mr. Hawn," he explained, "Assistance dogs can cost upwards of $100,000 to train, and individuals rely on their dogs. If your dog acts aggressively or bites one of the dogs, it could make the dog fearful, rendering it useless for assistance dog work." I assured Ed that I understood the magnitude of the situation. I then thanked him, hung up the phone, and commenced pacing around the cabin.

Booster got up and ran to my side, thinking we were going for a walk! He had no way of knowing that I was contemplating taking him inside an airplane to Baltimore to attend a conference packed to the gills with dogs! Booster loved other dogs, but too much! I knew he'd be fine at my feet on a plane, but going into a public building and acting like a gentleman was something else. Hell, I didn't know if *I* could act like a gentleman under such stress! I agonized and agonized some more about the opportunity.

Realizing it was indeed an *opportunity*, I decided to go for it! Booster was a service dog in training. He had passed his CGC test, and I'd received training at camp. With both of us having received training, I felt confident that we were credentialed to fly together on a plane. When the fateful day of travel arrived, Booster dawned his vest and walked with me into the New Orleans airport. We soon entered the plane and sat in the bulkhead seat, the seat of choice for many assistance dog partners. The flight was unremarkable. Booster slept, though I certainly did not. I was ready in case a cat fell from the ceiling, or a rabbit ran down the aisle.

When we landed, I summoned a taxi and braced for a fight. An elderly gentleman opened the taxi door for Booster, and he jumped inside without any ado. We arrived at the Baltimore Harbor and were soon checked into our hotel room without question. Could it be that as my attitude began to change for the better, my life followed suit? Was my pursuit of human and canine education responsible for empowering me, and hence my attitude changed? I pondered. The next day, we attended the conference. We sheepishly walked into the conference center and were directed to a second-story hallway leading to the conference room.

There were tables on both sides of the hallway. Halfway down the hall, two ladies with assistance dogs were juxtaposed, looking at items for sale on the tables. I was not about to thread the needle between two dogs and run the gauntlet for fear of canine interaction. How selfish it is for these ladies to create such a perilous blockade. I was an assistance dog virgin, so I sat my virgin ass down and waited for the path to clear. The minute I sat down, another lady entered with her dog and ran the gauntlet. Within seconds, her dog acted menacingly toward one of the other dogs. Ed authoritatively told the woman to leave with her dog. The woman blamed the other dog for inciting her dog, but Ed didn't buy it.

When the coast cleared, Booster and I entered the conference room. There were few seats left, and we sat between two Golden retrievers calmly resting at the feet of their trainers. I just knew Booster was going to ask for a date and misbehave . . . but he did not! I'd almost decided to leave, but I didn't allow my fear to prevent us from growing as a team.

At the end of the day, the women turned and asked me, "Would you like to join us for dinner?"

Like the idiot I was, I asked, "Are you taking your dogs with you into the restaurant?"

The reply was a resounding, "*Yes, of course.*"

With a trembling voice, I said, "Um . . . um . . . I don't know cuz my dog's never been in a restaurant before and he loves food!"

The women laughed and said, "What are you worried about? You'll be with two dog trainers."

Well, hell, I thought, *if they're up for it, I'll go along for the ride.*

I'll never forget walking along Baltimore Harbor en route to the restaurant with the two training angels and our canine partners. I wasn't so sure I'd made the right decision and would be up for the task at hand. Before long, we entered the restaurant without happenstance and ended up enjoying a great meal and tons of laughs. I even forgot that Booster was under the table along with the "Golden Girls." I told the trainers that it was weird, but when Booster wore his service dog vest, he seemed to know he was working. It must be psychosomatic, I explained.

The trainers looked at me and said matter-of-factly, "The dogs absolutely differentiate between work time and play time. When you put the vest on the dog, he knows it's time for work." I equated it with a police officer who partied on his day off but acted professionally when in uniform.

At the end of the dinner, I expressed my heartfelt gratitude. I'd lost my service dog virginity. Once lost, you never get it back! I was stoked! We flew home the following day, and a friend picked us up at the airport. I insisted that we go out to eat at a nearby restaurant. We entered as a party of three. Booster was content, resting beside my feet. I rarely ever entered a restaurant without Booster ever again and was so happy that I could live my life with Booster by my side wherever I went. I thirsted for more canine enrichment.

Remembering what I'd read about the ADI when I was in my cocoon in Arizona, I spontaneously picked up the phone, called the school, and talked to people that understood "dog." It was like sharing a new language. For the first time in twenty years, I felt passionate about something other than my addicts. I was going to go to California with Booster, come hell or high water.

Within days, I arranged to attend the seven-week service dog training seminar at Dr. Bergin's ADI and booked a room at the Flamingo Hotel in Santa Rosa, California. I wanted to get an education and help bolster my credentials with respect to service dog ownership. I jumped on a plane, with Booster at my feet, and flew to California, not quite knowing what to expect. The first day there, Booster found a credit card in the grass, and he carried it to the front desk in his mouth. Turns out the credit card belonged to one of the staff, and Booster was a hero. Of course, I already knew that, but it was awesome that others were realizing it. Most days, he accompanied me to class and faithfully lay at my feet. Other days, I hired students to walk Booster in my absence.

I was born into a middle-class family life from hell, yet I was fortunate enough to have gotten a great high school education. My mother worked at Tulane University in the days when women's salaries weren't at parity with those of their male counterparts. I'm not sure it's much different today. The cool thing was that if you worked full-time at the university for five years, your children could attend tuition free. We never quite appreciate that which is given to us, and in that vein, I took ten years to graduate. I later attended Howard University Law School and was elected to be the first-year class student body representative. I'm sure I was the first, if not the only, white student elected by the Black student body. It was an honor. Regretfully, I didn't complete my studies as I had a terminally ill parent that I had to take care of, so I resigned.

I never utilized my formal education. I'd often worked with my hands, doing odd jobs. For many years, I drove actors for local film production companies filming on location in Louisiana. My father once told me that he'd rather see me work with my head than my hands, but he knew I'd make it in life. I later built a mobile home park, meeting engineers and architects in the morning and operating cranes and bulldozers in the afternoon. That merger of aptitudes, using my education to meet professional people and yet being able to work side by side with blue-collar workers, was a gift. It was all education. They say if you like what you do for a living, you'll never work another day in your life. I enjoyed learning and building the business. It wasn't simply about money.

At the ADI seminar, I suddenly realized that I was experiencing the greatest educational experience of my life. I attended classes in wheelchairs and learned how different diseases affect the body. Some diseases impair mobility, some affect reasoning, and some affect both. I was taught to train dogs. They were eager to learn, and the finest of students! I was given a leash and a dog and told not to let go of that leash for seven days. It was called *the umbilical cord process*. Just as a mother is tethered to a fetus, I was tethered to a sweet female Golden retriever named Tatiana, who relied on me for food and nurture. After seven days of emotional and physical enmeshment, I walked into a gymnasium with my classmates. We were told to unleash our dogs, start walking around the track, and not to look at our dogs.

Amazingly, every dog walked beside its respective human partner. A bond of the finest glue had set in after a week's time. When the exercise was over, we sat down. I handed my leash and dog to my classmate and said, "Excuse me." I walked outside and kept on walking. *Oh my God*, I thought, it reminded me of my Booster never refusing to leave my side even though I had kicked him away and resented him. The umbilical cord exercise was more poignant for me than most others. My classmates had never kicked their dog away or shown animosity toward their dog. I had done so with Booster, and yet the net reward was the same! Canine love and loyalty is beyond reproach. Yes, I cried and walked, walked, and cried. I later returned to the gym, took my dog's leash, and looked into Tatiana's eyes. She jumped into my lap and smiled a beautiful smile—I think she understood that I *got it*.

I learned how to motivate a dog using treats as positive reinforcement, using food and emotional praise. I learned that the psychology used to motivate humans is often the same as that used to motivate dogs. At the midpoint of the seminar, the class was taken to a mall where you were given a list of tasks to perform with your dog while remaining in a wheelchair. You were instructed to take your dog into a department store, have him get a pair of socks off the shelf, and bring it to the register. You then instructed him to do an "up" and drop the socks on the counter. At that point, you had your dog bring your credit card to the cashier. Many such tasks were enumerated on an assignment sheet. Unbeknownst to us, we were each being watched by a *secret shopper*, who took notes about our performance. Of course, we had no idea that we were being followed. Later that day at the institute, we met the person who had followed us and listened to critiques.

I must share one thing that happened that day. I was instructed to go into a restroom with Tatiana and learn how to use the facilities partnered with my dog. Going into a restroom with a dog exposes the dog to a plethora of smells and possibilities. Luckily for me, the men's room was empty when I wheeled us in. I went into the stall with the wide door for the disabled and issued the sit command. I was in love with Tatiana by that time; she was my golden princess. I said, "Down, lil girl."

Tatiana refused to budge.

I said it again but more loudly, "*Down*, little girl." Tatiana, being the bitch that she was, just stared at me.

MY BOOSTER!

Again, I gave the command, "Go down, little girl . . . go down, little girl."

Suddenly, I heard feet shuffling and looked under the partition. There was a guy whose feet were standing in front of the urinal. "Where in the hell did he come from I wondered," wrongfully thinking I was all alone with my *lil girl* in the stall. I panicked when I replayed my words in my mind . . . *Go down, lil girl. Go down!* I jumped up, flung open the stall door, and looked at a very bewildered older gentleman. "Sir," I explained, "I'm in college learning to train service dogs, and this is my precious *lil girl*, Tatiana. Isn't she cute?" If it had been the Christmas holidays, he'd have thought I was another fruit cake!

On another day, we began working with at-risk teens. I was taken to a girls' juvenile detention center, where I taught young girls how to socialize and train service dogs. I knew absolutely nothing about working with such a populace, but the ADI instructor told me to be patient, step back, and let the dogs do their magic. Before long, the girls were emotionally attached to *their* dogs. They requested extra working time with the dogs! During a field trip to the store with the dogs, several of the girls asked me for money to buy snacks . . . for the dogs! Those girls found unconditional love. A few shared stories about their abusive parents, or worse, and I just listened. They hugged the dogs and afterwards shared myriad in-depth thoughts. The experience was as therapeutic for me as it was for the girls. We all have a cross to bear; just some crosses are heavier than others!

I remembered back to the day I hugged my Booster in Ajo, Arizona, when I *got it*. My life was changed forever, and I was now witnessing a similar transformation. The recidivism rate among participants in dog training prison programs is significantly less than for non-participants. Bonnie had introduced me to a "circle of education." I got the experience of working with dogs and at-risk teens. The teens learned to train the dogs (a future vocation), and the disabled got the dogs, using them to increase their independence in life. It was a perfect storm of benevolence.

During the second half of the seminar, you became an instructor and were called upon to utilize the training skills you'd just acquired. You taught a disabled person how to use the service dog they were going to  receive from the university. There was an elaborate personalitymatching formula used to select which dog was given to which disabled service dog recipient. It was all so fascinating!

I had to teach a young lady in a power wheelchair how to use the service dog the school was going to give her. I had to shake hands with a human whose hand didn't work. While I had done many things in my life, but this was different and powerful. For the first time in my life, I reached out to shake the non-working hand of a disabled human being. Her name was Elise.

During a class outing, Bonnie took us to a hardware store to learn how to pick a special carabiner clip to attach the leash to the wheelchair so it wouldn't get run over by a wheel and become entangled. I subsequently taught Elise how to attach her dog's leash to her chair. I also taught her how to back into an elevator with her dog in the proper manner. Failure to get it right would result in the elevator door closing, the dog remaining outside, and possibly getting lost or injured. This was but one of the myriad tasks I was entrusted to train.

At times, Elise was sad and started to cry. I had to deal with that, too. No, excuse me; I *wanted* to deal with that. I, too, had experienced tears of frustration in life, and I called upon the past to better the present. It was indeed a *present* for us both! When Elise later received the dog we'd selected for her, she was terribly disappointed.

She had her sights and heart set on another dog. To put it mildly, she was devastated. She cried so hard; I felt her pain. I knew the pain of

MY BOOSTER!

disappointment all too well and comforted her as best I could. At the end of each day, I relied on Booster to drain my emotional baggage and replace it with renewed vigor, as only he could do.

Meanwhile, back on campus, one of my classmates succumbed to the pressure. She explained that she had a low threshold of stress tolerance because of issues in her life. I had an exaggerated tolerance due to all I'd been through . . . a freaking war zone of an existence. I asked her to go with me for a drive. I drove, and she talked. She was in tears, and I listened. I stopped at a café, and we grabbed a soda. We embraced and held on for what seemed like an eternity. I opened up to her, and she opened up to me. Somehow, we merged our *selves* that day.

The next morning, I awoke with a mission in mind. I decided to take a photo of each of my classmates, and instructors, in action working with their dog. I wanted to present them with an 8x10 keepsake to remember the truly unique ADI experience and their dog. It's hard to say goodbye to your classmates but even harder to say goodbye to your dog! Really, your ADI dog becomes a fellow classmate and family member. We were all in it together and many students had a difficult time detaching. I was one of those. Though I had Booster in my life, I was going to miss my *little girl,* Tatiana, better known as Tattie. It was hard to leave her behind. I still have videos of my little girl, Tattie, and Booster jumping from bed to bed.

I took a slew of photos of my classmates, chose the most expressive poses, and had them enlarged. In addition, I had a wallet size made and inserted into a plastic photo keychain to which I attached a label that said, "Learning is the key." I looked forward to witnessing my classmates' reactions when I presented the gifts. For the first time in years, I'd made new friends . . . dog-loving friends . . . special friends. I was looking *forward* to something. I'd worried about going to California and being able to cope with a school experience, so I hadn't really looked forward to it with abandon. Giving gifts to my classmates was *One giant step for Davis: one giant leap for my life!* I remembered my Al-Anon teachings . . . serenity . . . *you only get to keep it in life by giving it away.*

One day in class, I heard that Bonnie had approached the State of California expressing her desire to found a college wherein students could learn about dogs. I often ask people to imagine Bonnie walking into some state office in the sere and yellow leaf of life. I can just hear the state employee asking, "May I help you, lady?"

"Yes, I want to found a college," Bonnie surely proffered.

"What kind of college do you want to start, lady?" would be the likely response.

She would explain, "It's going to be a college where people learn about dogs!"

I muse that they probably thought she was on medical marihuana before it was in vogue in California.

Bonnie literally mortgaged everything she ever worked for in life to accomplish her goal. Today, Bergin University of Canine Studies (BUCS) is the only accredited university in the world dedicated to teaching students Canine Life Sciences. Students have come from around the world, at great expense I might add, to learn from Bonnie at ADI and BUCS. Many of the students were older, seeking a more meaningful occupation, the import of which would make a significant difference in their country and the world. I inquired about entering the master's class as an old fart with physical and mental deficits.

My brother said it would be a horrendous waste of money. I'd learned long ago that if he said I shouldn't do something, then *I SHOULD* do it! He was the litmus test. He'd told me I shouldn't put mobile homes on my property, and it ended up granting me economic independence in life. When his negative thoughts erupted and spewed forth, I enrolled post-haste. I'd promised Booster that I'd share what he'd done for me with the world. I needed an education to keep my promise to Booster, regardless of what my brother thought. After all, Booster saved my life, not my brother! I contemplated attending the futuristic university, just as I had once contemplated suicide. My decision not to commit suicide enabled living. Contemplating furtherance of a canine-related education might enable *life* . . . a formerly unknown commodity.

After what seemed like an eternity, the summer seminar (a.k.a. boot camp) graduation day was rapidly approaching. Booster and I had befriended both man and dog, and before long, we'd have to part company. My brave new world would soon be coming to an end, and I'd have to return to my real world. I was transitioning from a world where I had lost my individuality and had no healthy relationships, similar to Adolph Huxley's *Brave New World*, in which he described the fear of losing individual identity in the science-oriented world to come. Suddenly saddened and simultaneously depressed, I was tired and found myself spending more of my time in bed with Booster than associating with my peers. Booster kept jumping up excitedly when he heard the other dogs frolicking outside with their humans teaching them a new skill set. I felt sorry for Booster; he got dealt a raw deal, having me for his human. I cried, slept, woke up, and repeated the process.

One day, my previously stressed-out classmate knocked on my door. My first inclination was to shoo her away. *Maybe she needs my support again*, I thought. I couldn't abandon her, just like I couldn't abandon Booster in the junkyard. I opened the door to a joyous smile and a hug. "Let's go celebrate," she bleated in my ear. "I'm so happy I completed the course, and I couldn't have done it without you. I want to take you out and have a few celebratory drinks. Let's bring Booster and Tatiana out for an afternoon on the town!" she said.

I reluctantly agreed, and within minutes, we took our canine dates to a local pub.

Booster and his golden honey behaved perfectly. My classmate instantly elevated my spirits, and we talked, talked, and talked some more. She said I was so strong, yet I felt so weak. She kept thanking me, and I kept telling her it was her strength from within that enabled her to complete the difficult course. In so many words, she turned the tables on me and said that I, too, have an inner strength that will get me through the days to come. After hours of intermingled melancholy and laughter, we left the pub and took the dogs for a walk. When we returned to the dorms, I told her goodnight, looked at Booster, and asked, "Ready?" He ran to my dorm door, jumped up, and hit the lever handle. The door swung open, and he jumped onto the bed in a celebratory fashion. Before long, we were both sound asleep.

Days later, I was on stage with Booster by my side. We were graduating! Our fellow graduates stood beside us with a mutual feeling of accomplishment. Together, we'd worked with dogs, disabled humans, at-risk teens, and others to acquire a specialized skill. Few non-participants could realize the amount of work and dedication invested at the ADI boot camp. We all paid to learn a skill to help the disabled live a better life. We felt proud. There was one attendee that rightfully should have felt prouder than others. That was my Booster! He'd broken the chains of codependency and got me motivated to attend the ADI seminar. I looked at my Booster smiling beside me. I looked into his eyes. He damn well knew what I was feeling.

Once we'd all received our diplomas and ADI graduate ID cards, we sat down on stage for the second part of the ceremony. The disabled attendees we'd worked with were going to be given their service dog. The dogs and their disabled partner graduate together. I wasn't ready for what I was about to witness. A young girl walked up on the stage with a beautiful Golden retriever that she, along with her dedicated family, had raised in their home for over a year. They were *puppy raisers* who sponsored service dogs in training until they were old enough to receive fulltime training at the university. The little girl looked at the war veteran on stage and said, "I love Missy. I walked her, and I used to talk to her . . . she's a great dog! She's really sweet. I want her to be yours now." The brave young child took the leash and pressed it into the veteran's war-torn hand. Within seconds, the auditorium was awash with tears, emotionally wracked by a tsunami of emotions. The killing machine of a man was crying profusely, effectively reduced to emotional rubble. I was shaking. As I write these words, there are tears of remembrance streaming down my cheeks.

Next, Elise was summoned upon the stage to receive her dog, Kate. She steered her power chair across the stage with a smile whose beam dulled that of the brightest star. This was the young woman who'd burst into tears the day she was so stressed out. She'd shared intimate details about her life as a paraplegic, living with a body that didn't work the way it should. Her mother had attended college with her so that she could earn her degree beside her fellow students. *What heroes*, I thought. I wished I'd had the strength, fortitude, and conviction that she had. Though Elise had legs that didn't work, she earned her wings that day. She soared!

When the graduation ceremony was over, I ran outside and hurriedly placed the 8x10s in their standing frames on the top of a table I'd purchased just for this purpose. As my classmates emerged with their friends and family, I told them that I had a little gift for them on the table. They walked up to the table and found their respective 8x10 photos and the accompanying photo keychain.

"So that's why you've been snapping all the pics lately," remarked one. "Davis, that's so cool," said another.

Then out of the corner of my eye, I saw Elise and her family coming my way. Elise had Kate do an "up" and grab the photo in its plastic frame and bring it to her. I walked up to her, picked up her hand, and it seemed like an eternity before I let it go. I had tears in my eyes and her mother approached me and thanked me for teaching her daughter and helping make it all possible.

When I first worked with Elise, I'd reached out to her dog Kate and shook the dog's paw. I then realized I hadn't shaken Elise's hand. I felt bad and reached out, not knowing how to shake a hand that can't "shake"! My hand soon squeezed her hand and my whole body was suddenly shaking! It became the best handshake I ever experienced in my life. Since that moment, I've never failed to reach out to a physically impaired person to shake a hand or make physical contact.

I looked at Elise, turned to her mom, and said, "Before the ADI experience, I'd never met or worked with a paraplegic. I didn't know how to approach such a person and would never have reached out to shake a hand that couldn't meet mine. Your daughter taught me far more than I taught her." I'd once placed Elise's legs in her wheelchair. Fate had forced her to expose her vulnerabilities and to trust others at an early age. Studies have shown that a service dog makes a disabled person more approachable. People more often remember the name of the dog than the name of the dog's disabled partner. I learned that firsthand at ADI. Rarely a day passes that I don't extrapolate something I joyfully learned at ADI.

Working with Elise taught me that there are others in this world who also struggle daily yet rise to the occasion. She unwittingly taught me that it's OK to trust, to be vulnerable, and to accept help from others. I remembered this when I reached out to physicians for physical and psychiatric help in the years to come. The very first day after meeting Elise, I somehow felt less different. If Elise could do it, then I damn well could too! I was confident that life would become a little easier for Elise with Kate by her side. I hoped the same bore true for me with Booster by *my* side.

At the end of the day, my leg throbbed terribly. I jumped into a bathtub, took the shower wand, and sprayed hot water on the affected area continuously for hours. I sent Booster to get me water from the fridge and bring my medicine bag. My classmates were gone, and I had no Tattie. We were alone now, just me and Booster. I often looked over the edge of the tub to reassure myself that he was still there. He never abandoned me. He never left my side on that bathroom floor. I shed a few tears that fell into a tub of contentment. Though I was in physical pain, I was struggling to handle the ever more disabling, torturous psychological pain. I reminded myself that if Elise could do it, so could I, especially with Booster by my side.

The next morning, I held Booster's service dog vest and said, "Dress," and he walked into it. Bonnie once explained that you dress yourself, and so should your dog. It's accountability. Everything at ADI was taught in the canine– human context. Getting dressed was yet another example. Yes, dogs can dress themselves. They can also help humans get dressed and change their lives forever in unimaginable ways. Just ask our veterans. In the US, more veterans die from suicide than battle; a far too-real ramification of post-traumatic stress disorder (PTSD). Almost every hour of the day, a veteran dies from suicide; twentytwo a day, to be exact. By having veterans with psychiatric challenges train dogs to assist physically impaired veterans, the effects of PTSD are diminished. The suicide rate goes down, and the veteran goes home!

It suddenly dawned on me that I, too, would be going home soon. Truthfully, I wasn't looking forward to it. I was, in fact, frightened. Even though I was newly emboldened, I was still fragile, having walked on eggshells for so long. Booster and I got into our rental car one last time. He jubilantly tugged open the door and jumped inside. I sauntered in, filled with trepidation. I was on autopilot until I turned the car in at the airport. Hours later, Booster and I were home. The cabin was empty and void. Judy Garland in *The Wizard of Oz* once said, "There's no place like home. There's no place like home." For *us*, no truer words were ever spoken. A home is what you make it, right? I'd turned my home into hell on earth. I now felt it might be possible to turn it into heaven on earth, with Booster's help.

In the days to come, I needed Booster to help me physically and emotionally. He balanced me when I couldn't touch my foot to the ground due to excruciatingly painful gout. He'd lie upon my leg when it throbbed mercilessly throughout the night. Booster opened the refrigerator and brought me water. He tugged the car door open and brought me my medicine bag. He turned light switches on at night when I had nightmares. When I had flashbacks of the knife coming at me, and I had a second to live, Booster responded to my screams. He'd jump up onto the bed and wake me. I instantly knew that I wasn't really being attacked . . . after all, there was a hundred-pound dog next to me!

Booster grounded me. Grounding is a way to calm an individual experiencing anxiety from a panic attack. The person is made aware of his surroundings. The resulting familiarity results in a sense of tranquility. He also let me know when someone was around. I always relied on Booster to enter my home, a hotel, and my car before I risked going inside.

Empowered by my ADI education, I started training Booster to become my service dog. Many people call a dog a *service dog* so that they can travel with their *pet*. I considered that to be selfish and abhorrent. I completed what I considered to be the finest service dog training course in the world. My instructor founded the service dog concept. Booster and I'd spent over a year together preparing for public access. The day would come when I'd take him in public without a trainer, fellow student, or friend accompanying me. I worried that I'd relapse into unacceptable and embarrassing behavior if confronted by ignorant humans shunning Booster.

The first time I took Booster into a public venue for training purposes, I was alone, and was scared as hell. I was no longer a student practicing under protected supervision or accompanied by peers. People stared at the man with the big dog. It was a department store in my hometown and two young kids started screaming when they saw Booster. It was as though a monster had landed from outer space. The manager of the photo shop told me to take the dog out. Rather than risk confrontation, I didn't say a word. I simply left. Booster had done absolutely nothing wrong. I thought, *If the children's parents had socialized their offspring as well as I'd socialized my Booster, the children wouldn't have reacted in such an asinine manner.* If I'd said anything, my PTSD would have kicked my ass, and I'd have instantly gone from calm to over the top.

Often, I couldn't remember the battles I'd fought. A friend who'd once accompanied me told me I wasn't the same person when the ramifications of PTSD kicked in. I had to learn to control myself in the face of human aggression. At the end of the day, I was quite depressed that I'd let Booster down. We failed to grow as a team. It took a lot of practice to successfully incorporate my ADI lessons into personal, real-life lessons. Over time, the number of confrontational episodes lessened, as did the severity of the events. Booster solicited attention in public venues the likes of which I'd grown accustomed to, and even started to appreciate. After all, he was my Booster!

After I eventually learned to control my emotions, I often had fun when I turned the tables on confrontational store employees who challenged me when entering a venue with Booster. Once in Flippin, Arkansas, I went into a major department store on Halloween. The employees were dressed in costume and sure enough confrontation greeted us upon entering the store. Zorro bounded over. "Hey, mister, we don't allow dogs in the store," screamed the young hero, saving humanity from the presence of a dog.

"He's a service dog," I explained to the pestering human, presuming he couldn't read it for himself though it was plastered all over Booster's vest.

"Is he a real service dog?" he implored.

MY BOOSTER!

I intentionally replied, just loudly enough to attract universal attention, "Hey, kid, he's a real service dog, but you ain't really Zorro, so would you please get the hellllll out of my way so I can shop and spend my money?"

The young man consequently tucked his tail between his legs and slinked away. By that time, a goofy-looking security guard approached the scene to also save the day!

"I need to speak to the manager," I explained. "Where's the manager?" I asked firmly.

Before he could answer me, the store manager bounded over like an overweight St. Bernard dog!

I explained, "Sir, this young man challenged me upon entering your store simply because I'm disabled, accompanied by a durable piece of medical equipment called a service dog. All eyes are upon me, and I'm the center of attention. I do not appreciate it, but really, it's not his fault . . . it's yours! You have signs proclaiming 'service animals welcome' because your company lost a huge lawsuit years ago, and it was part of the settlement. In fact, your store lost a subsequent service-dog-related lawsuit which required a dedicated number to be placed on all front doors, explaining, 'If problems call 1-800 . . .' Mr. Manager, you failed to properly train this young man and subsequently subjected your company to yet another potential lawsuit. today! You owe us both an apology."

After the manager muttered a feigned apology, people smiled, and I shopped unimpeded. I detested confrontation, relished solitude, and often feared for my safety when I was alone. Seemed like every time I let my protective force shield down, my head rejected the notion and found it totally unacceptable. Gratefully, I knew Booster would let me know whenever anyone approached and that provided solace. Really, I couldn't have stayed in my home if not for my Booster, my friend, my medicine, my rock!

After a while, it dawned on me one day that Booster had no canine companionship. He was totally happy with me being the center of his universe, but I wanted more out of life for him than I did for myself. One day, I got on the internet and looked for a Labrador puppy, a girlfriend for Booster. I saw the most incredible photograph of a dog resembling a Weimaraner, but it was a silver Labrador. Booster had fertilized my tenuous return to life, and I wanted to plant another seed. I decided to double down and write myself an additional canine prescription. Booster and I would both benefit!

I called my friend Charles and said, "Hey man it's a beautiful sunny day let's go to North Carolina."

"Huh!" came the response.

I giggled and explained that I thought my Booster was lonely. For once, I wanted to be *his* booster! Charles was always up for an adventure, and he loved Booster as if he were his own. He wholeheartedly agreed that Booster deserved a canine companion. The very next day, Booster, Chuck, and I jumped into my truck and headed out to North Carolina. We visited a Labrador breeder whose facility was absolutely breathtaking. In fact, it took your breath away every time you inhaled! If ever there was a puppy mill, this was it! I wasn't dismayed; rather, I was more determined than ever to rescue a canine soul. My need to rescue the wounded bird kicked in and I chose the neediest looking silver Labrador puppy. I named the silver girl Grecian, like the hair dye Grecian Formula . . . get the gray out!

While perusing the premises, I happened to see a beautiful white, block head female lab puppy. I inquired, and was told, "Her name's Penny, she's my favorite, but I'm willing to let her go." Every *THING* had a price in a puppy mill. Sure enough, I drove home with the two puppies. Penny remained Penny, as I couldn't strip her of the only dignity she had growing up in a puppy mill. My family was quite literally growing by leaps and bounds. I couldn't be any happier. That's an incredible statement coming from a tortured soul. I thought about the mythical character Tantalus, who reached out for fruits on trees and water, but the trees and water continually moved away. I felt as though I was a modern-day Tantalus; happiness sometimes seemed obtainable yet was always out of reach.

My life with a trio of Labradors blossomed. I continued to train Booster to perform service dog tasks and to behave properly in public, as I also aspired to do. All the while, he would romp and play with Penny and Grecian in his off time. Booster was happy. I learned to appreciate happiness from the dog I'd once shunned. Grecian and Penny were Booster's harem. Grecian was a diva, and Penny was absolutely the most

MY BOOSTER!

gorgeous block head Labrador bitch on the planet. She needed no jewelry as she was a jewel herself.

One day, I came home to find Booster and Grecian but no Penny. The trio was inseparable. Flags went up immediately. I searched for Penny, but she was nowhere to be found. I searched in panic for the entire day but never found Penny. The next day, Charles came over on his own accord. He called me in the afternoon and said, "Dave, I found Penny. She's dead in the woods."

I spontaneously erupted like a volcano spewing emotions. I drove to meet Charles and my dear Penny. She had a hole in her chest that looked like a bullet hole. Logically, I speculated that a local yokel might have shot her. I gathered Penny in my arms and took her to my veterinarian Dr. Beacham. I explained I needed to know what had happened to Penny. If there was a canine murderer in my neighborhood, I needed to know about it. Later that day, he called and said it wasn't a bullet wound. It was more like a puncture.

A few days later, I walked around my property and saw a large rock in the field. I had no clue where it'd come from. When I examined it, I saw a wire sticking out of the top. I suddenly realized that it was a remnant of the concrete slab that had once been part of my garage before Hurricane Katrina destroyed it. I'd bulldozed the slab and put the resulting rubble on the back of my pond dam to help fortify it. Penny must have run across the dam, slipped, and fallen upon the offending rock. She likely continued into the field with Booster and Grecian until the rock dislodged. She bled out farther down the road. I was crushed, just like the rocks on the pond dam.

I walked to the dam and looked at all the bric-a-brac. I suddenly realized that there were steel rods and shards of metal sticking out of the concrete rubble. It was a nightmare waiting to happen. I felt so stupid. In tears, I bent and broke every rod. I apologized to my departed Penny with every rod that broke away in my hand. They say time is a cure-all, but I've never forgotten Penny, though I've tried to do so to lessen my feelings of guilt. As a man who cried after killing a biting mosquito, shedding guilt is no easy task. I know Booster and Grecian missed Penny as much as I did.

Depression set in, but life went on. Later on, when out of town on a job site I passed time surfing the web. I started looking at lab puppies for sale on the internet. I saw a beautiful fox-red, female lab that was just gorgeous. I wasn't particularly attracted to red-headed bitches, but these pups were simply beautiful. I called the breeder and impulsively spent that week's paycheck on a new puppy. Then I picked up the phone and called my buddy Charles. "I need your help, as always. I just fell in love with a redhead bitch."

Charles didn't know how to respond to that. He simply said, "Oh really?"

I conveyed my intention to buy a fox-red Labrador puppy from a breeder in Michigan. Charles, being Charles, readily agreed to pick up my redhead, aptly named Scarlett, from the airport a week later.

When I arrived home, I immediately drove over to Charles' house and met Scarlett. She was red as red could be, a fox-red pointing lab who'd been bred to hunt and point at game, and thus had a lot of energy and exuberance. She was a piece of work, sure to keep the others on their toes. She had more energy than a Jack Russell Terrier. I then drove home and held Scarlett in my arms for an hour. I then introduced her to Booster. He growled and walked away. Grecian, on the other hand, instantly loved Scarlett and nurtured her. It reminded me of an Al-Anon newcomers meeting. The pack barked a welcome and the new puppy reacted with serenity yet expressed trepidation of the unknown. Within an hour's time, the newcomer had melded, and the family had grown. We were one. The pack needed me, and I needed them. The dynamics of duality kicked in and blossomed. In a short time, I often saw Booster sleeping with Scarlett. He was the dominant pack leader, sometimes grumpy but always loving. He reminded me of my father.

That night, I slept with all the "kids" on my bed. I was hugged, kissed, embraced, and loved without question or agenda. Soon the kids were snoring and I'm quite sure I was too. My kids were accepting, grateful, and appreciative. They were energetic, enthusiastic, and wanting to please for altruistic reasons. This was a learning curve for me. It was one of the greatest learning curves I've ever experienced in my life's journey on earth. We were as one.

Every day the pack would socialize in the 5-acre fenced-in field adjoining my cabin. They ran, jumped, and leaped into the pond. They rolled in the grass and chased birds. Often, they poked their heads under water chasing the fish that somehow always got away! My pack celebrated life with the energy of a Red Bull energy drink addict! Some days, I watched one of the dogs lick and clean the other's ears. I'd learned at ADI that this was called allogrooming. I witnessed the dogs communicate with one another. When Booster chased Penny, Scarlett would jump up and down and bark triumphantly. She was the pack cheerleader. Over the years, Scarlett and Grecian became inseparable. I often joked that they were my loving, lesbian diva couple.

They didn't want to fetch a ball and rarely wanted to swim. They just relished being themselves. At first, I was bummed that I wasn't going to be able to train them to perform service dog tasks. At least, it wouldn't be easy like it was with Booster. As time progressed, I learned from Grecian and Scarlett that it's OK to be one's *self*. We don't all march to the beat of the same drummer, or perform in the same way, or to the same degree as others. Scarlett loved herself and was always happy . . . barking like a cheerleader, egging the others on at every opportunity. She and Grecian shared a special undeniable bond. I learned to value love in whatever form it took. I also learned to be supportive and accepting of others and cheer them on. It took me a long time to learn to accept myself for who I am. I'm still learning to love myself. I have Scarlett and Grecian to thank for that. Al-Anon taught me that you only get to keep it (serenity) by giving it away. I wondered when Scarlett and Grecian had attended twelve-step meetings! Animals are rightfully concerned with survival, and life enhancing activities.

The ability to incorporate unconditional love into one's life seemed to work for dogs. We tap canine unconditional love to help humans live a better life. Perhaps we can learn from animals to incorporate it directly thereby allowing dogs to live less human-encumbered lives! Time will tell if man can ever lower his nose long enough to see the world for what it truly is and needs to be. Booster lowered my nose and opened my eyes. I strive to emulate him to this day. Learning to *give,* in order to maintain serenity, is a great gift. It would never have been possible if not for Booster. I only had my life because of him. I was destined to lose it and had attempted to do so. With Booster's divine intervention, I relished the opportunity to salvage my life in a beneficial manner as opposed to wasting it in a moment's slash of a knife. With my Booster's help, I wanted to help others salvage their lives, as Booster had done for me. I wasn't sure how to go about it, but I was learning.

CHAPTER 7
THAILAND BOUND

One day, I read that Bangkok, Thailand, was experiencing horrific flooding. Having experienced the ramifications of Hurricane Katrina, I knew firsthand the emotional toll it took on people's lives, especially for children. After a flood, nothing is left. I knew Booster had a special place in his heart for kids. I also knew that I'd worked very hard to train him for public access. On a whim, I decided to fly to Thailand, to take Booster to visit flood victims. He'd pulled me from an emotional abyss, and I knew he could similarly help others as only he knew how. Once again, I had more faith in Booster than in myself.

I researched the requisites for getting a canine into Thailand. Proper paperwork and inspections coming and going were required. It was all quite reasonable. Within a month, Booster and I boarded a plane bound for Bangkok via Tokyo, Japan. I withheld food and water from Booster, knowing that if nothing goes in, nothing comes out. It's quite simple, really. Over twenty-six hours of flight, I urinated frequently—old man syndrome. Booster never once urinated on the plane, though I was prepared with absorbent pee pads should the need arise.

About halfway to Tokyo, I gave Booster an ice chip to lick as I had learned in a training course, but he wouldn't lick it. I became worried that he was dehydrated. I expressed my concern to the flight attendant, who was a dog lover herself. She brought a bowl of water, and my Booster refused to drink. At that point, I started to enter panic mode. The kind lady then said, "Wait a minute. I'll be right back." She returned a few minutes later with a new bowl of water, and Booster drank every drop. With a warm smile, she explained that she'd cooked a steak and put the drippings into the water. She instantly morphed from flight attendant to superhero.

After a few minutes had elapsed, she returned with another bowl. She explained that she'd cut the steak up and asked if she could give it to Booster, who was drooling non-stop. I've never seen a dog devour something as quickly in my life. The steak was gone in a nanosecond. Our superhero returned yet again and explained that she felt guilty. I asked her how that was even possible as she'd saved the day! She said she felt guilty because Booster got a steak, and I did not. She then asked me how I'd like "mine" prepared. Booster and I were the only ones flying economy who got to eat steaks on the flight! "Imagine," as John Lennon once said!

We were seated in the plane's bulkhead adjacent to an incredibly kind gentleman. He invited *us* to join him in the flier lounge upon arrival in Tokyo. The waiting line to enter the lounge was long, and I was waiting for an attendant to help me gain access to a relief area for Booster, who was surely ready to pop at any moment. Suddenly, Booster's rear end went down, and I hurriedly opened my computer bag and threw the pee pad under his body. He let go with reckless abandon. People watched, but nobody overreacted. I disposed of the pad, and we entered the flier lounge without further ado.

Upon arrival in Bangkok, I took a private shuttle van to Tui's Place, a small boutique hotel in nearby Pattaya, Thailand. I'd arranged for Booster to stay with me at the hotel. It was the first time in the hotel's history that they'd allowed a dog to stay with a guest. I'd explained my mission when I booked the room, and the owner expressed his desire to help me in any way possible. Once settled in, I made calls to arrange therapy dog visits. By the end of the first day, many visits were scheduled. One was perhaps a little more special than the others. It was an orphanage located in Rayong, Thailand, about an hour away. Upon our arrival, I was informed that all the children had one thing in common: either they had AIDS or were HIV-positive. **Coincidentally**, I was going to be demonstrating Booster's talents to disabled young people, just as I had trained to do at ADI. I knew we were in the right place, and instantly, divinely aware of why we'd embarked upon this journey.

At first, the children were afraid of the hundred-pound dog. He demonstrated his abilities, won them over, and ended up surrounded by adoring, hugging fans. It was a joyous sight to behold. The children never took their eyes off Booster. They were mesmerized. He, in turn, never stopped wagging his tail in delight. Booster taught the children what a dog can do to help the disabled. He pulled me in a wheelchair, opened a refrigerator and brought them a bottle of water, took my socks off my feet, fetched my shoes, and more. Booster was quite the entertainer. I put my cap on his head sideways in gangster-like style and the kids went crazy.

The children taught me that day how to live life on life's terms and still be happy. I'd lived a compromised life I'd *chosen* to live, insidious as it was, whereas these children lived with a potential death sentence through no choice of their own. I learned a valuable life lesson from the children that day, one I've never forgotten. It was like the circle of education I'd been fortunate enough to participate in at ADI.

When it came time to leave, the children all wanted to hug Booster. The scene was beautifully chaotic; exuberant smiles and laughter filled the air. The center's photographer rapidly spun in myriad directions, capturing special images of Booster interacting with the children. It was so emotionally powerful that I was a man without words *and* a man without tears. There were no more tears left to be shed at that moment. Subconsciously, I resigned myself to the fact that life was livable on life's terms. I will never forget that visit or the effort the center put forward on our behalf.

At the end of the visit, Booster and I were exhausted yet exhilarated. The day was just so special that I couldn't process my thoughts. Booster fell asleep at my feet on the ride home. He'd made me so proud. The fine folks at the orphanage thanked me profusely, but the real thanks belonged to Booster. We arrived at Tui's Place, traipsed into the building, and up the stairwell to our second-story room. I fed Booster his customary kibble and fell asleep early without feeding my face. I needed to lose a few pounds, anyway. I wondered who would snore the loudest! We had another orphanage to visit the following day and we both needed rest.

The following morning, we ate a nice breakfast, and I summoned our van to take us to a foundation that was home to over 800 needy or disabled children. This was going to be a huge undertaking, and doubt eroded my confidence for a moment. I looked down, and Booster was smiling, reassuring me that he was up for the challenge. Letting him, or the children, down just wasn't an option, so I perked up, packed up, and jumped into the van when it pulled up to our hotel. When we arrived at the foundation, a sweet lady met us and explained she had someone she wanted us to meet.

We walked into a nearby meeting room, where we met another sweet lady who was blind and had a mesmerizing smile. She worked and lived at the facility and went on to say that she'd had a dog for many years at the facility, but it'd died, and she was too old to get another one. "It wouldn't be fair to the dog," she elaborated. "I heard there was a dog coming to visit, so I had a friend take me on his motorcycle to a pet store. I hope it's OK if I give your dog a toy."

I was in shock when she told me that. I could just see her at age eighty on the motorcycle, yet she could see nothing. She was blind from birth yet saw to it to bring Booster a present. She reached into her bag and presented Booster with a stuffed race car. She then gave him a squeaky ball. Booster grabbed the ball and squeak it did! He was so ecstatic. She then reached out and hugged the dog she'd longed to visit. My Higher Power was working overtime. I was instantly overwhelmed by what life had to offer. There was goodness in the world, after all.

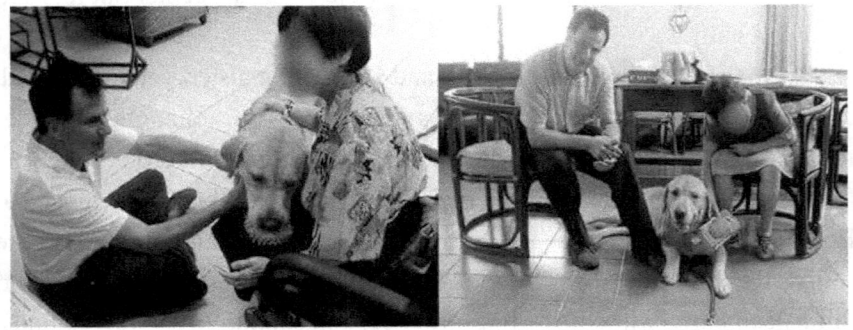

MY BOOSTER!

After a long, lovely visit, it was time to greet the children. We walked into a classroom and were suddenly awash with the sweetest of children. Their teachers assisted each one as they wanted to greet, touch, and hug my Booster . . . and  that day, he was *their* Booster too! These children were much younger than the ones we had met the day before, so it was more like a therapy dog visit than a service dog demonstration. That was fine with me, as I was still sore from the previous day's activities. I was amazed at how quickly the children accepted Booster as he sat, patiently enjoying their affection. *There's indeed beauty in simplicity*, I thought.

All good things eventually come to an end and the day to leave was at hand. The flight home was unremarkable. Once we got home, life settled down quickly. One day I drove to the post office and nonchalantly plucked a package notice slip out of my PO box. I opened the package, and all hell broke loose as if I'd been struck by a Russian nerve agent. I lost it like the day I'd accepted Booster into my life in Ajo. That package had surreptitiously been delivered by a Higher Power. The same power that had delivered Booster was at it again. Like water raging downhill from a mountaintop rooted in heaven above, tears gushed. It was another spiritual gift bestowed upon my lost soul.

In slow motion, as though frozen in time, I spent an hour in the post office looking at twenty of the most beautiful, love-inspired pages ever bestowed upon man. Written in a language of innocence, composed by deity pure minds, the documents weren't proofread, but rather, read like proof. All the symbols, words, and objects expressed love and gratitude, composed by souls of the purest gold. The authors surely weren't practiced, yet they wielded a homogenous mixture of earthly and heavenly wisdom. I was in the wrong venue for such a happening—I should have been atop a mountain in Nepal, holding another man's hand, one belonging to the Dalai Lama. I emotionally melted like a "Candle in the Wind," as alluded to in the Elton John song. Princess Diana would have donated tears afforded the honor to do so.

The director of the foundation in Rayong, Thailand, sent me drawings crafted by the Thai children that Booster had visited the month before. The drawings were of Booster, scripted with his name and words like "love" in English and Thai. I doubt any human alive today hasn't worried about dreaded cancer or infectious diseases, and I hurt for young souls facing the harsh realities of life at a no-longer innocent age. Once, I had been guilty of bankrupting on life, whereas these children, far braver than I, possessed such valiance and joie de vivre, living life on life's terms. The Thai children took the gift of crayons, turned them into love cannons, and fired back at me with ordnance possessing the efficacy of karma. This was a *Booster shot* of epic proportion.

LOVE . . .

. . .รัก Rạk

CHAPTER 8
FAMILY LIFE MINE THEIRS OURS

Meanwhile, back at the ranch, watching my pack interact was like watching circus performers under the big tent. Each dog's performance contributed uniqueness to the show and no two shows were alike! There was nothing in life I'd rather do than lie in the grass on a sunny day and play with my canine kids. I'd fire off tennis balls in machine-gun fashion, and they'd return moments later. I'd watch my canine kids paddle in the spring-fed pond. They loved the pond, but they also loved the water moccasins attracted to the water on a warm day. Every single dog had been bitten at one time or another by a poisonous snake and rushed to the animal emergency clinic that'd saved Booster's life. They'd always get bitten in the mouth because they snapped at the snake. The only dog that deviated from that plan of attack was Booster.

While walking in a field one day, Booster ran in front of me. He pounced on a water moccasin just as I was about to step on its head. He was bitten on the paw and took my "hit." I felt so guilty once again. Booster limped home, and off to the emergency clinic we went. Often, when a dog is bitten by a venomous snake, the immediate risk is swelling. A collar can choke a dog as his head swells. Luckily, I'd removed all my canine kids' collars long beforehand. A canine cop once told me he'd had a German Shepherd when he was in high school. He came home one day to see his beloved dog hanging, his collar stuck on a chain-link fence barb. The dog had jumped up and his collar got hooked on the fence. After I heard the sad story, I bought break-away collars that snap apart in such an event. Those collars lasted two days. The kids tugged at each other's collars, they snapped as designed, and ended up in the field. It was not a good investment!

MY BOOSTER!

As time marched on, I devoted myself more and more to my canine family members. The more time I put in, the more serenity and healing I derived. One evening, in boredom, I surfed the internet for Labrador stuff. I saw a wonderful photograph of a man in Tennessee with a wheelbarrow containing twelve white Labrador puppies for sale. I instantly fell in love, just like before. And, just like before, I dutifully called my buddy Charles and another road trip spawned. The next day, Booster, Charles, and I met the man and his wife. They introduced me to the female pup they'd chosen for me. She was one of twelve, born into what must have been a canine Catholic family. How else could one explain twelve offspring? I stared at the cutest of powder puffs. She was a fat fur ball bundle of joy that never stopped bouncing around.

I put her on the ground, and Booster wanted no part of it! He growled at the offender, just as he had when he'd first met Scarlett. I pulled him away. The fat little puppy was so cute. I held her in my arms, and she kissed me all over. She slimed me up and down and I loved it! I called her Puffy because she looked like a big, fat powder puff. My veterinarian later called her Piggy because she was so fat. Later in life, she retained her weight, though given far less food than her siblings. A study I read at BUCS attested to the fact that up to 25% of Labradors have a gene that makes them retain weight; I have no doubt that Puffy was among that select group. After driving around a bit, we headed home with Puffy asleep in my lap and Booster with his head on my thigh. His head warmed my leg, and it seemed to help the throbbing that I had grown to accept. When I returned home, I realized I had to go through the housebreaking ritual once again, but this time there was no interference or dominating counterproductive agent directing from the sidelines on a couch, no addict interference. Puffy quickly learned what was expected of her and soon bonded with Booster like an inseparable Siamese twin. It was such a beautiful sight to see them play together. Booster would play-growl with a ball in his mouth when Puffy approached him. He'd drop it just to tease her. As she went for the released ball, Booster would snatch it up, much to her chagrin! It was a sight to behold! Puffy's displeasure was Booster's delight!

Around two years later, Booster viewed Puffy from a different perspective. He adored her *heat*ed perfume and welcomed the opportunity to get to know her more intimately. They didn't seem to connect for some reason, and I don't mean psychologically. I sought veterinary advice, and Puffy was artificially inseminated. A litter of mini-Booster powder puffs was born. I sold the pups at a low price to loving homes, often to families whose dogs had died and whose children were grieving. As best they could, they'd explained the concept of death to children who were hurting. I was so proud to help the families comfort the hurting souls of their innocent children.

One family has stayed in touch over the years. I remember the morning I responded to an emotional SOS distress call. The gravity of the 911 call was immediate. Loving parents had recently taken their children to the veterinarian to put down their family dog. The parents enrolled their children in an advanced life lesson. They were at a loss how to handle their children's grief. Their children had lost their best friend, the only pet they'd ever known since birth. I hurt as much for the parents as the children. The parents were hurting for their children while simultaneously suffering from the loss of their dog. The canine–human bond has no age restriction. I've been told by many the only time they saw their father cry was the day they put the family dog down.

The patriarch of the family dictated the requirements needed to be met to consider a radical approach to heal the unique emotional dilemma. He threw a Hail Mary pass into the end zone of uncertainty. "We want a large, male Labrador puppy, white in color. I'm sure you don't have one, and you live 100 miles away." He wasn't prepared for my response.

MY BOOSTER!

"I've got just the puppy you're looking for." My Booster became "their" Booster that day, as he'd sired a litter of pups containing a beautiful, fat, white male puppy that I loved. I was tempted to keep him but knew it wouldn't be fair to the pup to deny him admission to a loving family, so I told the father I would meet the family halfway at a rest stop on the highway. I wouldn't enable anyone by doing all the work. After all, I was now an Al-Anoner!

Whether due to hope or helplessness, the father agreed to the deal. I met the most beautiful family the next day. The children were immaculately dressed and selflessly willing to meet a new pup. Like the Thai orphans, these were children dealing with life at an early age. They did a better job of coping than I did at an advanced age. Perhaps they could one day sit me down and tell me how they did it. I wanted to learn with open ears, no prejudice associated with age. I watched the children meet the pup. Hearts opened, canine and human, and a symbiotic, juvenile relationship was born. A shred of normalcy returned for grieving children and lost parents. The pack went home that day with optimism for a new beginning.

On yet another occasion, a day that will live in infamy, as President Roosevelt would have expressed it, I received a call that changed my life and validated my very existence. "Hello, my name's Joseph. I saw your ad in the newspaper . . . Labrador puppies for sale, father's a service dog.

"I'm nineteen years old. Last year I dove into a swimming pool and shattered a disk in my neck. I was instantly paralyzed. I was sure I would die, but someone happened to see me under the water, motionless. I'm a quadriplegic and have limited mobility. I can move my hand and fingertips a little. I went to Shepherd's Center in Atlanta, Georgia, for rehabilitation. They suggested I might be interested in getting a service dog. I told them I'd like to train my own. "Mister, do you think I could train my own service dog? I trained dogs in 4H when I was younger . . ."

After regaining my composure, I instantly felt that I had a responsibility to be honest yet encouraging. In my guarded response, I shared that I had almost taken my life once, and my dog Booster, had done things for me I couldn't do for myself. I further explained that Booster nor I had any training; it all resulted from the unique canine–human bond.

"Joseph," I prophesied, "I truly believe you can train your own service dog if you build the bond. I have puppies I know genetically will make the finest of service dogs."

Later that week, a van drove up to my cabin. A side door opened, and a wheelchair ramp was extended out. A handsome young man strapped to a power chair emerged. "Hi, I'm Joseph," came the greeting in a soft yet confident voice. I walked up, grasped his non-working hand, and shook it excitedly. I momentarily flashed back to my meeting Elise at ADI. "Hi, I'm Dave, and this is my Booster," I blurted out as I petted Booster on the head. "If you look over there, you'll see his pups, all excited to meet you!"

MY BOOSTER!

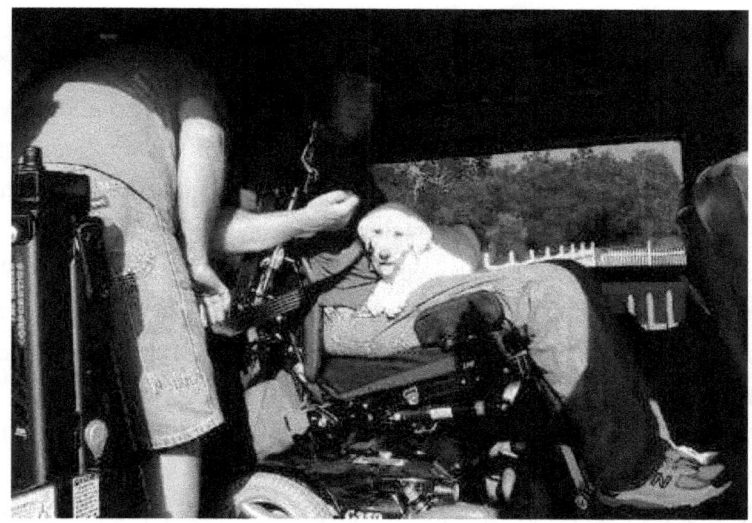

Joseph propelled his power chair toward the kennel and came to a stop. I opened the kennel door and took each puppy, one by one, and put each in Joseph's lap. After he had played with each puppy as best he could, I suggested he might want the large male puppy. He looked at me and firmly stated, "No, I want that female over there."

"Are you sure?"

He looked at me and said matter-of-factly, "Yes, I'm sure."

I'd never charged much for my canine kids, as money wasn't the object. I wanted to help people incorporate canine love into their families. So, I explained I was asking $350 per pup but I would accept $100 as I had so many puppies and I needed to find them homes. While I wanted to give him the puppy, pathos wasn't an option on this glorious day. Being disabled myself, I was keenly aware that people with disabilities are dependable, hardworking, and want to be selfreliant as possible. A disability doesn't disable pride. When I put the female puppy into Joseph's lap, he powered himself back to the van and told his uncle, "Pay the man!" He was all smiles as the two exited the driveway in route to a new beginning, for both the puppy and Joseph. I resolutely hugged Booster with reckless abandon, my soul refreshed.

About a year later, I got a call from Joseph and asked him how he was doing.

He enthusiastically blurted out, "Jill and I are doing great."

I then replied, "You got a girlfriend, man?"

His response was of astonishment. "NOOOO Dave, I named my dog Jill." When I asked why Jill, he explained that the first rehab specialist that worked with him at Shepherd's center was named Jill and he named his puppy in her honor! OMG, tears once again welled in my eyes when I heard those words of tribute. I then asked how Jill was doing and he said, "When I send Jill to the fridge to bring me water, she brings water. When I tell her Gatorade, she brings me Gatorade." My tears turned into torrents at the end of the line, though I did my best to hide my emotions. I told Joseph that what he'd accomplished was far greater than anything I'd ever done. I told him I profoundly meant what I'd just said.

At the conclusion of the call, I immediately called the newspaper in Joseph's hometown. I explained they had a hero in their midst. "A young quadriplegic got a Labrador puppy from me and trained his own service dog with his fingertips! Can you imagine such?" I asked. The following week, the story ran with Joseph in his power chair with Jill, and Booster and I proudly by his side. Joseph later explained that his friends called him after reading the article. He said they told him they "didn't know Jill was all that!" Joseph not only taught Jill, but a whole lot of humans as well. Education begets education once again!

On yet another future call, Joseph shared heartfelt thoughts.

"Dave, there were three major events in my life. I got Jill, got married, and had a daughter ... became a father."

"Wow! I didn't know you got married and had a child Joseph. Congratulations!

Truly, congratulations. You deserve that and a whole lot more."

"When I met you, I didn't want to live. I just laid in bed and let people dress me and days went by. I got Jill and had to do right by the puppy. I had to feed Jill, play with her, teach her. I had a newfound purpose to live."

My silence on the end of the line was more powerful than any verbal communication.

"Dave, the greatest life-changing event of the three was getting Jill."

I was at a loss for words. *How could I possibly formulate a response?* Wanna guess what happened next? A tsunami is a drought compared to the

MY BOOSTER!

glacier meltdown of my emotions at that instant. Was I becoming an emotional basket case, or were my emotional synapses on the mend? Life changed for both Joseph and me due to divine, miraculous canine intervention. There simply were no words forthcoming. When I recovered from the moment, I said, "I hope you don't tell your wife that Jill was the most important of the three events in your life." He replied, "Oh, she knows Dave."

Recently, I had the honor of taking Joseph, his wife, and their daughter out to dinner. It was an amazing reunion, twelve years hence Joseph showed me a video on his cell phone of Jill performing tasks. When Joseph said, "Flashlight," Jill searched and brought it. When he told her "Shoes," she returned with his shoes. The requests went on seemingly forever and Jill never missed a beat. I was totally amazed. I had never, ever, accomplished such in my life. It was a testimony to mutual love and canine–human bonding. I'd written about my experience meeting him and I asked his wife to please read it out loud at the dinner table. I wanted Joseph's permission to include it in my book and wanted to be sure everything was as it was supposed to be. As his wife was reading, tears started rolling down Joseph's cheeks. I saw myself in Joseph at that instant. Booster's progeny, Jill, had done for him what Booster had done for me.

Roughly two weeks later, I awoke to a text message that rocked my world. It was written by a valiant soul filled with overflowing love and gratitude. I couldn't handle it. After reading it, I sat on the floor and called all my dogs to my side. I held, petted, cried, squeezed, and cried some more. The Chernobyl disaster, when the USSR nuclear reactor melted down, paled in comparison. I hurt because I felt another's pain so acutely. And while I wanted to reach out and help, I felt powerless to do so. I read the beautiful text so many times that I almost had it memorized.

Hey Dave,

Just wanted to let you know that I had to have Jill put to sleep this afternoon. I can't talk about it, but I wanted to say thank you for providing me with a reason to get out of bed at first, and a best friend for the past 12 years. I truly couldn't have asked for a better companion. I always hoped I'd never see this day but here we are. Honestly when I got her, I didn't intend on out living her, but that damn dog made me get up every day and keep going. Now I have a wife and daughter that will keep me going. Words cannot convey how much that damn dog changed my life, and many others for that matter. She truly was the best friend through good times and bad, she's seen me at my worst and also at my best. I wouldn't be here had it not been for her. From the bottom of my heart, THANK YOU!

Joseph

Even the President of the United States found solace attributed to canine companionship. I once read that during the Cuban Missile Crisis, advice poured in from all directions. Research was conducted, but no perfect answer prevailed. As the white house hawks flocked to bomb the hell out of Cuba, young President Kennedy summoned the white house kennel master and requested that his dog be brought to his side.

Few humans have held life in their hands as Kennedy did that day. He resolutely petted his dog as Secretary of Defense McNamara exuded unparalleled wartime rhetoric. Kennedy didn't succumb to the venom any more than my pack did when confronted by water moccasins. At the end of the day, the young president, like a dove, took the softer approach. He ordered a blockade of Cuba, avoiding a response of unimaginable consequences. The Russians in Cuba had orders to retaliate in the event the US launched its bombs, and the Cubans had already amassed far more firepower than we were aware of. The argument can be made that the president made a calm decision that day due to the calming influence of his dog. As John Kennedy petted his dog, kinetic emotional energy flowed from his body, through his arms, and into a soul capable of processing emotions like a liver purifying the bloodstream.

Life-changing stories like these gave meaning to my life and validated breeding puppies for a higher purpose. The merriment associated with the cute puppies substantially added to my recovery and learning to live life

MY BOOSTER!

on life's terms. One morning, I awoke and realized that my litter of eight pups was down to two male pups. I'd taught them both to open the refrigerator door and perform service dog tasks. One was large, like Booster, the other smaller. When I swept the kitchen floor that day, the larger one was afraid of the broom. The smaller one was confident and bold. I decided to keep the smaller one and sold the larger to a family in Arkansas that rented a cottage from me. I saw that pup grow up into a beautiful large dog like Booster. I always second-guessed my decision that morning. *"Should I have kept the larger one and not sold it instead of opting to keep the smaller one?"* In honor of the program that had become my steward in life, I named the smaller pup Al-Anon and later took him to Al-Anon meetings, sometimes along with Booster. I often joked that I called him Al in public so as not to embarrass him. Really, I was proud of him, as he excelled in service dog tasks, and I was proud of the Al-Anon program.

As time went on, a storm of resentment fomented within my soul. I resented the fact that I couldn't go to my condo in Florida simply because I had a canine partner, one that had literally saved my life. It'd been over a year since I'd sent out a letter asking why pets weren't allowed on the property. Long story short, I found an attorney to help me gain access to my condo. I surely wouldn't go anywhere without Booster. I'd trained Booster for over a year, and there was no reason he couldn't accompany me.

The law was on my side, or so I thought. The law allowed service dogs and emotional support animals (ESA) to go into no-pets housing. I crawled up the mountain of the gods and properly asked permission at a blue-blood board meeting only to be rebuked by board lord Lucifer: "You know what? The last man who asked for permission to have a service dog moved!"

I later talked to that man, who had lived at my condo development for over twenty years. He had a bout with severe depression and asked for permission to have his prescribed service dog. When this was denied, he ended up moving away. He told me, "Lucifer publicly embarrassed me in front of my fellow condo owners. He knew how to do it so skillfully." Incredulous! Lucifer was more than just an exit cavity of the human body. He was a cancerous growth located therein.

After my lawyer formally asked for permission on my behalf to have my service dog, Booster, in my condo, I kept getting letters from the blue bloods' lawyers requesting more and more documents. I was asked for medical records with doctors' statements under sworn oath. This was before any mention of a potential lawsuit. It became obvious to all that the condo board was stalling. The board never said yes, but they never said no. They had the finest legal counsel paid with blue dollar bills and, no doubt, political connections. Before long, I was involved in a federal lawsuit. I was dragged over the heated coals of depositions and ridiculed. I burst into tears, to the relish of Lucifer, who showed up to witness my anguish. Lucifer wasn't part of the defending legal squad. He was simply there to add his kerosene to the fire, spewing arrogance with every motion of his body. I felt sorry for his kids, who had to live with such a father. I was sent to doctors to be psychologically dissected without anesthesia and made to feel like a piece of shit waiting to be flushed down life's toilet.

They sent me to one hired gun shrink, who interviewed me. Toward the end of the session, the jerk threatened, "Let's go ahead and bring your crack addict into the room." My heart stopped. I panicked, shook, and was instantly nauseated. The Hippocratic Oath he'd purportedly taken when he became a so-called doctor became the *hypocrite* oath. I was mentally paralyzed. That emotional atomic bomb set me back in life. I never again fully trusted mental health "unprofessionals." I needed all the help I could get but could no longer trust such humans. Booster would never have done such a horrid thing. My trust in canines was fortified and etched in granite.

My fears grew with each passing day, and I often held Booster in my arms for hours. I hurt, had been maimed by my codependency and the addicts I'd brought into my life. Why were seemingly educated people adding to the funeral pyre? It was as though the blue bloods were as afraid of a dog as I was of a drug addict with gun-toting friends who had a vendetta to settle. In callous, lawyerlike fashion, the blue blood beasts asked for medical records, photographs, my very DNA of existence. If they could have subpoenaed my heart valves, they would have done so without equivocation.

I'd sought the aid of health professionals, both physical and mental. Orthopedic specialists X-rayed my throbbing leg and determined that I had a hematoma from the camper that had fallen on my leg years ago. It had since calcified. It was obvious on an X-ray. The excruciating pain I often experienced when I touched my foot to the ground was something that wouldn't show up on an X-ray. It prevented me from walking and occurred at unanticipated times. Mental health doctors explained I had PTSD. To this day, when I drive at night, if the windshield fogs up, I shake and must pull over. My mind instantly flashes back to the hot night in Florida in my truck when my crack addict lunged at me with a knife. I'm still scared to enter my home, my car in a parking lot, or a hotel room without having my service dog venture in before I do.

I had concrete evidence of that which I already knew and had legitimate physical and mental disabilities. That wasn't enough, however, to turn cold, blue blood red and warm. There would never be enough. Empathy and understanding for another human being ceased to exist. The judge granted a summary judgment in what I considered to be the "connected" aristocracy's favor, stating that I'd only sought professional help once or twice before filing a lawsuit. The judge, who I never got a chance to appear before, questioned why I had waited to get help and only received a few treatments before requesting that Booster be allowed to enter the forbidden blue zone of my condo that I dutifully paid a mortgage on but could not use.

The noble prince of the IAADP, Ed Eames, told me he had been blind for years. Blind is blind. If he had gone to the doctor five years after losing his eyesight, it wouldn't mean that he hadn't been blind all along. I'd not been allowed to discuss my life. I'd been under total control of my addicts for decades, never allowed access to help. It was never, ever possible before. To have sought help would have compromised my life. A National Institute of Health statistic states that battered women more often die from leaving the abuser than from staying in the dysfunctional relationship. I totally understood that incredible finding.

The judge justified my inability to access a court of law because he found that the board never said no. That is true. The board's legal defense kept asking for more and more documents while craftily running up defense costs at $350 an hour. It's all about the money in the US, and Americans know it. The board would never in a million years say yes. So basically, I was left to start over and probably should have, but I had other ideas brewing. My lawyer should have, as he later acknowledged, made the board simply say yes or no. What really hurt, and still does, is that the decision effectively fed human growth hormones (HGH) to bullish condo board members nationwide as legal precedence. My lawyer later appealed, but the appeal met a similar fate. The bluebloods controlled all. Cuba's Fidel controlled the infidels and so did the equally "compassionate" condo board.

I've been told that my lawsuit cost over $100,000 to defend. The blue blood money worshippers didn't likely incur any portion of that expense because they had an errors and omissions liability policy that covered their liability for their decisions in the event they were sued. To my delight, they would have to answer affirmatively in the future when asked if they'd ever been sued before. Like a dog cleaning its anal sac, dragging its posterior across the floor, the bluebloods' shitty-ness left a trail. Their greatest error was being born into families that worshipped the dollar more than the animal–human bond. The lesson learned all boiled down, once again, to money, like most everything else in the United States.

The way I should have handled it was to ignore the bluebloods. They would have had to evict me and paid the cost to evict a homeowner. Insurance companies don't fund costs associated with evicting tenants. The condo association would have had to raise thousands of dollars by passing special property assessments. It's not about right or wrong in the US. It's about who has the money to win. I never got my day in court as an American living in the supposedly greatest democracy in the world. I could have accepted losing my court case (though I doubt I would have given the profundity of evidence that I had to present). What I still can't accept is not being given an opportunity to gain access to the courtroom. I was also at fault for obtaining a lawyer who had little disability law experience. Goliath had reared his powerful blue head. The powerful judge of OZ had spoken.

Sometime after the court decision, I called the condo rental office and reserved a rental. Many of the condo owners participated in a rental program in which the blue bloods used a sub-corporation to pimp out units to earn extra income. I called the *madam* in the office and reserved a unit, much to their chagrin. On judgment day, I arrived with young Al-Anon in my arms as a service dog in training. I had my service dog training

MY BOOSTER!

credentials, having been trained under the tutelage of *the* Dr. Bonita Bergin.

When I walked into a homeowners' meeting with Al-Anon, the blue bloods once again turned purple. A fat, Pillsbury Dough Boy of an ex-marine looked at me and said, "Don't we have a court ruling?" he haughtily bleated.

I said, "Yes, you do, but that concerns a disabled man and his service dog. I'm here today as a service dog trainer with a service dog puppy in training."

"Well," Pillsbury Porky said, "we may have to call the sheriff's department."

I proffered my cell phone and said, "Here, please use my phone. Are you going to call them, or am I?

"By the way, it's a misdemeanor offense in the State of Florida to interfere with the lawful training of a service dog in public venues."

Porky shut up and probably later went to lunch and pigged out.

On a previous occasion, when I'd gone to my condo without Booster, I'd gone to Blockbuster Video. I'd rented a few movies, and on my way out, I saw Porky. As I entered the security gate to the property the guard stopped me. He looked intently at, and in, my truck. I instantly knew something was amiss.

"Hi, what's up," I asked.

"Mr. Hawn do you have your dog with you?"

"No, but I sure wish I did. Why the search to the nth degree?"

"I got a call from Porky saying he saw you at the video store with your dog." "Yes, I sure was, and we looked for movies *together* inside the store as permitted by Federal law which *some* do not abide by.

"He warned me that you might try to sneak your dog onto the property." "Thanks for explaining. You're just doing your job, I understand."

When I got home, I sent Porky a thank you card in the mail that read, "Thanks for putting your life on hold to worry about mine . . . Much love, Booster."

After that, I tried to live a life and earn a living as best I could, even though I often experienced writhing pain in my leg and fear for unknown reasons when least expected. I started working as a bookkeeper for a man in my town who took a crew of guys to perform maintenance work in factories. Decked out with hard hat, safety glasses, and steel-toed boots, I took my camper to rural communities with Booster riding shotgun. I reluctantly left him in my camper until I returned home every day. I had to earn a living. Booster would just have to understand.

One day, when a six-week job was completed, I brought Booster onto the worksite. My boss, my friend, was embarrassed. I explained the ADA and asked him to trust me. Soon Charlie, the plant foreperson, arrived. I had Booster decked out with a hard hat, glasses, and a small lunch box hanging from his neck. Charlie smiled and said, "I can't wait to hear *this* story!" All the guys loved Booster.

I demonstrated his skills to folks who had never envisioned that a dog could do such things. He fetched water and brought my shoes. He took my socks off and turned light switches on. If I rolled my index finger to the right, he rolled to the right. When I rolled it to the left, Booster rolled to the left. He was soon part of the crew. He was a ***real working dog***! Booster soon became known as *Bootie*. The guys joked, "Dave done got him some bootie!" For the record, it was the best bootie I ever got! Booster helped me release more endorphins than *any bootie* else!

Booster attracted folks from all walks of life as a puppy and continued to do so with each passing day. I learned *something* from every soul he introduced me to. The dog I once shunned was *still* changing my life. He insidiously instilled his canine qualities in my soul. I didn't know it at the time, but that was the unequivocal reality of the day. He was, after all, my Booster. As time passed, I got more involved with life. I learned slowly to live life on life's terms. As one might imagine, it wasn't easy for me. I'd acquired canine-related street smarts, and now I realized I needed formal education.

MY BOOSTER!

CHAPTER 9
SELF-INVESTMENT BUCKS FOR BUCS

When it came to making large investments, my brother always chimed in. I indeed had an ace in the hole. Whenever he said I shouldn't invest in something, I immediately knew I should do it! He and my sister both threw nickels around like manhole covers! I couldn't imagine living my life like that. I pondered attending BUCS to get a master's degree in Canine Life Sciences. When I shared that with my brother, his response was, "What a waste of money." When he joked that I was "barking up the wrong tree," I instantly had my green light! I learned to invest in myself and with self-confidence. Booster taught me confidence and that there were no strangers in life. Scarlett cheered me on. Puffy taught me the value of loving for the pure and simple purpose of loving. Al-anon, the program and the dog, kept me focused on self! My Yugo life was becoming a Lamborghini smorgasbord. I revved my engine, released the brake pedal, smoked my tires, and spun out into the real world to get a glimpse of what many others took for granted.

I excelled forward in a g-force never before experienced and never looked back. The Al-Anon program taught me *if you let go of the past, it will let go of you.* My life's Lamborghini had no rearview mirror. I picked up the phone one morning and informed the university that I was packing my bags, and Booster and I would soon be there! Forthwith, I arranged for an au pair to live with my pack and made all the arrangements to better my life. While I'd have to travel to California for weeks at a time, several times a year, I knew I could handle it with Booster by my side.

When I ultimately stepped onto the university grounds, I felt like I'd returned to Oz. I felt like clicking my heels and saying, "There's no place like home, there's no place like home . . ." I'd lived in suburbia, inner-city New Orleans, Washington, DC, and a log cabin in the woods, yet I felt more at home, more accepted, more at ease at *my* university than anywhere on the planet. I experienced global warming among my classmates faster than Al Gore envisioned it environmentally. Bonnie Bergin, the university's president and Wizard of Oz, hugged me upon arrival. Yeah, yeah, I cried a little once again, but these were sweet tears. Bonnie had worked with the disabled all her life. She had a PhD in education and life itself. She was nonjudgmental. Just as I'd learned from my pack of dogs, she learned from her pack of students. Bonnie truly considered education a two-way street.

One day, there was dissention in the classroom. I had an emotional overload and walked out. A fellow student, an empathetic soul as most are in the BUCS family, ran to find Bonnie. I was walking away from the university, and I heard a faint voice calling, "Davis, you're walking in the wrong direction." I turned and saw none other than Bonnie herself. We found a green space and sat on the grass. Bonnie simply explained that the university needed me and Booster. The school was a premature baby on life support, fighting for accreditation, and the students were the umbilical cord. Bonnie explained she needed students who had life experience, who wanted to learn and better the lives of others. I instantly warmed, like a victim of shock encapsulated in a warm blanket. I was needed. Really?

Wanna guess if I cried? Wanna guess if I have tears in my eyes as I share these words? Many worldwide regard her with such high esteem. Oprah Winfrey once invited Bonnie to join her on stage, and subsequently presented her with a large check to help support her humanitarian work. At the outset of her career, Bonnie taught in Asia. One day, she saw a donkey helping a man with no legs to cross the street. She suddenly had an epiphany that dogs could contribute to the betterment of the disabled in more ways than just leading the blind. Much to the amazement of condescending peers, she founded the service dog concept. I'd be willing to bet that some of her friends at the time were like my brother . . . proselytizing what a waste of time, money, and resources her idea was.

In her sixties, Bonnie mortgaged everything she owned to found a college where people from around the world could obtain a comprehensive caninerelated education. Students were empowered to develop their unique thoughts, goals, and aspirations to make the world a better place.

She envisioned students learning to motivate dogs to help society in new and novel ways through the creation of canine programs. One such program was Paws for Purple Hearts, in which veterans with psychiatric issues train dogs to help other veterans with mobility impairments. Another program utilized dogs to smell and locate the mealy worms that were decimating the beloved California grape crops, adversely impacting the wine industry. The students, the programs they developed, and their contributions to society were diverse, yet predicated upon a common denominator of love and the wanton desire to utilize unique canine attributes to help others.

At BUCS, students can earn an associate degree, bachelor of arts, or master's degree. It's a liberal arts college offering a wide variety of courses, all canine-connected in some way. I learned about the history of dogs in society, the psychology of the dog, facts about various breeds, human disabilities, veterinary medicine, how to use the internet and research medical journals . . . and much, much more. I learned how dogs are trained to detect bombs, agricultural products, dropping blood sugar levels, impending seizures, and far more. Veterinary school is tunnel vision, an educational experience solely concentrated on learning to better the health of the dog and animals. In addition to existential learning, I was also given hands-on dog training lessons taught in a canine–human format. You don't hit a child and you don't hit a dog. You don't choke a child and you don't choke chain a dog! I was taught positive methodology at its best. Once, when I walked into the classroom, Bonnie grabbed my shirt sleeve and yanked on it so hard I almost fell over. The class shrieked with laughter. I thought she'd gone mad as I jumped away. Bonnie matter-of-factly turned to the class and asked, "Did you see what he did? Davis jumped back when I pulled on him. He had an incredulous, bewildered look in his eyes. Perhaps he was resentful?" She then summarily explained that when humans yank on a dog's leash, they often create the same scenario in the eyes of their adoring dogs. When you pull on the dog's leash, you are teaching your dog to resist you. Perhaps that's where the expression "don't yank my chain" comes from! Bonnie went on to say that she hoped to never see a dog's human yanking a leash, or employing a pronged choke collar on campus. Students were stunned, enlightened, and instantly aware that they were at the right venue to learn what they could learn nowhere else in the world. Bonnie pulled me that day . . . into her heart . . . as I experienced her hands-on passion to educate. She coupled passion with compassion as she partnered her love of dogs with an equal love for the disabled and her students.

One day, a child psychologist entered the classroom. He explained in detail how he worked with three-year-old children. I wondered what this was all about. After all, I was sitting in a classroom with twelve adults and none . . . may I repeat . . . none of us had kids! Even Bonnie herself had no offspring. No, it wasn't a rainbow festival, and no one was named Dorothy! It was more like an Essence Festival . . . the essence being that not all humans procreate for validation or other myriad reasons. Some studies suggest that single individuals, childless couples, or gay couples, have dogs in their family unit as substitutes for children. To me, children scream and dogs bark . . . there ain't a hell of a lot of difference. Some people grow up to be role models, whereas others become killers. I'm sure parents are devastated when their child takes another's life. I would feel the same if my dog did such.

Bonnie explained that a dog has a mental capacity equal to a three-year-old human. She told her students to work with the dogs using the psychological methodologies that worked for three-year-old children, write a paper relating our findings, and turn it in by morning. *How cool*, I thought!

At BUCS, dogs were partnered with students, socialized, and taught to perform service dog tasks. Eventually, the trained dogs would be placed with a disabled human at a BUCS graduation. One semester, Bonnie gave us an assignment to train our dog to do a complicated task or a compilation of several simple component tasks. I was the first student called upon to demonstrate what I had trained Booster to do, so I invited Bonnie and the class to join me on the second-story balcony. Then I looked at Booster and said, "Car." He ran down the steps, opened Bonnie's truck door, jumped inside, and found my medical bag. He then jumped out and ran to bring it to me. I told him, "Bring it to Bonnie." Booster looked into my eyes and followed them to Bonnie. He subsequently bypassed me and put the bag in Bonnie's hand. I'd introduced Booster to Bonnie's truck door during class breaks. He knew which vehicle to run to as it was the only one with a tug rope attached. I beamed with pride.

Back in the classroom, my fellow students were upset. I was accused of raising the bar. "Davis, how in the hell are we supposed to teach our dogs to do something like that . . . now Bonnie will expect the same from us!" I wasn't sure how to take that and simply stated, "Guys, you're here to learn. I'm sure you can do something far more intriguing." With Booster by my side, I was learning to believe anything was possible in life. I might even learn the task of living.

On yet another day, a day I will never forget, I entered the classroom and saw a fifty-something-year-old lady in a power wheelchair. My disabilities class instructor, Marcia, had invited her to lecture to our class. I'd previously learned at the ADI summer seminar to greet and communicate verbally and physically with severely disabled individuals. This lady fell into that category. She was my age, and it could well have been me. I walked over to her, put my hand on hers, and not so simply said hello. My fear of rejection was ever-present; however, I'd never encountered a disabled person's rejection. With each such new encounter, my self-esteem and self-worth escalated.

The lady had Lou Gehrig's disease, Amyotrophic Lateral Sclerosis (ALS). I'd learned in a previous disabilities class that it's a motor neuron disease that insidiously impairs the nervous system, ultimately resulting in death. As students, we took our seats with freedom of movement in a manner previously taken for granted. That was about to change . . . forever. May I please borrow a Kleenex from a reader at this juncture? Please?

The amazing lady lived nearby and propelled herself in her power wheelchair along the sidewalk to get to the BUCS campus. She entered the elevator on her own accord and arrived at the school promptly as scheduled. She had a projection screen attached to her power wheelchair. When she looked at an object on the screen, it spoke the name of the object. She shared with the class that she had once been a corporate, big-shot lawyer, plying her trade around the world. She was one of *those*. An inexperienced lawyer had failed me in my attempt to enable my Booster to live with me in my condo in Florida. An experienced condo lawyer had skewered me. I was a 360-degree victim of life and had little ability to

MY BOOSTER!

appreciate a drug dealer or a lawyer, as I often held both in the same contemptuous regard.

She explained how her disease had transformed her life. With my Hooverlike floodgates of emotion wide open, she shared the ramifications of her life's transformation. I was about to have another emotional breakdown as I understood transformation and accompanying helplessness, though in a far different context. Just as I was about to lose it, she explained she was GRATEFUL FOR HER DISEASE! I thought I'd been daydreaming. I didn't remember getting drunk before class and I wasn't a diabetic slipping into a euphoric, diabetic coma the likes of which I'd studied in class the day before. With honesty, wanting clarity, I raised my hand. I simply said, "Repeat . . . that . . . please." She gave the same answer.

I looked down at Booster and asked him to do an "up" and a "hug." He did as I asked and soon straddled my lap with reckless abandon. I squeezed Booster because I was in the eye of a storm and needed his help to get through it. My broken soul was preparing to truly encompass something I might not be ready for. My only defense was holding Booster in preparation for the pending volcanic eruption of emotional lava that surely did flow. I was allergic to emotion and was about to be bitten, subjected to impending shock. Life's water moccasin was about to inject its venom. I was mesmerized and simultaneously hypnotized. I didn't move, and neither did Booster. He sensed the energy flowing through my body and into his empathetic soul.

The selfless lady further explained that she'd been so busy in her corporate existence that she never really realized the important things in life. She'd zoomed through the years, earning money and recognition. She expressed resentment for missing out on the finer things in life due to loss of definition. Lou Gehrig's disease was the lighthouse to her soul, redefining the beacons in the later years of life. The gift she instantly bestowed was a spontaneous desire within me to find a way to be half as successful and accepting as she was. Like a TV infomercial, "Wait, and yes, there's more!" I had never really listened to the preacher when I went to church as a child. I had been in church because I had to be there. Now, however, I was at BUCS because I *wanted* to be there. I'd invested in an education, and by God, this time I really got one!

She went on to share that after all she'd been through in life, she currently lived on five pennies a day. Her story was as unique as her soul. She extrapolated upon her statement by saying that she lived on five pennies of *energy* a day. If she wiggled to get dressed, she would expend two of her daily five-penny allotment, and she would only have three pennies of energy left—not enough to go watch her grandson play baseball with his team in the park. She succumbed to being bathed and dressed to preserve the energy to go to the park.

From that moment forward, every time I saw a penny, I thought of this truly unique learning experience. A penny isn't worth a penny anymore, they say. I agree. It's priceless! I remembered the day I lost a "Penny" (my dog). I never got over it! It's funny how life works when you work it. "Keep coming back. It works if you work it, so work it 'cause you're worth it!" I'd often chanted hand in hand with strangers at countless twelve-step Al-Anon meetings. I suddenly got it like never before. After meeting the miraculous lady, I never saw money in the same light. In fact, I totally disrespected it and those who hoard it, simultaneously squandering what really matters in life. As I built my trailer park, I used every credit card, balance transfer, and coupon I could find to invest in my business. The conservative retired couple who'd run my business for me during turbulent times called credit cards "shovels" as, in their eyes, they would bury me in debt. I laughed at the conservatism as for me money meant little the minute I left the BUCS classroom that day. The heroic lady lecturer's success in finding what truly mattered in life lit a fire deep within me; unparalleled, spontaneous combustion. I pitied those who threw nickels like manhole covers rather than invest them in continued learning in some form to help the less fortunate. Then I took that learned philosophy, traveled the world, and learned to assimilate while respecting other cultures and appreciating *differentness*.

As a direct result, I devalued the import of money in my eyes and, because of that, I invested it in my business with reckless abandon. I used money like play money on a Monopoly board. I built a business and later sold it for millions of dollars, even though I'd once lived a week on a 5-

pound bag of potatoes when my government food stamp allotment ran out. By all rights, I, more than most, should have valued money and the security it affords. I have friends and family members who are conservative with money, aka tight with a buck. To some degree, they rely on structure in their life for guidance, a concept I never knew. I was always doing my own thing. I'd always needed freedom to explore, as the poet Robert Frost expressed in his poem "The Road Less Traveled," and rarely spent my time following others' dictates in a structured environment. Thus, I was fortunate to have Booster, Bonnie, and BUCS as mentors to teach me the important investments in life and to have confidence in one's own abilities to net the greatest return on investment (ROI). It was better to have learned late in life than to have never learned at all.

    A dog and a unique education changed my decade's long, devastating lifestyle. To this very minute, I am committed and eternally grateful to Bonnie Bergin and Bergin University of Canine Studies. I guess I'm like a disease they can't get rid of! I attend graduations and stay in contact. In my heart of hearts, I hope Bonnie sees me as a disease in the same light that the wonderous lady with ALS saw her disease. I see myself as a blood transfusion recipient of Bonnie Bergin's blood. All that she worked for in life was invested in BUCS and by proxy into me. I travel the world aspiring to do the one thing Bonnie expects of her students . . . the one thing . . . *change the world through utilization of the canine–human bond.* Let me simply, succinctly state that I love Bonnie and BUCS . . . for she and her/our university, along with my (other) *Booste*r, truly transformed my life forever. The life I once tried to end, I now cherish.

    Truthfully, I loved each and every class. It was amazing. I learned so much. BUCS provided a wide parameter education, not tunnel vision, and I was grateful for that. I credit my Booster with giving me my life back. It was a new beginning. Without ADI and BUCS, I would never have been able to grow my relationship with Booster nor develop the knowledge necessary for us both to realize our full potential

    Service dogs are taught to "settle" down when in public venues. Over time, my life also seemed to settle, but I did not. I still looked over my shoulders everywhere I went. I often searched for my addicts' names on the internet to know where they were and what they were up to. I never truly let go of my past. Fear was unmistakably tattooed upon my soul. Does a slave ever forget his past? I couldn't! I relied upon Booster to minimize fear in my life whenever possible. I continued to send him into my car and home before I entered. If I heard strange noises at night, I'd shake Booster and provocatively ask, "Who is it???!!!" Booster always perked up, looked around, sniffed the air, and resolutely listened. On the occasions he would bark, I became defensive and grabbed my phone, ready to dial 911 at the slightest provocation.

I always knew that someday I'd come home and find one of my addicts sleeping inside. History repeats itself. In the past, my addicts disappeared for a month at a time. I returned home some days to find one of my addicts, with an equally lost soul in tow, sleeping inside the cabin. If the door was locked, my addicts broke a window and went inside or slept in an old car in the yard. The only certainty in my life was uncertainty! Whenever I had the chance to leave my home, I felt safer in some ways, yet more fearful in others. I knew I wouldn't be subject to the ghosts of the past confronting me elsewhere; however, new ghosts lurked in the outside world.

The only solace I had was Booster. He was my one and only "nice" constant. I felt safe, loved, and more self-assured with him by my side. Booster accounted for 90% of my healthy social interaction. I really didn't want to make friends or risk meeting new humans and taking them into my confidence. With Booster by my side, I didn't have a choice as he attracted people, and conversation inevitably ensued.

CHAPTER 10
LIFE ON AN EVEN KEEL, BAHAMAS BOUND

One day, I decided to take a cruise to the Caribbean. I wasn't capable of going alone. I invited the retired couple that had managed my trailer park and, of course, I took Booster. From the moment we stood in line waiting to board the ship, all eyes were *onboard*. Passengers stared at Booster and the man with the dog. Every few steps I took, hands extended, and people asked, "Can I pet your dog?" With the calming effect of Booster by my side, I no longer caustically replied, "It's *may* I pet your dog," as I was now less miserable in life. I was grateful that Booster drew the attention away from me. I was in the limelight because I had a dog, but it was somehow different. The inquiries fired weren't directed toward me, but rather toward Booster. I began having what I called "safe conversations." People shared happy stories about their lives and their dogs.

The cruise line set up a nice box for Booster to deposit his used water and food in. It was filled with the most sterile, non-peeprovocative material on earth. The problem was he had no clue what the hell it was... playpen, work of art, or mini golf? Try as I might, I couldn't get him to use the box. I even went so far as to urinate on a pair of my socks and throw them into the mysterious box. Booster just looked at me as if to say, "Gee, this is getting more fun by the minute!" He tried to return them to me! I didn't want him to explode, nor did I want him to drop a bomb on the ship in front of everybody.

I used the internet and emailed a dog trainer, and she suggested taking a wooden match with a red head and putting into his rectum. Truthfully, I almost lit a match to touch it to my Booster's ass to get him to poop. I was so desperate. Months later, I learned some trainers at dog shows put the head of a red match into a dog's rectum because the sulfur works as a sort of enema, resulting in a bowel movement. My Booster almost went up in flames! No shit!

I went looking for real grass. I asked the florist onboard if she had any grass (no, not weed) or smelly flowers. She replied she didn't. I explained my dilemma, and she kindly shared, "In my country of Romania, I was a veterinarian." Yep, another **Coincidence**. In a heavy European accent, she further stated, "Takes deez dog up on zee top deck and put heez nose againss da wind and he will do his buzness." At 3 a.m., the drunks on the ship's walking track went to bed. At 6 a.m., the senior Olympian fast-walkers emerged to strut their stuff. I threaded the needle and took Booster onto the front of the top deck (canvas poop bag in hand) and put "heez nose to da wind." Within a minute, he peed on the pee pad enough to put out a wildfire. I then rinsed the area with a rag and water I'd brought along, and onward we went . . . but not for long. Booster's hips sank, and the most wonderful, voluminous pile of used dog food hit pee pad number two. Did I say *NUMBER 2*? Cuz it surely was! Booster relieved himself AND ME at the same time. Miracles never cease! He found the poop deck!

Before long, the ship docked in Freeport, Bahamas. We all went for a walk in Port Lucaya. A Bahamian gentleman greeted us and offered us a free meal if we agreed to tour a time-share. You know the drill. Our Bahamian friend took us to the Island Seas Resort. It was a *no-pets* resort, but I was assured I could tour with my service dog Booster. As we toured the property, Booster made friends. I had him pick up litter, do an "up" and drop the litter into trash bins around the property. Though they didn't offer Booster a job, they did offer to let him accompany me if I elected to buy a time-share week. I didn't buy a $12,000 week from the salesperson, but I did buy a week second-hand on eBay for a few hundred dollars. The

MY BOOSTER!

decision to attend the presentation changed my life. I had no way of knowing how life-changing that decision was. "Keep coming back. It works if you work it, so work it 'cause you're worth it!" the twelve-step Al-Anon theme song resonated within my psyche.

The following year, Booster and I returned to Island Seas Resort. Since I'd bought my membership online instead of from a salesperson, I wondered if the promise to allow my service dog on the property would be honored. We flew into Freeport, and the taxi driver took us to the resort with no issue at all. We walked into the resort's lobby, went to check in, and reminded them they'd said I could bring my service dog. The lady behind the counter said, "Mr. Hawn, do you remember when you demonstrated your dog's abilities to me and my children when you were here last year? My children took your newspaper story to their school and told their classmates that 'We met THE Booster; we met THE Booster!'" She then stated, "Of course, you and THE Booster are welcome here at Island Seas." I almost fainted!

The next day, the shuttle bus transported me and THE Booster to the straw market. I demonstrated Booster's ability in Port Lucaya as tourists and Bahamians alike looked on. I wanted to practice my newfound trust in humanity, which my Booster had introduced me to. A Bahamian police officer walked up to me and said, "Sir, I know what you're doing, but please be careful around the children." He was worried that the big dog might bite a child. I was happy to see a police officer taking his job seriously! I then booked a tour of the island with a local tour company. It was the same company the resort contracted with to provide the shuttle service to and from the port.

The following morning, the tour bus came to pick up the passengers for the tour. "No mannn, you can't bring tha dog on the bus mannn" the driver explained with the beautiful Bahamian accent.

"But sir, it's a service dog and I need him for medical reasons."

"No mannn, he might bite somebody, and we'd lose our insurance."

"All of your passengers are from my timeshare resort, and they've been playing with my service dog all week. May I speak to the owner of the company, pleaseeee?" The driver called his boss and politely handed me his phone. I explained to the boss, "I, too, own a business, and would never want you to lose you insurance, but I would like a few minutes of you time." He graciously agreed to listen.

"A service dog is, by proxy, part of the human body. If you are blind, the guide dog is your eyes. If you're deaf, the hearing dog is your ears. You can't separate your body parts in order to go on a tour bus. I am disabled, and as such, I am a minority. One of my heroes in life is Rosa Parks. Do you know who she was?"

"Of course, I know who Rosa was, mannnn."

"The United States has a dismal civil rights record. Minorities were made to ride in the back of the bus. Rosa was a minority because her skin color was black. Discrimination predicated upon the pigmentation of one's skin was ignorant, wrong, and disgusting. I, too, am a minority because I'm disabled. We wrongfully made a minority ride in the back of the bus because of their skin color. I'd gladly take Rosa's seat in the back of your bus. But what you just did to me today, sir, was far worse because you just kicked the minority off the bus all together! But I know you don't have a discriminatory bone in your body, sir. You're in the tourist business after all. This is a new concept and I understand that. I want to thank you from the bottom of my heart for taking time out of your busy workday to take my call and listen to my words."

"No problem, mannnn."

Before leaving the resort, I called a newspaper reporter and suggested that we do a story so I could thank Bahamians for being so hospitable. When the lady reporter arrived, I introduced Booster, and demonstrated some of his skills. She took plenty of photos and attentively listened to my words of gratitude. It was a joyous meeting. A few days later, the story appeared in *The Freeport News*, "Visitor Applauds Service Received." I was sure the fine folks at the resort would see it as Freeport is a relatively small community.

Months later, I searched "disabilities Bahamas" on the internet and learned there was a Disability Awareness Week in Nassau. I called lots of phone numbers to obtain information. I was instructed to call a lady by the name of Sheila Culmer. She was the president of the Bahamas National Council for Disabilities. I spoke with her after what seemed like a century of effort. She was a delightful Bahamian woman who explained that she'd been fighting for years to get a law passed for the disabled but had all but given up hope. She then graciously extended an invitation for my Booster and me to attend the Bahamas Disability Awareness Week activities. I called my blind friend, Toni Eames, and asked her to accompany me to the

Bahamas, and she accepted the invitation. Sheila arranged for me to appear on a television show called *Bahamas at Sunrise* as well as to speak at the Native Golden Gates Baptist Church in Nassau. I bought plane tickets to fly to Nassau with Booster, intending to visit my newly acquired time-share in Freeport shortly thereafter.

All airlines that fly to the US must accommodate service dogs coming and going. It comes under the jurisdiction of the US Department of Transportation. However, once you land in a foreign country, you're subject to the foreign airlines' discretion. This trip, I bought tickets to Nassau. I arranged for pet-friendly housing, but I had no idea how I was going to get to Freeport. Because I was used to living life on the edge, I decided to *wing* it and take each day as it came. I figured I could take a boat if I had to.

We arrived in Nassau and needed a taxi to take us to our resort. I was prepared to beg for access but wasn't called upon to do so. Our entourage was greeted by the resort manager, who explained that he and his wife waived the no-pet restriction so we could attend Disability Awareness Week. I looked into the man's eyes and thanked him for his kindness. He shook my hand, then reached out to pet Booster, who immediately rolled onto his back. Booster soon received a belly rub and visitors at the resort rushed to greet the friendly dog. My fear momentarily melted. With Booster by my side, I was Superman, with no kryptonite existing on the planet!

The next day, Booster, Toni, and I met Sheila. The resort arranged for a taxi to take us to the church. We were invited to demonstrate a service dog's abilities to a group of disabled Bahamians attending the Sunday service. Booster and I entered the church and met the preacher. I explained that I'd never addressed an audience before, and I had *issues*. He held my trembling hand and said, "All will be fine." A reassuring calmness entered my body, as though I was on a morphine pump. We were led to a front-row seat and shortly thereafter summoned upon the stage. Booster opened a refrigerator and brought water. He removed my socks from my feet and then brought me my shoes. I looked out over the audience, many of whom were disabled, and I saw frightened faces. I instantly thought, *In Bahamian culture, dogs are used for fighting, not helping the disabled.* The audience feared the 100-pound dog!

MY BOOSTER!

The preacher then asked me to speak to the audience. I was hesitant, but then a cloud of serenity enveloped my less-than-confident self, so I stood and walked to the podium with Booster. I needed his support. He was my rock. I was nothing without my Booster. As I surveyed the audience and witnessed eyes as big as saucers, my mouth involuntarily opened, and words started coming out.

"I see fear in this room this morning," I said. "I respect fear. I have dreams at night of a knife coming at me and I have a second to live. I experience flashbacks of an assault from a previous confrontation. I'm tired of almost dying night after night after night. I want you to know that I respect fear. I'm afraid of dreamed events that seem real but are not. You're afraid of a 100-pound dog and that's far more real. People fight dogs and a 100-pound dog can do some damage. I get it! But I want you to know that I read in your newspaper this morning that you've had over ninety murders in Nassau this year. None of them were committed by a dog! Perhaps you have more to fear from the person seated beside you in this room than the dog seated in front! It's man's inhumanity to man that you need to fear. My Booster will work for me for the rest of his life without a cent in payment."

The audience grew silent. Booster and I took our seats. I looked down, afraid to look out at the audience, not knowing how my words had been received. Surely, I'd offended people or said the wrong thing. Booster had made all the right moves, as he always did. I was the one who'd likely blown it! Instantly, I thought, *I've let my Booster down.* I felt sad as I kept petting Booster with uncontrollable zeal, my face focused down, awash with uncertainty.

The preacher walked up on the stage and took the podium. He started into a parable about a dog. He changed his planned sermon for the day. It was unrehearsed and genuine as could be. I marveled at the parable that unfolded spontaneously as a result of Booster's impact upon the faithful. I thought about how Booster had never let me down. He, too, was faithful, and I renewed my vow that day to share him with the world and never let *him* down. Hercules had his hair, and I had my Booster! His confidence and love insidiously permeated my life. I was changing, but I didn't realize it. My disdain for my fellow man lessened. I hadn't blown it after all. My words, partnered with Booster's talents, had been well received. Yep, teared up in the moment.

When the church service was over, Booster and I walked outside. Toni and her guide dog Keebler joined us for a short walk to stretch our legs. Within moments, we were greeted by well-wishers from the local US embassy. "That was really something" said officials who came to greet me and Booster.

"We love everything about the Bahamas except for the fact that they don't have a disability law for the disabled," I said.

We'll never get a disability law passed in our country; we've been trying for years" chimed Sheila rather pessimistically.

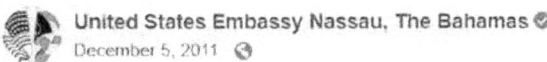

United States Embassy Nassau, The Bahamas
December 5, 2011

On December 2, the Bahamas National Council for Disability (BNCD) launched activities in observance of its annual Disability Awareness Week with a one-day forum focused on "Independent Living and Legislation for All". The theme for the week of activities is "Differently Able" with the focus of raising awareness of disability issues, addressing the fundamental rights of persons with disabilities, and the integration of the disabled into the social, political, economic and cultural areas of society.

NASSAU.USEMBASSY.GOV
2011 Press Releases | Embassy of the United States Nassau, Bahamas

On December 2, The Bahamas National Council for Disability (BNCD) launched activities in observance of its annual Disability Awareness Week with a one-day forum

MY BOOSTER!

focused on "independent Living and Legislation for All." The theme for the week of activities is "differently Able" with the focus of raising awareness of disability issues, addressing the fundamental rights of persons with disabilities, and the integration of the disabled into the social, political, economic, and cultural areas of society. (Bahamas Local, December 6, 2011.)

Later in the day, we feasted on wonderful clam chowder, fried conch, and conch salad. I held off on ordering lobster, saved it for dinner! I loved seafood and the Bahamas, a perfect combo platter! After a meal fit for a king, we took a taxi to a local radio station, where Sheila and I talked about how a dog can help a disabled individual. I made note of the fact that service dogs become handicapped if they don't have public access. "Why does a blind man have to beg to go into a restaurant or a hotel with a guide dog?" I asked. Though I wasn't blind, and Booster wasn't a guide dog, I kept reminding myself that this society was unfamiliar with service dogs. It was a foreign concept in a foreign country. Most people have heard of guide dogs for the blind, and that familiarity was useful in introducing the service dog concept.

The following day, Sheila arranged for us to appear on a television show. I was so excited, yet Booster was far more used to celebrity status than I was, so he simply snoozed with his girlfriend, Minnie Mouse. We later visited Bahamian schools. The first school we visited was  the Stapledon School for the Mentally Disabled. I was impressed when I saw a newspaper reporter in attendance, accompanied by a cameraman. I asked the children how many were afraid of my 100-pound Booster. Almost all the children's hands shot to the sky. I asked if anybody had a dog at home, and several raised their hands. I asked if anyone let their dog come inside, and a few hands went up. The Bahamian children, like the adults in the church the day before, were apprehensive when it came to associating with the 100-pound dog. I then stepped back and let Booster do his thing.

The children's enthusiasm was hard to contain. It was heartwarming. Booster showed the children how a dog can change human lives. I then explained that rather than fight a dog, perhaps you might want to train it to help your elderly grandmother. Booster performed as teachers and the press looked on. At the end of the school visit, I asked the children a question. I immediately thought, *What a stupid question!* I commenced beating myself up for asking it. *What a dumb ass question!* I had asked frightened children, "Does anyone want to pet Booster?"

The children ceremoniously screamed YES, and hands reached for the sky in unison. They jumped up and ran to Booster's side. I suddenly felt claustrophobic, as I could no longer see daylight. I was surrounded by children, all reaching out to love my Booster with resounding adoration. During the commotion that ensued, one child looked at me and innocently asked, "Why are you crying?" "Because you guys are so special," I said. It was just a single solitary tear, but I couldn't hide it from the astute student. My emotions had once again surfaced. At that moment, I knew I was changing internally. After thanking the children and the teachers for having invited us, we returned to the resort.

The following day, we visited another school. The children were impeccably dressed, the norm in the Bahamas. They were focused on Booster and listened attentively to what I shared. The questions posed were truly remarkable for children of that age group. One young man was reluctant to pet Booster, but the teacher sensed that he wanted to. Perhaps his peers might have teased him about it? The teacher accompanied him to Booster's side. She petted Booster several times, then nonchalantly joined her hand with his and they petted Booster simultaneously. The canine-human bond was perfected. That teacher was indeed put on this earth to teach. I was

MY BOOSTER!

simply in awe. The teachers said that they could use a dog like Booster at their school, a facility dog.

The next day, we went to the airport, filled with doubt that I was going to be permitted to bring Booster into the plane. My backup plan was to take a ferry boat. Booster and I waited in an area as far away from the airline staff as possible. True to form, Booster made friends while waiting. When the time came to board the plane, I presented my boarding pass, grabbed Booster's leash, and bum-rushed the plane. I sat in my seat with Booster at my feet. The flight attendants were beside themselves. The pilot came down the aisle to talk to me. He explained they don't fly dogs inside their aircraft. I asked him, "You wouldn't fly a blind man with a guide dog?"

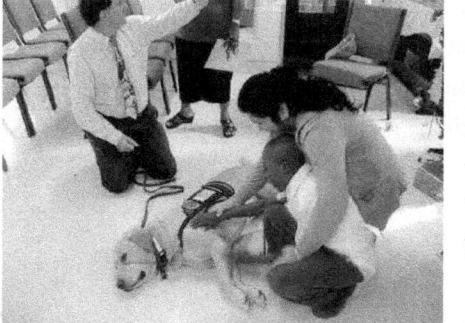

He said, "I know you aren't blind, sir."

I countered, "Yes, sir, you are correct, but my specially trained service dog balances me when my legs don't work. He helps me with mobility and helps ameliorate the horrific effects of PTSD."

The benevolent captain looked into my eyes and said, "Sir, I will fly you, but I ask that you send me information and documentation so I can explain to my supervisors why I elected to fly you today." He wrote down his personal email and that of his superior on a napkin and handed it to me.

Booster's aura was working full force. I was proud. I was trusted because my Booster acted professionally and was trusted! When I returned home, I sent the captain and his supervisor information about service dogs/assistance dogs. I also sent them copies of newspaper stories in the Bahamas featuring school children hugging Booster with Bahamian teachers singing his praises, stating that they could use such dogs in their schools. I included clips from television appearances we'd made.

A newspaper story appeared in Nassau within days of the captain's brave decision to help a fellow human being. At first, I was a little embarrassed that I had caused such a fuss in a country that had treated me so kindly. Bahamians didn't deserve to be inconvenienced by my problems in life. Sheila later called me, congratulating me on making history in the Bahamas. I didn't know what the hell to think. I looked at Booster, smiling up at me. It was as if he said, "I told you all humans aren't bad. They may not be as good as a dog, but they ain't all bad!"

Bahamasair eases travel policy curb on animals who help people with disabilities

Traveller with Post Traumatic Stress allowed to take dog on board

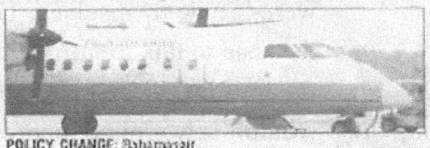

Seven years later, a different Bahamasair pilot challenged my ability to fly with a service dog. It was rather embarrassing, but I was used to dealing with those who were out to save the day by protecting the world from a service dog. I instructed the pilot to refer to the Bahamasair operations manual and to call the magnificent captain who'd helped me in the past. The hassle pursued, but ultimately, we took our seat on the plane. What happened next defied belief!

When I returned home, I did what I always did, documented, and created dialogue in hopes of keeping such transgressions from reoccurring. I wrote an email to the CEO of Bahamasair, evidencing the value of service dogs in society. In addition, I explained I was disrespected and treated wrongly simply because I was assisted by a durable piece of medical equipment, my specially trained service dog. "Once the passengers were seated," I explained, "The captain exited the cockpit with his cell phone in hand. He took several pictures of us as ALL my fellow passengers looked on in disbelief. I was photographed like a criminal being booked for a crime in a jail house! My service dog and I acted with the utmost professionalism, whereas your captain did not . . . and in violation of the Bahamasair's operations manual."

The following year, I returned to Island Seas with Toni, her blind friend Lyn, and their guide dogs. Toni and Lyn wanted to go on the tour bus ... the same bus that had denied my boarding the previous year. We bought tickets. When the bus arrived the following day, we were beckoned aboard. I hesitated and said "No, please call the business owner and ask his permission for us to board the bus." I spoke to him on the phone, and he succinctly said, "You are welcome on the bus, mannnn." I looked at Booster, and once again, tears flowed. The business owner's response resonated deep within me. No guns were ever pulled, and no harsh words were spoken. Mutual respect, coupled with education, resulted in a treasured response. Our trip to the Bahamas was a life-changing event. I wasn't happy among human beings in my own country, much less foreigners in a land other than my own. I was insecure. Rather than hit a time clock and work beside others, I'd most often elected to work alone. I harbored more prejudice against myself for *being* different than I did others for *looking* different.

Going to the Bahamas and speaking publicly was a great challenge. In fact, it was one of the *greatest* challenges I had faced in my life. As it turned out, it was a *great* experience, as I learned so much from the acceptance I received from the Bahamian people. I was accepted, and they listened to little ole me share what I'd learned from a dog. In a culture where the love of dogs is often secondary to an interest in fighting them, I'd connected. I returned to my Freeport time-share every year. I always called the newspaper, visited a school, or wrote letters to the prime ministers.

Months later, I was chatting with my friend Peggy on the phone and mentioned I had a time-share credit. I needed to use it or lose it. It was a beautiful time of year, and Peggy suggested we go somewhere in New England. We found a unit available in Vermont and booked it a few days later. I told Peggy that there was a very special place called Dog Mountain we needed to visit while we were there. Peggy, being Peggy, joyfully smiled and clapped her hands and said, "How cool," before I even had a chance to explain its personal significance.

Dog Mountain was the inspirational creation of renowned artist Stephen Huneck, whose life very much paralleled my own. Stephen was lying in a hospital bed in a coma when his wife, Gwen, visited him with one of his beloved dogs. Stephen awoke from the coma and credited his dog for the metamorphosis. He subsequently devoted his artistic talents to painting dogs, depicting spirituality and virtue. Some of his paintings depicted dogs as canine angels with wings. My Booster was similarly a canine angel.

Stephen also built an amazing dog chapel where dogs could come and go through a doggie door in the middle of the night, if need be. I had visited the chapel years before when Booster was just a pup. Even at an early age, Booster confronted death, so a dog chapel was especially meaningful for a dog whose life was saved on numerous occasions. Peggy and I somberly read many of the notes written by dog lovers across the country who sought to immortalize memories of their cherished canine family members.

MY BOOSTER!

Unfortunately, Stephen succumbed to depression and committed suicide when the economy took a nosedive, and he couldn't pay the employees he loved so dearly.

With Peggy's support, I later did a newspaper interview with his wife, Gwen, and explained that I would have surely followed in Stephens's footsteps if not for Booster's impact on my life. She smiled and said, "Stephen was always painting (isolated) and rarely got to experience the love of those who admired him and his work." Tears spontaneously flowed from my eyes because I might have suffered the same fate "but for" the intervention of a dog that I initially shunned. I, too, had wanted to isolate, but Booster kept pulling me back to people; isolating just wasn't an option. As my relationship with Booster blossomed, so did my life for years to come, though it took me years to see the import. To this very day, I live life based upon the principles bestowed upon me by my Booster.

CHAPTER 11
PROJECT FIDELITY

For two years, I travelled to California to attend my BUCS master's classes. Bonnie asked us to keep an open mind with regard to what we'd do for a master's thesis. I was a Bonnie disciple if ever there was, but I knew what I was going to do for my thesis. I wanted to prove that a codependent woman suffering from battered woman's syndrome could transfer her codependency from the batterer to a dog. A batterer's feigned love would succumb to the unconditional love of a dog. I envisioned taking battered women from their shelter to visit other likely battered souls, equally hypervigilant and seemingly helpless. The women could perform self-sustaining service work by rescuing shelter dogs whose lives were also at risk due to no fault of their own. I planned to teach the women to train the dogs to become therapy dogs. The dynamic duos would enter hospitals, nursing homes, and hospices to learn what true appreciation and unconditional love really were. That's what Booster had done for me. It was personal.

One night, while living in the dorms, I happened to read a magazine article entitled "Havana Dreaming." It alluded to the day that Americans could once again travel to Cuba. Cubans were trapped on an island, unable to travel freely, but so were Americans with respect to traveling to Cuba! Booster had been the impetus for my mental freedom and the ability to communicate with others. I laughed out loud as I thought, *I bet a dog could do what humans could not . . . promote communication leading to fidelity.* I knew in my heart if anyone could promote love, harmony, and fidelity, it was a dog, particularly Booster.

That night, I didn't experience a dream in the form of a life-threatening PTSD-related flashback. I dreamed I was in Havana, surrounded by strangers wanting to pet Booster. I was in Havana demonstrating Booster's skills to an educated populace that'd never seen a dog perform tasks that could help the disabled. That dream became an obsession. The

MY BOOSTER!

time for my thesis project selection was rapidly approaching, and I was as conflicted as the relationship between the United States and Cuba. How do you choose between helping people suffering the same torment you once suffered and bringing together two populations suffering a decades-old, dysfunctional disconnect?

I knew Booster was the one diplomat in the world that could uniquely project fidelity between the United States and Cuba. Booster had an uncanny ambassadorial ability to meet, greet, and convey unquestioned, unconditional love. He was the canine equivalent of John Lennon. With reckless abandon of established norms, I decided to board the *Starship Booster* and go where "no man has "'successfully' gone before" . . . at least not a regular US citizen (for decades). I was determined to go to Cuba to project fidelity. My thesis proffered dogs are a social lubricant, a social bridge that can bring people together in a unique way. With that thought in mind, I conceptualized Project Fidelity to project fidelity between two countries that couldn't seem to do just that, despite many ambassadorial attempts made by many humans from around the world.

It was about this time, ***coincidentally***, that President Obama encouraged people-to-people cultural exchanges between US and Cuban citizens. If you were conducting research in conjunction with an accredited US university, coupled with the likelihood that your findings would be published, you'd be given the almighty permission to travel as a free man to visit other humans living 90 miles away in Cuba. A problem still existed, however. BUCS was not yet accredited. It was a fledgling university seeking government accreditation. *Why do humans make seemingly easy things so damn complicated?* I pondered. Dogs encounter obstacles but go about their lives unfettered by their canine cohorts. They form packs as they know there's strength in numbers. Humans often distance themselves from others, and even take provocative postures, often resulting in war.

I put my Project Fidelity idea on hold while I pursued my studies. My thoughts returned to helping battered women overcome codependency with canine help. It was fruitless to go into Cuba to proclaim the merits of a dog if I couldn't publish my findings without subjecting myself to prosecution. According to *Wikipedia*, the US already had the highest incarceration rate in the world. I didn't want to further that statistic! I remained in my quagmire until Bonnie made an announcement in the classroom one day. With a radiant smile, she explained BUCS had passed the requirements to be certified by ACIS, an accrediting council for US colleges. **Coincidentally** . . . BUCS had earned accreditation at the perfect time. Accreditation enabled me to start working wholeheartedly on Project Fidelity. I was being stalked by My Higher Power! *Perhaps My Higher Power is also codependent?* I mused.

I took my recently acquired BUCS research skills and delved in head-over-heels to learn anything I could about Cuba. Specifically, I wanted to ascertain what was required to get a dog, my Booster, into Cuba. Not so surprising, a country that didn't allow its citizens access to the internet or the freedom to travel published little information on the web. There was a lot of history regarding the Cuban Missile Crisis, but little else. I did learn, however, that Canadians traveled to Cuba and extolled its virtues. I subsequently read a story about a Canadian man who ventured into Cuba about the time his beloved dog Spanky died. He felt sorry for the Cuban street dogs and wanted to help. He founded the Spanky Project and arranged for Canadian veterinarians and donations to flow into Havana, and also started a spay and neuter program that became very successful.

I called the man one day, and he gave me the name of his associate, a Canadian lady living in Havana who was working as a translator. He also gave me the name of a man I could trust to be my guide. Before long, I was communicating with them both via email. The communication was limited by file size. Often, my emails were rejected for odd reasons. I didn't know if it was due to a primitive Cuban internet or Cuban Big Brother listening in. I didn't care; all I wanted to do was give Booster an opportunity to do his thing.

MY BOOSTER!

I had an inherent fear of communism. When I was in first grade, I was taught to jump under a desk in the event the Cubans launched the missiles. If I was in the hallway when the civil defense siren sounded, I was to lie in the corner, clasp my hands behind my neck and look away from the flash. Students across America were taught to *duck and cover* to protect themselves from nuclear fallout. Years later, I listened to Walter Cronkite on the nightly news, "Another 100 American boys lost their lives to the North Vietnamese 'communists.'" I was afraid to enter Cuba, was advised by my therapist not to go, yet I trusted Booster with his therapeutic and ambassadorial abilities.

I couldn't find any information about bringing a dog *into* Cuba. Rescue groups had gotten dogs out. There was no US embassy to call to glean information. I called the Cuban Interest Section in Washington, DC, and was never able to get through to a human. I later called the New York Cuban Mission and talked to a secretary who had a friend who worked at the Interest Section. She gave me a private number to call. When I spoke to her friend, she said she knew a diplomat who always traveled with his dog to Cuba. That spark ignited my hope within. I sent her a fruit basket and a warm thank you.

Eventually, I had enough information to design my project, but I'd all but given up on getting Booster into Cuba. I'd researched in vain for months as to how to get a dog into Cuba, whether the Cuban authorities would allow it, and what was required, if it was possible. I found a Canadian tour company, Cuba Educational Tours, that took Americans into Cuba. They wouldn't allow a dog on their Cuban tour bus, nor would Cuban hotels allow a dog inside. I was screwed, hurting, and bummed out to the max. I signed up for the tour and decided to go without Booster and just conduct research on canine-related topics in Cuba. After all, I needed to graduate, come hell or high water.

A few days before my departure date, I got a call from a classmate, Dailyah. We were both misunderstood souls. We'd become BUCS buddies who spoke as we pleased, whether the other person wanted to hear what each had to say or not. I often criticized Dailyah, and she'd criticize me. It was an honest dialogue between educated adults who were open-minded and appreciated intimate respect without injecting emotional drama. Dailyah's words that night resonate to this very day. "Dave, you're a great guy, but you're nothing without your dog!" I was shocked to hear that, but she was right! It was all about Booster, not about me. If I had to swim to Cuba with Booster on my back, I was now determined to do so.

That night, after being told I was nothing without Booster, I remembered the Bahamasair pilot who'd helped me. His email address was still on file, and it popped up when prompted. I emailed the captain, not knowing if the email address was still valid. I gingerly asked if it might be possible for Bahamasair to assist me with my university project entitled Project Fidelity. Bahamians value education and send their children to school in clean uniforms dressed in pride. I suspected that the fine captain might be sympathetic and supportive. He knew firsthand my devotion to Booster and education, as well as my appreciation for the acceptance I had been afforded by Bahamian society.

I got an email response from the captain the very next day, stating, "Bahamasair was familiar with you and Booster; therefore, I don't envision a problem flying with us." What a compliment I thought … a testimony to Booster's professionalism!" The email further stated, "If you decide to fly Bahamasair, please advise me of the date and time, and I will advise my colleagues, to ensure that you and Booster have a delightful experience with us." He didn't say "you and your dog." He remembered Booster's name!

I was in absolute awe. I was simply a man with a dog. In shock, I once again exuded crocodile tears. It was overwhelming. The love of a classmate, a pilot from another country, Canadians, and Cubans all culminated to help me pursue my passion in life. *What the hell was going on?* I wondered. *Why do people need drugs to get high when life provides such a stimulus?* I finished reading the captain's email and somehow kept it together long enough to compose an email to the Cuban guide who had offered to help us. I asked him if he, his wife, and their son would babysit my most valuable possession in life, my Booster. He empathetically offered to help and agreed. He explained his wife would take a week off from work and take care of Booster. Yeah, yeah, tears streamed. *Why is this goodness happening for undeserving me?* I asked myself over and over. *Is there **really** such a thing as goodness and karma?*

MY BOOSTER!

I rapidly focused on getting ready to fly into the unknown. I bought canine antibiotics for the Cuban dogs, and crates to house them. As I was limited to two suitcases, I used the brain My Higher Power (MHP) had given me and packed in layers. Starting with a large suitcase, I put half of a large crate inside, with half of a smaller case inside it, and then packed half of my clothes and necessities therein. I repeated the process with suitcase number two.

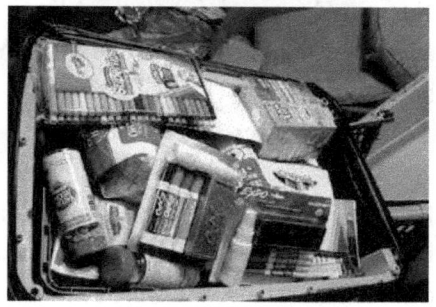

The following morning, I contacted my veterinarian and rushed to his office to have Booster inspected. He completed the United States Department of Agriculture APHIS form for the international transportation of an animal. I also had him complete a separate pet travel form I'd found on the internet that was written in Spanish. I assembled copies of shot records, not knowing if the Cubans would accept US papers or the fact that Booster had received the three-year rabies vaccination. Many countries, and even my local county, required *annual* rabies vaccinations to be administered. In a BUCS veterinary class, I learned that the one-year rabies vaccine was identical to the three-year rabies vaccine. It was a matter of the one-year versus three-year warranty period. Requiring annual rabies vaccinations was unnecessarily overdosing dogs. I read that a veterinary school was conducting a study that hoped to prove that the rabies vaccine afforded protection for seven years.

The more documentation I had, the better. If the Cuban authorities wouldn't allow Booster into Cuba, I would fly home. I was extremely worried, however, that they might quarantine Booster in who knew what facilities, or possibly destroy him if there wasn't a quarantine option available. True to form, I started to beat myself up. *Why would I risk my*

Booster's life to facilitate my education? Am I a monster for even allowing such a possibility to transpire? What did Booster do to deserve such a horrible human partner? I jumped through the hoops of mental mind fields, expecting to explode at any moment. Under pressure, both real and perceived, I hurt. I hurt. I hurt. I was on my mental roller coaster once again, seeing the sky one moment and hell the next. Adrenaline and hurt coexisted.

Three days later, I boarded a plane bound for Cuba via Miami, then Nassau. Upon arriving at the Miami airport, a smiling Bahamasair ticket agent saw me, walked up, and said, "You must be Mr. Hawn, and this must be Booster."

"Yes, ma'am, he is my Booster," I responded.

We soon boarded the plane and shortly thereafter landed in Nassau. During our two-hour layover, Booster entertained children and adults alike in the waiting room. We were instructed to board the plane first and sit in our assigned seats. We were seated in the middle of the plane, sequestered. The seats in the front of us and behind were blocked off to protect fellow passengers from a dog and to limit possible complaints.

Once we were seated, passengers started walking down the aisle. People clamored to sit next to the friendly yellow Labrador that was by now their personal friend. Booster smiled and his tail wagged. The flight attendants, possibly frightened by the sight of a hundred-pound dog, were simply too astonished for words. I could read their body language, "People want to sit *next* to a *dog*?"

The plane took off with hands petting Booster. Seat belts restrained passengers' waists, but their adoring hands were out of control. I was so happy. DID YOU HEAR THAT? I WAS HAPPY! My happiness was soon joined with tears. Once again, Booster brought me to tears. We landed in Havana at José Martí International Airport. When I entered the airport, an official-looking man in a blue coat and tie grabbed my arm and said, "Come with me."

I started shaking uncontrollably. *I'm going to jail! What will become of Booster when they haul me off?* The aficionado looked at me and said calmly, in almost unintelligible English, "I'm the airport veterinarian, and I must inspect your dog. I have a yellow Labrador, too!" He could never know how frightened I was. I started petting Booster until I thought he'd lose his hair from friction. Booster subsequently drained my emotions as only he could do. I was so frightened.

A victim of my emotions and trapped in Cuba, I had no US agency to turn to for help and no therapist to rely on. I simply had my Booster. Inexplicably, they say that death often becomes a pleasurable experience. Somehow, I, too, was enveloped in a protective cloud of serenity as Booster behaved as he always did; he wasn't fazed. His projected calmness reassured me that my emotions were out of balance, out of check with reality. Friendly smiles radiated throughout the airport as heads turned to see the yellow dog carrying the universally known Mickey Mouse. I lived through what I was sure would be an end-of-life experience.

The veterinarian then explained that he had a private practice and surreptitiously invited me to visit him at his clinic in his home. He gave me his contact information and asked me not to tell anyone about his wonderful invitation. Cubans feared government repercussions from interactions with foreigners, especially Americans. He then offered to help me roll my two suitcases through customs. I looked at him and said, "I have *drugs* in my luggage." He was mortified. But then I explained that I'd brought jugs of antibiotics for dogs as a donation to the Spanky Project, but I now wanted him to have half of them. He escorted me through customs and pointed to the suitcase that didn't have drugs. It was opened and inspected but the other was not! **Coincidence?** More likely *Connections* I assumed, but never learned.

I left the terminal and wasn't prepared for what came next. There were hundreds of Cubans surrounding the airport. I was in the midst of a riot, or so I thought. The truth of the matter was that they were waiting for cargo shipments from relatives in the US to arrive. They were desperate for goods. It was a first of many lessons learned in Cuba.

A man walked up suddenly, introduced himself, and said in broken English, "You must be Dave. Hello, Booster!" He took us to meet the Cuban family who would host Booster. We walked in, and Booster begged for attention, which he promptly received. He then walked over to the man's wife, with Mickey Mouse in his mouth, and ingratiated himself. Their teenage son then entered the room, a bit apprehensive to greet the

100-pound yellow monster. He didn't say a word. Booster took charge and brought Mickey to greet the young man. Before long, the boy was throwing a ball, and Booster kept bringing it back. The canine– human cold war ended as fast as it started! I took photos but was politely asked not to share them due to fear of reprisals, a quickly developing theme.

Plans were made, I petted and hugged Booster goodbye, and then my taxi driver took me to my hotel. I met the tour director and fellow tour mates. Most were female teachers from California. That night, I learned that the hotel bartender earned more in one night from tourist tips than a doctor did in a month! We were all listening to a pianist play the grand piano. Suddenly, he began playing a new song, "Imagine," by John Lennon. I instantly thought about my BUCS thesis paper that sported a photo of Booster dressed as John Lennon with the subscript *imagine*. I nearly fainted. My Higher Power was still stalking me as though checking off a score card!

At the end of the evening, I entered the elevator to go up to my room. It was old fashioned, like almost everything else in Cuba. The man pulled the metal wire gate shut and rotated a wheel to encourage the old elevator to rise. He welcomed me in English. I'd learned Cubans weren't allowed to talk to tourists in the streets. If they were caught doing so, they risked going to jail. I asked the man if I gave him a list of questions pertaining to dogs, would he answer them? I went up to my room, composed a list, then returned for another elevator ride. The following night, he stopped the elevator between floors and answered all my questions. He handed me a piece of paper with notes scribbled across the page. It was done in secret. I was truly in a communist-controlled population where severe consequences were meted out for those who dared to question or violate the established norm.

The next day, the Canadian tour company reviewed our itinerary. They'd put together an impressive array of things to see in Havana. The first day, we visited the Latin American School of Medicine. I met the administrator, the head doctor, and explained that we often use dogs as a form of medicine in the United States. I further explained that we train mentally impacted veterans to train dogs for physically disabled veterans, and the suicide rate plummets. The United States is known for being an aggressive country, perhaps especially in Cuba. The doctor immediately looked into my

MY BOOSTER!

eyes and said, "Better dogs than bullets!" I've never forgotten his words of wisdom, with which I wholeheartedly agree.

Then we visited a large, urban hydroponic gardening project sponsored by a German organization, which the Cubans called Organopónicos. We were taught about growing healthy food. Most of my tour mates walked aimlessly through the fields, taking in the flora and fauna. As others walked the fields, I elected to visit my canine comrades. Myriad dogs and puppies languished in the fields, much like the Cuban workers stymied by a social system that rarely rewarded productivity. The farm workers loved the farm dogs and had given them all names.

I wondered if any of the Russians from years before had brought their dogs to Cuba. I learned at BUCS that researchers tracked the historical migration of man across continents based on DNA samples taken from modern-day canines. As humans traveled, they took their dogs with them.

The Cuban workers cooked us a meal that was the best I had in Cuba. The food in Cuba sucks as the government doesn't have money to do a lot of importing, and much of the farmland lay idle due to lack of incentive to work it. Are you going to pull a plow in 100-degree heat for $25 a month? I learned quite quickly from a Cuban, "The government pretends to pay us, and we pretend to work." At the end of the meal, we all left a little token of appreciation in the form of a tip. Most of the ladies left one Cuban Convertible Peso (CUC), but I chose to leave two. Suddenly, a hand reached out as one lady rescinded her tip and said, "You don't want to spoil it by leaving too much . . . they'll expect more in the future." I was pissed, as I wanted to show gratitude as *I* knew how to do it, not based upon someone else's preconceived notion. So, I reached into my pocket and put another CUC on the table! She stood up and marched off. She couldn't take away from zero!

Years before, when the Russians withdrew their support from Cuba, it was called the Special Period. Life was difficult. Cubans often had no electricity. Many ate animals to survive. I was told that cats were eaten more often than dogs. That day at the garden represented the second *special*  *period* when a life-sustaining gratuity was selfishly rescinded. Canines just don't act like that; they exude unconditional love, not selfishness. I was glad I was traveling accompanied by a dog! My life had once been below zero, but I learned confidence day in and day out with Booster by my side. I handled confrontation that day for the first time in a long while. I was changing, for the better!

Days later, I was in the country town of Vinales and saw an elderly dog suffering on the sidewalk in the hot Cuban sun. A Cuban man helped me chase and capture the helpless *lassie* while his friend brought a cart to carry us to the local veterinarian. The old gal's mange-laden body didn't have a hair on it. She had no coat to protect her from the sun's heat. I'd learned at BUCS that a dog's coat can help cool a dog. Many dog owners shave their dogs during the summer, thinking they're making the dog cooler when they're in fact exacerbating the situation by exposing the dog's skin to the sun's rays. I paid for treatment and left the beautiful dog in loving hands that promised to take care of her.

That night, I decided to go to Chinatown for a bite to eat. Booster jumped into the taxi with Mickey Mouse in his mouth. When we arrived, Booster jumped out, and we walked to a nice Chinese restaurant where we enjoyed a surprisingly good meal. Street performers dressed up as a dragon performed a well-practiced routine. An hour into my meal, I heard a man crying out, "Señor, Señor." I looked up and saw my former taxi driver carrying Mickey. He leaned over and gave it to my (grateful) Booster, who grabbed it instantly. He explained that he'd gotten home, saw the toy I'd left in his taxi, and came looking for me all over Chinatown!

MY BOOSTER!

Cubans don't have money for gas. That man drove an hour round trip to return Booster's toy. I stood up and gave him a hug. I took out my wallet and gave him $20! I'm sure my selfish tourmate would have had a heart attack right then and there if she'd seen that! It was another restorative moment in my life. Perhaps, for some, it was nothing; for me, it was everything. It meant the world to me. This man chose to project fidelity in the most simple, purest manner. I was ready to go home. The benevolent taxi driver took Booster to his foster home. I hugged Booster goodnight, then the driver took me to my hotel. He refused to take any additional money.

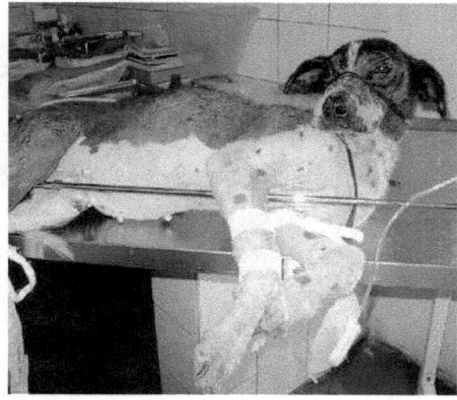

Later that night, I walked down the main tourist street in Havana. It was like Bourbon Street in New Orleans.

The frightened young man said, "Tell him you know my family."

I explained that we'd met when I was demonstrating my dog in the street the day before. The callous cop wrote his name in a book and sent him packing. I was the most scared I'd ever been in my life. It was worse than the airport scenario. Grateful for my freedom, I walked back to my hotel. A Canadian man explained that I was never in any danger of arrest. It was the Cuban. They aren't allowed to talk to tourists on the street. If they're caught doing so, their name goes into a book. If caught doing it again, they're subject to going to jail! I had no idea. I'd walked that street during the day with Booster and performed service dog tasks many times, and large crowds often surrounded us. It resembled a large drug deal going down.

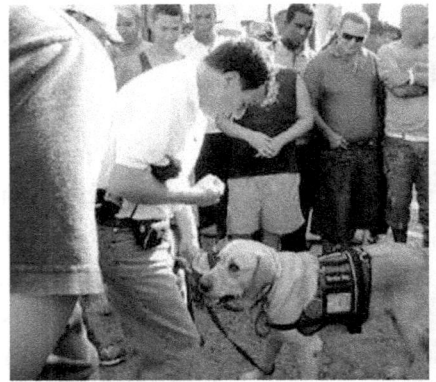
Crowds gathered; the police watched.

We were being watched.

That bitch scares me. She's hairless!

Hemingway looks my way!

A few blocks away, I started talking to a college student. Within minutes, a Cuban police officer came up to me and asked, "So, how do you know him?"

MY BOOSTER!

*My Booster witnessed Cuban dogs networking.
One watched while the other got the goods.*

I knew damn well the Cuban police and government officials had seen the throngs of Cubans talk to me with Booster in the street. There was always a police officer or five on any given corner. I postulated that the Cuban officials allowed the Cubans to talk to me in the street because it was a form of education. I worried they might think I was trying to promote democracy by using a dog as a ploy. At that time, a US contractor was convicted and lay in prison for allegedly trying to promote democracy by bringing in satellite phones piece by piece. He was purportedly part of a US government operation. I am quite sure I was on the radar screen and given enough rope to hang myself.

Cubans are smart. They probably knew I was coming before I got there. No one would ever need to question *my* conviction . . . or would they? I went to Havana with purity of soul and purpose. I went like a dog . . . living in the here and now . . . not burdened by the past, nor plotting for the future. I often went to bed at night shaking, wondering if the communist government would get the wrong idea and imprison me. I shook and called out for Booster in the middle of the night to comfort me, but he wasn't there! It was dreadful. My therapist was right. I wasn't prepared to handle it. I just couldn't cope! *Oh, MHP help me*, I prayed!

With the help of the Canadian Spanky Project, I was introduced to the president of AINCI, the Cuban group for the blind. He asked, "Why might you want a guide dog when you can use a cane?"

"Fifty percent of the benefit of a guide dog," I explained, "is the emotional component, the comfort provided by a dog.

"Sir, I'm sure you've cried in darkness in your bed at night. I've often done the same. The cane doesn't lick you on the face, lie on your chest, and let you know life will be OK. You're never alone in darkness when you have a best friend, conveying unconditional love, by your side 24/7."

He got it!

The next day, I visited the president and vice president of ACLAFIM for the disabled. After talking for an hour, Booster demonstrated some of his tasks and they were amazed. The Canadian lady translator said, "Dave, have Booster remove his socks from his feet for him." I thought, *Great. If anything goes wrong, I might not be able to leave the island. Why did she volunteer without asking me?* I was on the spot, and I looked at Booster and said, "Socks/tug." My Booster ran to the man, removed his socks, and gave them to him! I half-jokingly counted the man's toes to establish the fact that they  were all accounted for. My unsubstantiated fear would prevent Booster

MY BOOSTER!

from growing or using the skill set at which he was so adept. I had to work more on reducing my fear.

We later visited the president of Aniplant, the organization for the plants and animals of Cuba. The president, Nora Garcia, expressed a desire to have such a dog when she retired. With her help, I ended up on *LIVE* Cuban television and *LIVE* radio! They had good things to say about the American and his doctor dog (a term used by a Cuban child in the street who met Booster).

One day, I found myself with time on my hands. I remembered the Cuban airport veterinarian and decided to call him. He invited me to meet him for lunch in a park. I went, got Booster, and took a taxi to the park, as instructed. Then I sat on a bench, waiting for my new veterinarian friend to arrive. Beside me sat the bronze statue of a man who looked familiar. *Bam!* I was struck by instant awareness as I realized I was seated next to none other than John Lennon! I freaked the hell out. Booster and I were in the outskirts of Havana, **coincidentally** seated next to John Lennon in Lennon Park. I really was being stalked by MHP. There was no doubt about it! I started shaking and grabbed Booster.

In the sixties and seventies, Cubans weren't allowed to listen to American rock and roll music. If they were caught doing so, they were subject to going to jail. Many Cuban youth would listen in basements with headphones on. Some would quietly play American rock music, knowingly subjecting themselves to potential imprisonment. Eventually, someone explained to Cuban officials that John Lennon's message of peace, harmony, and *sharing all the world* was synonymous with the communist message of equality. According to communist doctrine, everyone is equal. According to the reality exhibited in communist countries, including Cuba, everyone is equal, but some are *more* equal than others!

My veterinarian friend arrived, and we shared a warm embrace. I explained I was being stalked, and he laughed. He explained that the day Fidel Castro dedicated the park, people came from around the world and threw flowers at the statue. By the end of the day, the statue could not be seen as it was buried below 6 feet of flowers, pollinating love. I could only *imagine*! I asked my new friend to take a picture of me and Booster seated with our buddy John. While I wanted to include him, it would have subjected him to potential repercussions. I'm quite sure he would have declined, in order to preserve anonymity in the tough, communist culture of the day.

Later, we were invited to my new friend's home to visit his veterinary clinic. Booster had a chance to meet his yellow Labrador. The gentleman later invited us to visit his home the next night. I met his wife and sons. His brother was visiting from Miami, where he'd traveled to during the Mariel boatlift. It was a complete circle of sharing and unconditional love. I wouldn't expect anything less from a man dedicated to helping downtrodden Cuban animals. I've often said you can trust a human who loves an animal. The converse is certainly true, as well. I was making quality friends in Cuba very quickly. Ironically, my Cuban veterinarian friend later won an immigration lottery and is now living in southern Florida.

One day, while walking in downtown Havana, I happened upon a street dog that came running up to me. He was a cute little dog, half Coppertone-colored and half furless mange. He seemed overly friendly. I surmised tourists had fed him scraps, so he was quite well socialized. I sat on the dirty pavement, and he jumped into my lap. He then licked my face! I know it doesn't sound sanitary, but a dog saved my life so for me, dogs can do no wrong! Every moment of my life was an *extra* because of a dog. I sat there for twenty minutes, basking in the Cuban sun, playing with the

MY BOOSTER!

dog, when I was suddenly blindsided by emotion. Like a ton of bricks falling from a mountain top, I was hit with another epiphany.

I, too, had once lived an aimless life, seemingly abandoned. I'd been all alone and had struggled to survive against all odds. When I looked into the little dog's eyes, I saw myself—I, too, had once found myself in the gutter. I broke down and started crying, cradling the dog, oblivious to the fact that the rear half of his body was hairless and blackened with 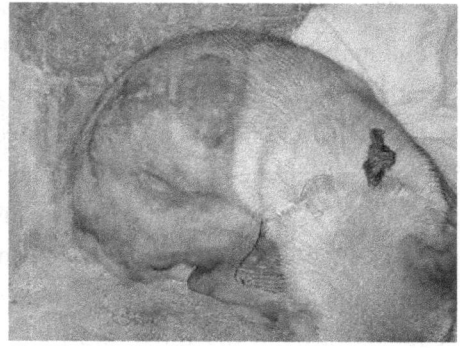 mange. I'm not sure what happened next. I was lost in rays of reflection. All I remember is looking up at a Cuban teenager with a pedal taxi. "Señor, señor, are you alright?"

Shaking, I told him, "I . . . I . . . wantttt to help the little doggggg."

Rather than question my sanity, which would have been the right thing to do, he ran and got a burlap sack out of a garbage pile. He went to the little dog, wrapped him in the sack, and cradled him in his arms. "Get in," he said, "I'll take you to a veterinarian." Within minutes, we were at a veterinarian's office, but it was closed. My friend's clinic was way  across town and also likely closed. It was getting late, and I was getting worried. The young man read my expression and said, "Don't worry, my brother's a barber and he loves dogs." Barber or Mickey Mouse, I'd have taken help from any available source at that moment. He peddled *us* across Havana, and we ended up at his brother's apartment. Only MHP knew where! He walked in, explained to his brother that I wanted to help the dog and the brother put the mangy little dog in a corner of his living room. He then tethered him with a leash.

I gave the brother some money to get food and vitamins for the dog. What seemed like an eternity later, the younger brother peddled me back to my hotel. I walked up to my room, showered off the slippery slobber, and fell asleep on the bed. I didn't need to count sheep to get to sleep—I could count dogs! When the time came, I'd now had two to get out of Havana.

The following day, our tour brought us to an inner-city Havana elementary school. I'd arranged with the tour organizer in advance to conduct a service dog presentation featuring Booster. The tour group entered the school, and my eyes landed on the pic of Booster I'd sent days before, telling the children we would visit them and bring some fun toys. My guide's wife met us at the school as planned, accompanied by Booster. I was seated in the classroom when Booster enthusiastically came running in and planted kisses all over my face. The kids laughed as I fell backward. I looked around the room and didn't see any disabled children. I then explained that some people have disabilities, and a dog can help them do things they can't do for themselves.

I had Booster run to a small refrigerator and bring one of the children a water bottle. I then kicked off my shoes, and he brought them back to me. He then removed my socks. I tied a rag to a chair and asked him to bring it to me. Booster had never been trained to do that, but he was good at *generalizing*, and often applied his learned tasks in new and novel ways. I momentarily flashed back to the time I walked onto a plane and couldn't walk off due to a gout attack. The airline brought me a wheelchair, and Booster pulled me through the airport, never having been trained to do so.

The Cuban children, tomorrow's leaders, were learning a valuable lesson. I witnessed open minds, eager to learn from a new teacher . . . a dog! Toward the end of the visit, the children gathered around Booster to take a group photo. We spent more time at the school than planned and were off schedule for the rest of the day. *It was a small price to pay*, I thought, *but I'm quite sure my tour mates were starting to digest enough Dog 101 by this time!*

MY BOOSTER!

I later remarked to friends that children in Cuba seemed very mature for their ages. Whenever I walked Booster in Cuba, the Cuban children would run up to the big dog, pause, look into my eyes, and calmly ask, "Muerde?" (bite). I always answered, "Nunca!" (never!) Often, the kids then looked directly into my eyes and assessed my response. They were like little thirty-year-olds!

In a future visit to the island, I was invited to visit a school for disabled Cuban children. I walked into the school building and was greeted by children of all ages who clamored to meet the new visitor . . . and it wasn't me!

Instantly, Booster was inundated by love in the form of pets and pats to the head. The children immediately homed in on the fact Booster had a black sunken-in area on his head where a tumor had been removed. They pointed to his head and to the side of his face where he had no fur due to the side effects of radiation therapy (RT). The disabled children were sensitive to the fact that Booster was also disabled. They were so enthused they forgot to ask, "Muerde/Bite?" The instant bond was more beautiful than any rainbow I'd ever witnessed.

The dedicated Cuban teachers organized the children in a central classroom. I asked Booster to demonstrate his unique canine abilities. As the children watched the dog perform tasks, I looked at the kids in the classroom. They were equipped with modern medical devices to help them with their disability. I saw wires leading to modern cochlear implants for Deaf children. Others relied on new canes and crutches. Some sat in shiny wheelchairs. When the demonstration was over, I asked the kids if anyone would like to pet Booster. Hands flew high, and a tail wagged proud!

The Cuban teachers calmed the children with uncanny ease. It wasn't so much discipline as it was the children's respect for their teachers. One of the teachers brought three students at a time to meet and hug Booster. They all pet Booster with great zeal. Suddenly, a chorus of hands shot to the sky! They wanted to know if they could pet Booster again! "Keep coming back. It works if you work it!" I remembered the Al-Anon saying. Every time I shared Booster with others, and I do mean *every* time, life worked as it should. I often gained and learned more from the experience than those I'd come to visit. It made me think and think some more!

The Cuban government took care of its disabled citizens. The medical devices used to help the disabled were relatively new and in good condition. I never witnessed homelessness in Cuba, though I'm sure it exists. The only time I witnessed homelessness on trips to Cuba was when I had a layover in San Francisco and went walking in parks. I spoke with the homeless and learned that several were veterans unable to cope with the atrocities they'd participated in overseas. Our war veterans rely on a Veterans Administration Hospital. I wondered if Cuba provided better health care for their military. I remembered after Hurricane Katrina demolished the area where I live, the Cuban government offered to send hundreds of doctors to help. The US government refused the help.

MY BOOSTER!

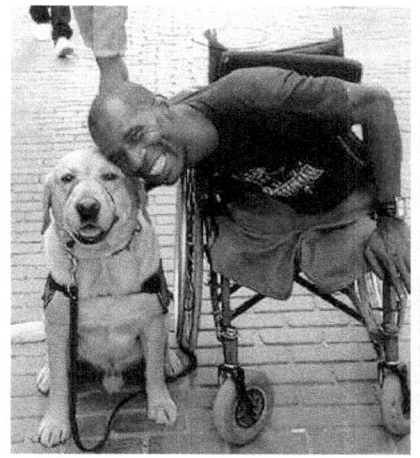
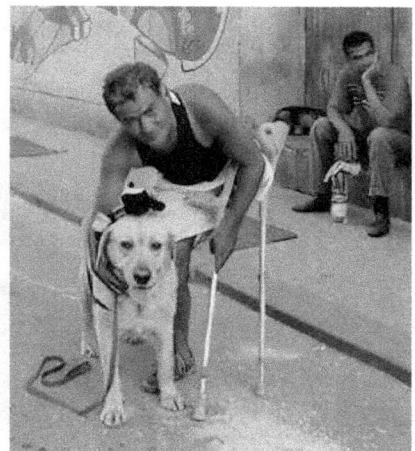

People clamored to pet the dog that came to Cuba to show how dogs can help the humans they love unconditionally. Like Cubans, Booster was born with dogs. I can certainly identify. Hemmingway knew he was dying due to his drinking. He was undoubtedly consoled by those who loved him unconditionally. He left behind his literary works and headstone tributes to his dogs. They are both still visited daily by people from around the world.

After spending weeks in Cuba, it was time to fly home. I had to get an exit permit for Booster. The Cuban government inspects animals before they leave the country. Of course, Booster would pass inspection, but my little street dog would not. The Cuban government inspects animals before they leave the country. I met with black brothers. He had no learned prejudice, and neither did most Cubans. The Black and white Cubans grew up together, they were symbiotic. They both struggled to survive in a poor country of equals.

It was obvious to all whose eyes were open that discrimination was hard to find in Cuba. Cubans had no ability to love money so instead they *love thy neighbor*, regardless of color. I found it captivating that communist Castro Nora and she said she would find a foster home for the little dog, and I could give her a little money for his food and medicine. Grateful, I retrieved the little Cuban dog from the barber and brought him to Aniplant's headquarters. By the end of the day, he was no longer the little shut down religion to consolidate control, yet the religious doctrine of love thy neighbor flourished, nonetheless. I'm sure some prejudice existed because we are all only human, right?

OMG, more tourists!

OM Headstones honoring Hemingway's dogs *G, more tourists!*

One day, our tour group was taken to visit Ernest Hemingway's home in Cuba. Lines of tourists flock to the house every day. As you enter the property, you're greeted by stray dogs and cats that never venture far away. They're provided for by Cubans interested in animal welfare as well as those affiliated with the Spanky Project. You witness a graveyard where Hemmingway's beloved dogs are buried. It's easy to imagine the old man drinking, writing, and petting his dog. He was aptly named Fidel . . . ity! I dared not name him Fidel for fear I might not be allowed to reenter Cuba if I disrespected the Cuban leader by giving his name to a street dog!

I'd one more task to attend to before leaving the island. Weeks before, I'd walked into the Cuban Artists Gallery on Obispo Street, where I always walked Booster. I purchased a teak wood bulldog's head carving and commissioned the artist to carve a Labrador dog's head for me. The artist agreed to have it ready the day before I was scheduled to leave Cuba. When I went to pick up my Labrador head, I was told that the artist was on his way. He was riding a Harley-Davidson motorcycle in the rain to deliver the carving, as promised. I was asked to wait awhile.

MY BOOSTER!

I crossed the street to a café and ordered a cup of Cuban coffee. A withered man in his elderly eighties approached me. I knew he was going to try to sell me something but wasn't in the mood as I was going over my mental checklist prior to departing the island nation. I waved my hand to fend him off, but he either didn't understand sign language or more likely chose to ignore it. He uttered words in Spanish that I didn't understand. He was trying to respectfully speak to the obvious American in English. He thrust four pages of lined notebook paper scribed in English into my hands! *This is going to be interesting*, I thought. I read it, sadly more out of curiosity than respect.

He was trying to verbally explain something in broken English about the writings. The more I read, the more fascinated I became. It was poetry. It was beautiful in context, intellectual in composure, and written in English! I got to the last page and saw a sentence that contained an asterisk. My eyes transitioned to the explanatory asterisk in the upper right-hand corner. I cried . . . yes, damn it, AGAIN! I damn well lost it. Yes, damn it, again! The asterisk was attached to the name JOHN LENNON! I had to sit before I fell. I held my head in my hands. I will never know what the man was thinking. Perhaps he thought I saw it as the most beautiful prose I'd ever experienced. If he had such thoughts . . . he was right! It was an affirmation by MHP that I had somehow learned from Booster how to bring fidelity into my life. You may say that I'm a dreamer.

They say three strikes and you're out. In my case, I had three John Lennons and a full house. I had visited the blind, physically disabled children and adults, befriended Cuban canines, appeared on live television and radio, allowed access to classrooms, and made enduring friendships through *people-to-people-contact* as envisioned by President Obama. While I'll never know if I was under Big Brother's surveillance by the Cuban government, I *do know* that I was under the surveillance of My Higher Power, documented by John Lennon. Booster had introduced me to spirituality the likes of which had never previously existed in my life. Talk about *people-to-people* contacts, Booster, BUCS, Canadians, Cubans, and even John Lennon himself were all implements utilized by My Higher Power to breathe life into my tattered soul. The life I once sought to end experienced a renaissance. God gave preachers a Bible; My

Higher Power gave me a dog. "What are you going to do with a dog?" my brother had once asked. I still had a long way to go to answer the question completely.

The day before I left, I took Booster to visit little Fidelity. We went to the Aniplant headquarters, and Nora greeted us with her customary smile. We walked in, and before I could even say hello, she put a cup of Cuban coffee in my hands. We sat and talked, and suddenly little Fidelity came running in. He cussed at Booster like a drunken sailor. *Yap yap yappy yap!* Booster maintained a detent with the finest of decorum. I momentarily thought I'd need to enact a new Cuban blockade. It was all I could do to hold them close enough to have a photo snapped. Later that night, we went to a nice little Cuban restaurant. The walls were adorned with graffiti written by visitors from around the world. Many of the inscriptions were from US visitors so, without hesitation, my Booster and I joined the pack! "Booster and BUCS were here," I scribed on the wall.

The minute I got home, I started working on a plan to bring Fidelity into my life. I couldn't bring him to the US on a Bahamasair flight because Bahamian regulations would not allow Cuban animals into the Bahamas. The Bahamian airline also had no cargo agreement with the Cuban government so Fidelity couldn't fly in a crate down below. I didn't have a clue if US immigration and customs would accept Cuban veterinary documents certifying Fidelity's good health when he was all fixed up and ready to fly the friendly skies. I reached out to Mexican and Canadian animal welfare groups. Somehow, the Mexican group had formed an alliance with a Canadian group to get homeless Cuban dogs into the hands of those who had met them and fallen in love with them throughout Cuba.

One day, I got an email from a Canadian animal welfare association Cats and Dogs International (CANDI). President/Founder Darci Galati informed me she'd been in contact with APAC-Varadero, a Canadian-Cuban animal alliance.

The two organizations had worked together to arrange for the Canadian airline Air Transat to fly Fidelity to Toronto, Canada. They'd heard about my love for a little Cuban dog. The airline was known for supporting animal welfare and flying animals for free to better their lives.

MY BOOSTER!

They asked if I would fly to Toronto and pick him up. My immediate response was, "Well, hell yeah!" However, I phrased it a bit differently. It took months, but eventually I boarded a plane to Toronto to get my little Fidelity, not knowing if he would clear customs at Chicago's O'Hare International Airport.

The plane from Havana landed at 3 a.m. in Toronto. I met a sweet Canadian volunteer who greeted the three people who'd come to claim their Cuban canine orphans. She drove us to the airport hangar where the dogs were waiting in their respective crates. All three adoptive pet parents had to clear their Cuban canines through Canadian customs. We were warned that the Canadian government would want tax money of some kind. *Be prepared* . . . it ain't just the Boy Scouts marching song!

I met the Canadian customs official, and as though on cue, he asked me, "How much is the dog worth?"

I looked him straight in the eye and said, "He isn't worth anything *economically*."

The gruff man then said, "Well, he must be worth *something*, or you wouldn't be here."

I responded, "You are correct, sir. Now that I think about it, between flights to Cuba, veterinary boarding and medical expenses, the dog's worth about negative $2,000!" My tact wasn't exactly the best way to handle the situation, I must admit. We compromised at a declared value of $100, on which I paid a small percentage. I paid Fidelity's "bail" and went with the others to collect our parolees.

One by one, the crates were opened, and each canine Cuban immigrant ran to its respective human. It was such a sight to behold ... an affirmation of the powerful canine-human bond. Fidelity was the last to be released. I was seated in front of his crate, and he took one giant leap and sat by my side. Once again, he kissed me like he'd done when our lives were in a gutter in Havana. The lady volunteer captured the moment in a photo.

This time there were tears streaming, but I remember every precious second. A variant of Robert Frost's poem, "The Road Not Taken" was in the making. Instead of the line "two roads diverged", it was "Two gutters diverged." Interestingly, as a young lady, my mother had Robert Frost as an English teacher. In her wildest dreams she could never have imagined this corollary.

Reunited with Fidelity, we were driven to my pet-friendly hotel in Toronto. I was sure Fidelity was quite hungry, having spent all day in a crate in Havana before being flown to Toronto. I was quite upset that the little dog couldn't have simply flown from Havana to New Orleans but for the US embargo against Cuba. The US-Cuba embargo, justified or not, hurt a lot of human beings. For the record, it also hurt a little dog that embodied fidelity. I put Fidelity on a leash, and he balked right away. The Cubans were to have introduced the little feral dog to a leash and walked him in Havana. Had they indeed done so or was Fidelity as rebellious as the Cuban leader Fidel? Later, I carried "little Fidel" in my arms up to my room. I put food in my hands and fed him, then I cradled my palms and gave the little guy water. I wanted to establish the canine–human nexus by associating my smell, my "self," and the issuance of food. After feeding Fidelity, I decided to go down to the lobby to feed myself. I didn't want to abandon the little dog for a moment, so I attached his leash, and we "fought" our way to the elevator to descend to the oasis of the vending machines at 4 a.m. I found the life-sustaining machines and feasted on Coca-Cola and potato chips, traditional American cuisine.

We struggled our way back to the elevator. When the elevator door opened, Fidelity lurched forward, and I dropped the leash. He ran away at lightning speed and was suddenly out of sight. Our room was four hallways and turns away from the elevator door. I found my way to our room and the little dog was sitting in front of the door, looking at me,

MY BOOSTER!

wagging his tail. *Was it arrogance or pride?* I wondered. I opened the door, sat in a chair, and the little bastard jumped in my lap and kissed my face once again. I took him to the bathroom and washed his little ass and dried him with a towel. He jumped up on my bed and we both fell fast asleep.

In the morning, I fitted Fidelity with a Service Dog in Training vest. We took a long, combative walk around the hotel grounds. The once-feral dog slowly grew accustomed to wearing his official uniform. Before long, we were on the shuttle bus to the airport. Life changed forever for little Fidelity. He learned quite quickly to walk on a leash. He sat patiently on the escalator, which absolutely blew me away. We practiced "sit" and "wait" in the airport. As we walked, he insisted on stopping to greet new friends along the way.

Though Canadian airlines don't recognize service dogs in training, we boarded the plane with no incident. I'd given Fidelity several meaty dog biscuits prior to boarding. Cubans feed dogs ground-up cow organs mixed with boiled rice. It was fine caviar for a dog. Conventional dry dog biscuits would have been as appetizing to Fidelity as a brick, but street dogs rarely say no to any type of food. He expressed his desire for more by subserviently following me like a child following Santa!

When we landed in Chicago, the canine Cuban immigrant was confident as hell as he pranced off the plane in full regalia. He reminded me of a miniature Clydesdale as he trotted down the plane's aisle and greeted flight attendants and passengers alike. His vest sported both the Cuban and American flags "juntos" (together). My customs declaration attested to the fact that I was bringing a live animal into the country. We were sidetracked to the customs area. It was judgment day at the OK Corral! It was make or break at this point. I met a somewhat bewildered customs agent, who didn't quite know how to handle the situation. I didn't know if Cuban veterinary documentation and health certificates would be honored in the US, so I'd taken my newly arrived, Canadian tax-paying dog to a local veterinarian to obtain his Canadian health certificate. ***Coincidentally***, the veterinarian was a lady whose family had emigrated from Cuba years before. All bull "processed food" aside, we were allowed into the US.

My flight home from Chicago was delayed, so I had to walk off Fidelity's energy. That proved to be an insurmountable task. I soon learned to do what the little dictator demanded! Fidelity was understandably not used to walking on a leash. I'd learned at BUCS to never pull on a dog's leash as it breeds resentment. I flashed back to the day Bonnie had grabbed my shirt. When Fidelity wanted to go left, I went left. When he chose to go right, I obediently went right. If I'd chosen to fight him, the world would have known he wasn't trained enough to be flown in-cabin as a service dog in training. For the record, service dogs in training aren't summarily allowed to travel in airplanes in-cabin. Fidelity donned a vest that clearly stated Service Dog in Training. If he acted appropriately, I assumed we would be granted the privilege, and it *is* a privilege, to be flown together.

I took my little dictator to the airport bathroom to get some water. I cupped my hands, and the smart little dog knew he had refreshment coming, but I only gave him one handful of water as I didn't want him to urinate on the plane. Later that day, we were rushing to meet our departing flight, and without compromise, Fidelity insisted on going to the right when we had to go to the left. I gave in, not wanting to create a scene at the last moment. I was pulled into the men's room where I had given the little dictator water hours before. He was thirsty, and he *knew* where to get water!

My mind was on sensory overload. Like a miner panning for gold, I'd found the educational mother lode. I instantly recalled my BUCS class, where we learned that dogs have mapping skill. That's how lost dogs find their way home, sometimes all the way across the country! I remember as a young man learning about Charles Darwin's theory of the *survival of the fittest*. A little feral Cuban dog had just taught me a lesson that required educational synthesis. Fidelity was a street dog who navigated the streets of Havana in 100-degree heat. He undoubtedly knew where the dumpsters containing food scraps were located. He knew where the tourists hung out as he was incredibly socialized. I envisioned him hanging out with a sign around his neck proclaiming, "Will kiss for food" He must have known how to return to air conditioners that dripped water taken from the humid Cuban air, or the Malecon, where water splashed ashore and accumulated

MY BOOSTER!

in puddles. He was a great example of survival of the fittest. His intellect and mapping skills had allowed him to survive in a hostile environment.

In awe, I'd watched Fidelity find his way back to our hotel room the night before. I was standing in an airport bathroom with a dog that remembered where he'd found water hours before. Once again, I was learning from a dog. I also knew that if I hadn't attended BUCS, I never would have seen the reality of the day. It was such a novel way to see the concept of survival of the fittest in the real world. I was an old dog taught new tricks by a young dog, whom I surmised was only about a year old. I'd learned in my BUCS veterinary classes that you can judge the age of a dog by his teeth.

We eventually boarded the flight home with no problem. We arrived, and I introduced Fidelity to my pack. Issues arose when the little dictator learned he couldn't dictate to a pack with an already established hierarchy. Fidelity introduced aggression; a concept relatively unknown in my pack. Booster's son, Al-Anon, being quite the pacifist, took exception to Fidelity's aggressive ways.

Al-anon was far bigger, but Fidelity was faster and had street smarts. Al experienced a torn ear and a gash in a testicle due to Fidelity's aggressive ways. There was a coup d'état when my even larger Labrador Savior (Booster's other son) defended the little dog when others fought back against his aggression.

There were warring factions among the ranks. My little Fidel introduced strife not unlike that witnessed in Colombia in days gone by. He was a canine version of Che Guevara, a Cuban revolutionary associated with the Colombian rebel group FARC, Fuerza Armada Revolucionarias de Colombia. I had a nuclear family suffering from unwanted foreign aggression. "Fidelity Activist Revolutionary Canine (FARC)" had entered my formerly peaceful homeland

Within a few days at home, Fidelity learned to perform service dog tasks. He opened the fridge and fetched water. He learned to retrieve items. This was a firsthand lesson for me. I had a cute little street dog that could perform tasks yet proved aggressive to other dogs. When Bonnie first developed the service dog concept, she trained a shelter dog. She had been about to place that dog with a disabled human partner when the dog adversely reacted to a delivery driver. The shelter dog, like me, had emotional baggage. The delivery driver had a beard, and Bonnie surmised that the dog might have been previously abused by a man with a beard. That's when she decided it was better to train from birth when the *pages are blank.* We all have baggage in our lives. I have more than most! We're taught to train dogs in a canine–human context. Why would we then expect dogs not to also have emotional baggage? You must repeat a positive lesson thirty  times to try to erase one negative learning experience, and yet relapse is likely.

A short while after my return from Cuba, the Canadian tour company posted a synopsis of my trip to Cuba. The company's owner asked permission to write it as though I had written it myself. I happily granted permission. It was a very positive article, likely written to generate new business, appease the Cuban government, and paint a picture of socialist Cuba in a favorable light. The California bilingual newspaper *LaVoz* also ran an intensive article. It was published in English and Spanish. Months later, I contacted the New Orleans newspaper, *The Times-Picayune.* A reporter was interested in doing a story about a man who went to Cuba with a dog. It was a feature story in the Living section of the paper. The reporter did a great job and included myriad photographs. A few days after it appeared, the reporter contacted me. She said a high school classmate I hadn't heard from in over thirty years read the story and wanted to contact me.

I received an email shortly thereafter. My classmate and I caught up on the last thirty years. Suddenly, he opened his emotional floodgates and the

MY BOOSTER!

turbulent turbines of his life generated interest. I wanted to meet up personally rather than share emotions over the telephone. The following weekend we met at a popular New Orleans restaurant. Of course, I had Booster by my side. My classmate looked at me and asked, "You aren't going to try and take your dog inside are you?" I answered him by saying," I wouldn't go in without him! Hey, it's the law...they can't deny us access." Much to his credit, he went along for the ride without expressing his trepidation. I'm quite sure he was embarrassed at the thought of entering a restaurant with a dog. I told him we would be greeted

with greater acceptance than he might imagine. The restaurant's staff didn't bat an eye. It was a perfect experience. Our server greeted us and was all smiles. Within minutes, she shared her doggie stories and whipped out a cell phone to show us her pictures accompanied by her canine partner. Booster got a pat on his head and calmly remained at my feet, under our table.

I then shared a warm meal with a warm heart. My buddy explained that he'd worked with Search and Rescue (SAR) dogs as a hobby. He told me he had a loving wife, two daughters, a nice home and a great profession. After high school he'd gone into the US Navy and became a medic. He then went to medical school and became an orthopedic surgeon. He had life by the lower male extremities! (My words, not his). One day, his life changed forever. He had two daughters in college, a large uptown home, student loans, and a host of other debts. He awoke one morning with a vision problem. He had a detached retina and subsequently lost his eyesight in one eye. Without depth perception, he could no longer perform surgeries.

They say God never gives us more than we can handle, but I think in his case, the envelope was pushed. Even the affluent experience effluent.

I was not alone in dealing with life on life's terms. He understandably experienced acute depression. I never asked him if he "considered exit options," as I once had. I did ask him how he got through it. He looked me in the eye and said, "It was Messi," referring to his beloved SAR dog partner and canine companion. Once again, the canine–human bond sustained a human through difficult times. I had to believe we both had canine angels sent from heaven above.

Interestingly, rather than dwelling on our lives' horror stories, we started explaining how our dogs had helped us. My classmate's dog was by his side through thick and thin. There's something sustaining about a dog that's just different from a human. Often, our human partners don't understand the attachment to a dog. When a disabled person gets a service dog, the spouse or family member is out of a caretaking job and often feels jilted. They are no longer needed to the same extent as before. The service dog enables independence. We're often called upon to explain our canine connection. True to form, he shared that he didn't think his loving wife quite understood it all.

After a great meal, we parted ways. Years later, I emailed him and asked how he was doing. I learned that he'd just returned from a resort with his current Labrador. He explained that Messi had passed away years before. He'd opened his heart to a new dog that he had trained to be a service dog that helped him overcome deficits in his day-to-day life. He'd joined an orthopedic group practice and did consulting work. Most days, he brought his dog to work. To the credit of his human cohorts, his service dog was accepted as an equal partner in the group! Today, he rarely travels without his canine medicine, his Labrador service dog. Once again, I was able to maintain my serenity by giving it away. Booster changed my life years before and changed my classmate's years later.

One day, I opened my email account and found a wonderfully inspiring email from a Cuban man. It included a photo of him holding his dog while enjoying a day at the beach. He said he wished he'd had a chance to meet me and Booster while we were in Havana. He made me promise to contact him whenever I returned to the island. Somehow, he'd seen some of my articles and news stories on the internet. I was a little

MY BOOSTER!

suspicious at first as ordinary Cubans didn't have access to the internet at that time.

When I returned to Cuba months later, he met me at the airport. He took me to his home to meet friends and his beloved rottweiler. He introduced me to an internal medicine doctor who thanked me on behalf of Cuban citizens who could use a service dog to better their lives and help generate independence. I wasn't quite sure I could process the word *independence* in the same sentence containing the word *Cuba*. The Cuban Revolution resulted in Cuban independence from US government control and mafia domination, but the Cubans lost all independence when they couldn't leave the island for over fifty years, like rats stuck in a cage.

Upon my third visit to Cuba, I met him again. He'd developed a neighborhood betterment project to help the Cuban people. He introduced me to his staff of volunteers. That night I attended a party at his home, met US college professors, and got entrenched in rather deep philosophical discussions. Virtually all agreed that if the US-Cuba embargo ended, and Americans flocked to Cuba, the country would suffer as a result. Americans would ruin Cuba once again! I could just see the throngs of US kids in Cuba, sagging their pants, showing off their flowered underwear. Cubans are not allowed to do such a thing. I laughed at the thought of US kids asking a Cuban police officer, "Say what?" and being hauled off to jail, many learning the concept of discipline for the first time.

I then started thinking about helping Cubans to learn to train service dogs. In a country where the average monthly salary was $25, a lot of dogs could be trained at a far more reasonable cost than $50K each. The Cuban government gave scholarships to students from around the world to become doctors. I envisioned the Cuban government supportive of training "doctor dogs" and exporting them around the world as part of their communist model. To me it was a no-brainer. I could write a book about what happened next, but it wasn't pretty. As part of Project Fidelity, I gave scholarships to two Cubans to travel to BUCS. One was a man around forty years old, and the other a young lady around thirty. They were the adult children of some of Nora's friends. The Cuban government gave the students permission to leave the island but the US government, via the Swiss-run Cuban Interest Section in Cuba, wouldn't let the Cubans come. I wrote harsh letters and made a lot of calls, and the following summer the students did come. The Cuban man who purportedly loved dogs didn't want the smell of a dog in his room and commandeered the bathroom air freshener to spray his room, which housed his assigned dog. He didn't follow the rules, but he sure followed food into the kitchen and devoured it faster than his canine assignee. I withdrew my support and gave him a plane ticket to Miami to catch his flight back to Cuba. I should have made him walk . . . on all fours! The arrogant man demanded a non-stop ticket to Miami at twice the cost of a ticket with a connection. **Coincidentally**, there was a mechanical problem on the aircraft, and he did have to make a connecting flight the next day! Turns out, he'd been talking with Cuban friends in Miami all along and didn't return to Havana. I felt betrayed and used because I was!

The young lady did well in school. She truly loved dogs. I bought two expensive Golden retrievers for her to take back to Cuba to start the Booster Center, the first service dog training facility in Cuba. I supported her efforts, but when I later visited the dogs, they were heathens! One  chased children and passersby as they walked down a sidewalk beside the fenced yard. The first night I was there, one dog jumped up and stole the uncooked roast off the counter. Meat is a prized commodity in Cuba, but not for an entitled American dog, I guess! I was mortified.

I later spent thousands of dollars rescuing the dogs from Cuba. It was hard to get them away from the lady, who knew they were supposed to be placed with a disabled person in the future, anyway. It was terrible, and I paid a lot to make it happen. Today, one of the dogs is living with a family and has a swimming pool to cool off in. The other was adopted by a BUCS trainer and is doing great, working as a demo dog in a program to help veterans. There's a lot more to the story, as one might imagine, but this is the gist of events.

MY BOOSTER!

I tried so hard, and I never let anyone down. To this day, I have a sterling reputation on the island. I truly tried to help the citizens of Cuba, but at the end of the day, Cubans let Cubans down. I went to Cuba during the thaw in international relations. I have no doubt Booster sowed seeds of salvation. I returned many times. President Obama rightfully promoted people-to-people contacts. He couldn't possibly have known that people-to-canine contacts might have been far more successful. I picked up the slack, took Booster into Cuba, and made contacts that persist and grow to this day.

When I initially went to the island nation, I didn't speak a word of Spanish. I downloaded a translation program called Jibbigo onto my computer the night before travel. Once downloaded, you didn't need internet access. I knew I wouldn't have easy access to the internet in the communist country. The program helped me communicate with Cubans throughout Havana and the surrounding areas. When I returned to the US, I felt obligated to express my thanks to the program's originator. Booster had taught me the value of expressing gratitude rather than negativity. I emailed the program originators, explaining that their program added to my success in Cuba. I said, "By the way, it's a great country with wonderful people."

I got a rapid reply. "Thank you, sir, I am glad we could be of assistance. Thanks also for your nice words about Cuba because I am Cuban!" Again and again, My Higher Power taught me that there's no such thing as **coincidence!**

After we got home, I went to visit a friend. When I returned, I saw a tornopen box in my front yard. As I got a closer look, I started to shake. It was a box that *had* contained twelve or more months of meds and heartworm prevention tablets. They were gone. They're made to taste appealing to dogs, who must chew and digest the tablets. Ingest them they did. *Did one of my canine kids eat them all . . . or were they ingested by many?* I freaked out. *Were my "kids" poisoned? Were they going to die due to an overdose?* The company that shipped the MEDICINE included CANDY in the box in the form of a large, tasty dog biscuit. Dogs have a keen sense of smell. The delivery driver had set the package in the yard. My "kids" found it, smelled the biscuit within, and ate everything.

Devastated, I called a poison hotline. It was awful. Imagine if your children had done the same!

I called the company and queried a supervisor, "Lady why in the hell do you ship dog biscuits in boxes containing medicines?"

"I'm sorry, sir, but our customers look forward to the free biscuit and complain if we leave it out," she responded.

"Hey, lady, do you think they'd complain if they came home to a dead dog? If the VA or pharmacy sent you medicine in boxes with candy and popcorn, and your kids ate the goodies *and* the medicine and got sick or died, how would you feel?"

Try as I might, I couldn't convince the company to mend its ways. The best they would do was to put *do not include bone* on the order. I received another two boxes of candy-laced medicine because the warehouse shipped it out despite the instructions CLEARLY PRINTED ON THE LABEL ITSELF! I never ordered anything from the company again. Even their own pharmacists agreed with me. Such stupidity and callous disregard for the welfare of the dogs they purported to help floored me. I called the company on a whim just before publishing to ascertain if the insane policy had ever been rectified.

To my absolute astonishment, the company representative explained that they no longer ship bones in boxes. **Coincidentally**, the policy change became effective just days before I made what I thought was a pointless call. I asked to speak to a member of management and finally had discourse with a rational adult who understood my festering frustration. Turns out, she remembered my calls of yesteryear, pleading for policy change. She honestly explained that other customers had experienced similar happenings and upper management finally got the message. I no longer had a *bone to pick* with that company. NEXT!!!!

My life eventually settled down, but I had a difficult time adjusting to a lifestyle that no longer revolved around drama. It felt strange somehow. Years later, I received a call from my friend Sheila Culmer, re-elected President of the Bahamas Council for Disabilities. "Dave, we got our law!" Sheila exuberantly explained. "Dave, we received more notoriety and press as a result of you and your Booster than we had in the preceding twenty years." I was in shock. My Booster had passed away six months

MY BOOSTER!

before and wasn't by my side to hear the great news. I started trembling, unable to speak.

"Dave, are you there?" Sheila asked.

I managed to utter, "Uh huhhh." I breathed deeply in and out as Booster had taught me to do so many years before. With broken speech, I said, "Sheila, I'm afraid to ask, is service dog and guide dog access included in the new legislation?"

Sheila replied excitedly, "Oh, yes, Dave, it's all there!"

Damn it, the damn dam burst again, and I sobbed, so proud of my Booster's accomplishments yet so sad he wasn't around to share in the limelight of his success.

A few months later, I decided to visit my time-share in Freeport, Bahamas, once again. I invited a friend, Sharon, and her husband to join me. One fateful day, we went walking in the port area. Later that afternoon, I summoned a taxi to take us back to the resort. The driver refused to allow my service dogs, Boosted and Busted, to enter the taxi. I explained to the taxi driver that he was violating the new Bahamas disability law. He couldn't have cared less.

We walked to the nearby police station to request assistance for my assistance dogs. I asked Sharon to hold onto Busted while I ventured in with Boosted. Upon entering the small, modular police station, I was immediately verbally accosted by a police officer. "Get the dog OUT!" boomed the megaphone voice.

I then retorted, "He's a service dog."

Another officer added to the melee and shouted, "Did you hear what he said?"

Then a third officer chimed in and said, "You better get the dog out."

President Roosevelt would have referred to it as "a date that will remain in infamy." It was my Pearl Harbor Day. I was devastated. I exited the building before risking arrest.

I called Sheila, and explained what had transpired. She called me back later that same day and told me that she'd been in contact with the Assistant Chief of Police of the Bahamas. He invited us to attend a conference, ***coincidentally*** scheduled two days later, on the island of Freeport. When that day came, Sharon and her husband joined me with

Boosted and Busted. We meekly walked into a large conference room in a courthouse. There were roughly twenty chiefs of police from across the Bahamas seated in neatly arranged conference tables. There was also a video camera televising the conference for those chiefs located elsewhere who couldn't attend in person.

We were cordially greeted. I surveyed each face in the room, male and female, all adorned in brown suits denoting rank. I explained what had transpired two days before. "People worry about being attacked by a pack of dogs, but I was attacked by a pack of police officers, in a police station, in violation of your national law. What good is a law if the police violate the law? Who do you turn to? I'm not angry, but rather grateful to be able to share my education with a population willing to listen and learn. I'm so proud of your country for passing a disability-related law." I then explained that service dogs and guide dogs are an extension of a disabled person's body and can't be separated. I then demonstrated Boosted and Busted performing service-dog-related tasks, as seeing is believing. Before long, smiles and questions rapidly intermingled. The temperature once again rose in a police environment but this time it was due to the warmth of human kindness and understanding. The officers apologized and insisted on taking a group photo on the courthouse steps. To this day, I know that a disabled person accompanied by an assistance dog will be warmly received throughout the Bahamas. When we returned to the

MY BOOSTER!

Island Seas Resort, it was time for relaxation and socialization . . . for me and the canine kids, who had earned their wings once again!

A year later, Boosted, Busted, and I returned to Freeport with my friend Rocky. I once again called the newspaper and reiterated Booster's life story to a reporter at the end of the phone line. My first thought was that the person wouldn't care but then I reminded myself that this was the Bahamas, where I'd always been received so warmly. I often thought it was where the concept of kindness originated. I choked up as I told my story, and I could feel the warmth of the soul on the other end of the line. That warmth morphed into the following full-page story, displaying my Booster's photo: Tears, tears, and more tears.

Seeking positive change is important. Expressing gratitude is equally important and helps affect change. Whenever I gave Booster a treat, he expressed gratitude with a wag of the tail, a kiss on the cheek, and a boisterous bark. I learned from him to do the same, perhaps utilizing a different format!

CHAPTER 12
TESTING THE WATERS

As time went by, I enjoyed going on cruises with Booster. I'd often isolate in my cabin and walk him during less crowded times. Occasionally, I enjoyed sharing him with others, depending on my mood. Cruise lines always send myriad documents explaining one's responsibilities when traveling with a service dog onboard. Given the proliferation of fake service dogs taken into public venues by selfish, ignorant humans, I totally understood.

As a profoundly proud service dog advocate, I felt compelled to promote those who could not promote themselves. To attest to canine aptitude, I sent a photo of Booster urinating into his assigned box he'd learned to use so faithfully. I also sent photos taken of signage seen in a country visited on previous cruises. On the island of St. Lucia, the government posted signs with eloquent verbiage on public buildings. I not-so-humbly suggested to the cruise line that if any of their customers were from that island, perhaps they should concentrate on the humans and send them similar documents to sign. I further shared that "My Booster has a $50,000 education and knows when ... and where ... not to urinate." Whenever I was in a particularly sarcastic

MY BOOSTER!

mood, I added: "Booster really enjoys good music, especially the strings. Please don't worry; he knows to relieve himself before going on stage!!!" On one cruise, the staff posted a drawing of a dog's head and proudly placed it above my Booster's relief box. I subsequently adorned the wall with Booster's photos, taken around the world. I often included a section entitled: "Reference Letters." I then attached the following letter received from Carnival Cruise Line's Office of the President:

Carnival

Feb 1, 2007

Mr. Davis Hawn Mississippi

RE: HOLIDAY, 11/11/06, M21, 2N431.6, 005030541B

Dear Mr. Hawn:

Thank you for taking the time to contact us regarding your cruise vacation aboard the HOLIDAY. Knowing our success depends on guest satisfaction, we appreciate the opportunity to respond to your kind words. It's such a pleasure to hear from guests who enjoyed their cruise vacation so thoroughly. Carnival strides to provide each of our guests with an excellent product and superior service. We appreciate you taking the time to tell us we accomplished our goals.

To show our appreciation, we would like to extend a special gift for your next cruise. Please contact the Guest Relations Department 45 days prior to sailing at 1-800-929-6400 and we will arrange to have a Bon Voyage gift in your cabin upon arrival.

Thank you again for taking the time to contact us. We look forward to welcoming you and Booster back aboard soon.

Sincerely, Susan Cohn
Special Adviser,
Office of the President

It was always an experience cruising with Booster. From ballrooms to beaches, to parks, to city streets, he always had an entourage. He adored people from all walks of life. I wish all humans would emulate him. "What a Wonderful World," as Louis Armstrong wonderfully expressed it in his worldfamous song!

On one cruise, my Indonesian cabin boy asked me if I had a picture of me with Booster. I happened to have one taken on a previous cruise (the photo on the cover), and I gave it to him, thinking it was likely a souvenir of sorts, due to the novelty of having a dog onboard the ship. On the last day of the cruise, I heard a knock on my cabin door. When I opened the door, my cabin boy presented me with a rolled document of

MY BOOSTER!

some sort. I knew it wasn't an eviction notice, but I had no idea what to expect. I gingerly accepted the document and slowly unrolled it. Suddenly, I was in the flash zone of an atomic bomb of emotion. My eyes automatically panned up to meet the young man's eyes in disbelief. I was dumbfounded; totally speechless. I instantly thought, *How kind a gesture this is*.

Cruise ship employees work an uncanny number of hours, and this young man spent his time off drawing a sketch of me and my Booster.

"WOW, you have no idea how much this means to me. Thank you for sharing your talent. I can't wait to frame it and hang it on the wall in my home," I told him. "I hope you like it sir," he said with a confident, toothy grin.

I uttered, "You're amazing," and handed him a tip. There was no gratuity worthy enough. I thanked him as best I could, given the emotional state that I was in.

On yet another cruise, I took Booster to the beach. I threw his ball out into the ocean, and he jumped into the waves to fetch it. Other cruise goers asked to throw the ball too, and it was quite a festive occasion. Later that night, back onboard the ship, Booster began to unceremoniously vomit. He was sick, really sick. We were helpless in the middle of the ocean with my beloved Booster. I called the front desk, asking for help. The angelic staff arranged for a veterinarian to see Booster at the next port of call in Roatan, Honduras. I prayed until I couldn't pray anymore that Booster would make it through the night. I surmised that he'd ingested a dangerous amount of salt water.

When the ship docked, I took a taxi with Booster to the veterinarian's office. I must admit I was in tears as I entered the clinic. It was clean and modern looking. Booster walked unsteadily on his feet. Before long, he was on an examination table. I can't remember what was said as I was truly out of it. My emotions were all-encompassing. The veterinarian exuded confidence and empathy. He gave Booster a shot and reassured me that he'd be OK. He also asked if he could take a picture of us together.

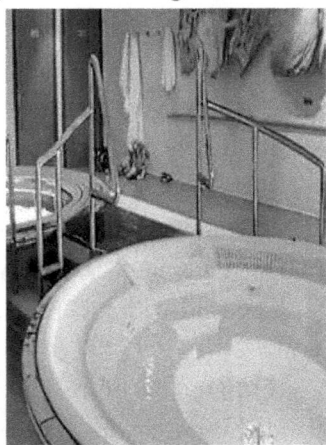

A year later, I was scheduled to attend one of the veterinary conferences. I emailed the Honduran veterinarian and invited him to attend. I explained how much he had impacted my life that day and I'd never forgotten it. He returned my email and said he might attend the conference, too. I then offered to provide plane tickets for him and his wife to fly to the US to attend the conference. It was scheduled to happen until his backup veterinarian canceled out at the last moment and he couldn't go. *What a bummer*, I thought.

Years later, I took Booster on a cruise and bought the thermal package. It gave you access to a beautiful glass room overlooking the sea while sitting on a heated ceramic tile chaise lounge. It was a perfect place to read, relax, and in my case write a book. It also provided a large, multi-person jacuzzi, and several smaller ones. I entered the thermal suite with Booster who sat in the far corner while I used the jacuzzi. He later sat stoically beside me when I was in a chaise lounge.

That afternoon, I was summoned to meet with one of the ship's officers. "Sir, I'm sorry but you can't enter the thermal suite with a dog." He declared authoritatively.

The officer was worried about how sanitary it would be to have a dog near the jacuzzies. Rather than get angry as I would have done in the past, I laughed out loud much to the gentleman's bewilderment. When I regained my composure, I frankly stated:

MY BOOSTER!

"Sir, my service dog was 50 feet away from the Jacuzzis that are filled with chemicals that burned my eyes. They undoubtedly have body hair from myriad human bodies from, as the traveling chef Anthony Bourdain would have said, 'parts unknown.' Some might be black, some blonde, red, and even curly. You're worried about a dog hair floating fifty feet through the air and entering the jacuzzi, really? Your Jacuzzis are filled with sterilizing chemicals that burned my eyes. My service dog Booster has been under the dinner table on every cruise I've ever taken, including this one, and you aren't worried about his hair going into people's food and being ingested."

His retort was that the cruise line's home office had made that decision. They refunded the fee for the thermal suite. I then emailed the home office and carbon-copied a governmental agency. When I spoke to an official in the home office, I was told it was up to the ship's discretion. That really infuriated me... *Round robin, good cop/bad cop, here we go.* I went back to the ship's officer and explained what I'd been told. Somebody wasn't being truthful as to who had made the discriminatory decision. I explained that I'd be filing a complaint with the US government, and since the ship sailed from a US port, it was likely subject to the ADA and the provisions therein. I was pissed off and pissed on!

Two days later, I was once again summoned to the officer's office. He explained that it took some time to sort it all out. He then apologized and said:

"Mr. Hawn, this is a learning curve for us. I apologize for the misunderstanding and inconvenience. You may use the thermal suite with your service dog Booster, and it'll be free of charge for the remainder of the cruise. We are also issuing you a $100 credit on your ship account as a goodwill gesture. I also invite you and your service dog to join us at the officer's table in the dinner theater tonight, to watch the acrobats perform in the cirque du soleil show."

As if that wasn't enough, that I then asked him to do me a favor. I explained that the pool boy had voluntarily brought Booster water on a hot day and the cabin boy always greeted him nicely. I asked, "Sir, would you please summon those two gentlemen to your office tomorrow so I can thank them for their kindness? I'd like to acknowledge them in your presence and give them each a $50 gratuity. What goes around comes around. The $100 you gave me, I would like to give to them!"

Once again, my BUCS education, coupled with my Booster-instilled social skills, crafted a wonderful social interaction. I loved Booster and began to love myself. There really aren't words to describe the transformation that took place. As the photo evidences, we were both happy. My life changed in *epic* proportions!

CHAPTER 13
MY DEAR PEGGY

Before long, it was time to fly home. When we arrived, canine madness ensued. The other canine kids were ecstatic that we were home. It'd taken years, but I finally had tranquility in my life and a home life as it's meant to be.

One day the phone rang. It was my friend Peggy. She invited Booster and me to visit her. I looked forward to spending time with Peggy. If ever anyone had life by the *cojones* (balls), as they were called where she lived in McAllen, Texas (fondly referred to as northern Mexico), it was she. With three pensions and a home paid for in her early fifties, she was set for life. They say if something seems too good to be true, it likely is! Such was the case for Peggy. She'd recently been diagnosed with breast cancer . . . for the second time! She'd successfully battled the disease roughly ten years before and rued the fact that she hadn't elected to have radical mastectomies.

After her first bout with cancer, she enrolled at BUCS to get a canine-related degree so she could help veterans cope with PTSD. She was a veteran unknowingly about to face the greatest battle of her heroic life!

Many people think PTSD is simply a gateway to getting a disability check. I never chose that route, but probably would have qualified. I had once thought our troops were soft, until I read that more veterans die from suicide than battle. I quoted that suicide statistic to a gentleman in the French Quarter of New Orleans. He said, "Sir, you don't have to tell me that. My son came back from battle and committed suicide six months ago."

He then related a story about how he'd met a young soldier the night before, dressed in fatigues. The soldier was in tears, and the man asked him why. The soldier explained that he'd been pickpocketed and had no money to have a good time and meet some young ladies. He further stated that he was going to "off" himself (die by suicide).

"You're going to kill yourself because you can't have a good time?" the man inquired.

The soldier matter-of-factly related that he was going to die by suicide because he couldn't live with himself any longer. The valiant soldier had befriended a young Afghan boy and had tossed a ball back and forth with him almost every day. He explained, "The boy was like a stepson. One day, the Taliban strapped a bomb onto the boy, and he came running into our camp. I saw him, raised my rifle, and had to shoot him. I can still see his brains exploding. There's no pill you can give me; no medicine can erase it. The only freedom I'll have from the pain is to kill myself."

On another occasion, a man explained that his son drove military trucks in convoys. The drivers were told to never stop, for if they did, the enemy would pounce on them. The Taliban, or enemy of the day, would throw children under the tires or tracks of the vehicles. The man's son looked down into his vehicle's mirror and saw a child's head crushed, barely attached to the lifeless body that had been so vibrant moments before. He'd run over the child and was wracked with pain from the emotional scar for years to come.

I wondered how many people knew what we were subjecting our youth to. I'd been so naïve to automatically assume our heroes were soft and I'm sure I'm not alone in my wrong assessment. I was wrong, dead wrong.

What I'd experienced in my life paled in comparison, yet still took a toll. My mind often played tricks on me. At night, I often had dreams and relived the event of the knife coming at me. Driving down a highway on a dark, hot night, the windshield often fogged up. My hands would start to shake, and I'd have to pull over. I'd pull Booster close and hug him tightly. It's an emotional reaction to the night in Florida when the physical confrontation took place, and my truck's windshield had fogged up.

Peggy and I fought the mental ramifications of events wrongfully processed by the human brain. Her greatest battle was yet unfolding, as she was diagnosed with Stage IV breast cancer. She hurt and I hurt. Breast cancer threatened to take away one of the few humans I wholeheartedly loved and trusted without compromise . . . as much as a dog. Life sucked again.

Ironically, it was Peggy supporting me more often than me supporting her! She was a valiant warrior, and I was a wimp.

Peggy appreciated my willingness to share intimate details of my life to help others. I explained to her that I didn't care what others thought of me. I shared the saying I'd heard at an Al-Anon meeting: "What other people think of me is none of my business." I further explained that every moment of every day was bonus time, as I should have rightfully died long ago. My willingness to expose my fragilities was predicated upon my relationship with my Booster. He'd helped *me,* and I was determined to help others with him by my side.

One day, when Peggy and I were talking dog 101, it dawned on me that she could help others just as I strived to do.

"Hey Peggy, you know you're my Veteran hero in battle and life. You can connect with other Veterans and women suffering from codependency and abuse far better than I can. Let's do a newspaper story in your hometown and share how our service dogs have changed our lives."

"Oh my God, I don't know if I could do that. I don't want my neighbors thinking I'm a WAC (Women's Army Corps) wack job!"

"I totally respect your feelings, its just you're so special. You're my Peggy! "From the moment we first met at BUCS, you inspired me. You opened up and were so supportive. You impacted my life. I know in my heart you can do the same for others."

Silence permeated the line. Peggy, being the warrior she was, selflessly responded, "To heck with it. If I can help others cope with the shit I've dealt with and promote service dogs I'm down dude!"

Before one of my visits to Peggy's home, I picked up the phone and called the *Monitor Newspaper* in McAllen. I explained that I had a service dog I credited with saving my life and changing it for the better. I then shared that I had a close friend who was a war veteran, a McAllen hometown heroine, who had an important story to tell. After sharing myriad details, the reporter suggested we all meet at the McAllen airport upon my arrival.

The day I arrived, she greeted us and watched in awe as Booster pulled my luggage cart for me. She took lots of photographs of Peggy with her dog, Tara, and me with my Booster. She then accompanied us to Peggy's home. The lady reporter was indeed a lady, respectful and empathetic. I knew she'd do a good job and present the story in a positive light. Within days, the feature story appeared in the newspaper.

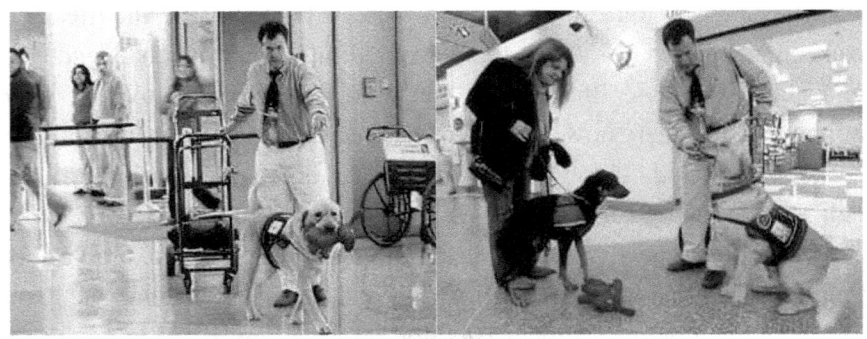

Service Dogs Aren't Just for the Blind Anymore

That night, Peggy and I went out to dinner in a Mexican restaurant to celebrate and unwind. We entered with our service dogs and were told we couldn't bring the dogs inside. We explained that they had to allow us into the restaurant with our service dogs; it was the law. The assholes took us into the backyard, turned on a light hanging from a wire, and tried to seat us at a rickety old picnic table. I lost it! My PTSD outperformed Peggy's that night!

"Look, is this where you stick the gringos? You kick disabled people, minorities out in the field to get eaten by mosquitoes?" I wasn't going to get eaten alive due to PTSD like I'd experienced hiding under my house years ago. "Look, Poncho," I said disrespectfully, "it ain't gonna happen in the good ole USA!" I looked at Peggy and screamed, "Follow me!"

Peggy looked frightened. I walked us into the middle of the restaurant and stood there while I dialed 911 on my cell phone. The local sheriff's department responded when I said things were getting out of control and going to the dogs! Two officers arrived and listened to my story. I had to calm down. If I appeared agitated or spoke loudly it would give them the rightful excuse to remove us from the restaurant.

With all eyes in the restaurant focused on us, I explained, "I came to this nice restaurant with my Veteran friend Peggy, not expecting to put her through battle again. The waiter ejected us from the restaurant and lead us to a picnic table in the back yard. We are both disabled and accompanied by professional service dogs."

"Sir, I will explain that the law provides access for those accompanied by service dogs but I can't force them to serve you."

I firmly stated for all to hear, "Officer, I totally understand. I simply ask that you take a report, so I have evidence when I file the lawsuit. I needed documentation in the land of the undocumented! I was pissed.

I looked at the staff and said, "I've never wanted to own a Mexican restaurant but, in this case, I would take great pride in owning this place due to the large fine you will pay as a result of breaking the federal law. I'll feed dogs inside, and humans in the backyard where you took us." I then took a breath and asked them to call the owner so I could speak with him. The owner subsequently apologized, and we were seated in the epicenter of the restaurant.

The next day, Peggy asked where I wanted to eat. Wanna guess where I chose to have lunch? We drove to the restaurant where we'd eaten the night before. As we started to walk in, I told Peggy to stop. There was a newspaper machine near the front door. Our story ran that day and was referenced in the header of the front page. *Wow*, I thought, another **coincidence**. "My Higher Power sure has a sense of timing," I told Peggy. I bought a copy, and we walked in. The daytime manager greeted us and evidenced learned behavior like Fidelity had years ago! I proudly and defiantly opened the newspaper and showed him the feature story. "I prevented your staff from breaking the law last night, and I know the restaurant owner is grateful." We received a complimentary dessert, which we savored like never before.

I looked at Peggy and said "I'm proud of you. I love you." I then turned to my Booster and Peggy's service dog, Tara, and hugged them both. I said in fairness, as I'd learned to do at BUCS, "And I love you two equally." Peggy smiled her radiant smile I loved to see. "You're really something, my friend," she said.

I responded, "And you're really my best friend, second only to my Booster!" She smiled an even bigger smile.

On another occasion, I called Peggy and asked her if she and her service dog, Tara, would like to attend the Association of Professional Dog Trainers Conference in Covington, Kentucky. We both loved to bone up on our canine educations at every opportunity. Peggy enthusiastically agreed to join us. We subsequently flew to Kentucky and met at the hotel, had a nice dinner together, and retired to bed early. After grabbing a quick breakfast in the morning, we went outside and hailed a taxi to take us to the conference. We calmly approached the driver, but he adamantly refused to allow us to get in because we were accompanied by our service dogs. I struggled to maintain my composure. *Here we go again*, I thought. *Play it again, Sam!*

I explained repeatedly that access was required by law. I soon realized, to express it politely, that I was urinating in the wind. I told him, "I'm calling the police and you are not going anywhere!"

I dialed 911 before things got out of hand. My Booster and I stood in front of the taxi, preventing him from leaving. Peggy said she was going to grab another taxi and I nodded an acknowledgment. Within minutes, a police officer arrived.

MY BOOSTER!

"Officer, I'm attending a conference with a friend. The taxi driver refused us access because we are both partnered with service dogs to help overcome disabilities in our lives."

"I understand sir" the officer responded.

The officer explained to the taxi driver, "You must transport a passenger accompanied by a service dog unless the passenger or the dog are unruly. If you don't want to allow a dog into your taxi, perhaps you should perhaps find another vocation."

I asked the officer to please give me a police report item number. The taxi driver then curtly stated, "Get in."

I responded, "Do you really think I'm going to get into the vehicle with you after what just transpired? For one thing, I wouldn't feel safe, and secondly, I'm not going to reward you with payment for violating our national law!"

The officer, to his credit, waited until another taxi arrived to take us to the conference. I later got a copy of the report, wrote a letter of thanks to the responding officer, and sent it to his superior. Astonishingly, I received an email response from the officer. He thanked me and explained that his uncle was blind, and he knew all about the access laws for assistance dogs. He also proffered that he was equally upset and was glad he could help. What a **coincidence** that I was lucky enough to have that particular officer respond to my call.

COMMONWEALTH OF KENTUCKY

SYNOPSIS:

Complainant was refused service from cab driver due to his having a service dog. The dog was clearly marked and licensed.

DATE AND TIME OF OCCURRENCE:

10/21/2012 at 16.28 hours INVESTIGATION:

Mr. Hawn suffers from a disability and has an 8-year-old companion/service dog. The dog had proper credentials, was wearing a vest identifying him as a service dog. In addition to the vest, the dog was leashed and well behaved. Mr. Hawn attempted to enter a Community Yellow Cab #XXX that Mr. A was driving. Mr. A adamantly denied Mr. Hawn entry into his vehicle. Mr. A told Mr. Hawn that he would not allow the dog in his cab. Despite Mr. Hawn explaining that the dog is a service dog and that the Americans With Disabilities Act prohibited him from denying service because of the service animal, Mr. A still denied service. A vehicle parked behind the cab prevented Mr. A from backing up, and Mr. Hawn stood in front of the cab with his dog while waiting for police. Upon arrival, myself and Spc. C explained the law to Mr. A, and that he could not refuse such service. Mr. A explained to us that he was afraid of dogs and that he was unaware of such a law. Mr. Hawn elected to wait for a different taxicab company.

When I caught up with Peggy at the conference, she looked intently into my eyes and told me she was proud of me. She further explained that she'd fought her battles in the army and wasn't emotionally capable of handling confrontation due to her PTSD kicking her ass.

I totally understood and appreciated her frankness. It'd taken years for me to be able to resolve conflicts without excessive confrontation. I had my Booster to thank for that.

Peggy then snapped a photo of my Booster embracing me at the conference.

I cherish it dearly.

MY BOOSTER!

CHAPTER 14
THE ENEMY WITHIN

The following year, I arrived home from Thailand and was informed that my Booster had been brought to the veterinarian because he had a sore jaw. The diagnosis was temporomandibular joint disorder (TMJ), muscular pain associated with the hinge that connects the jawbone to the skull. My Booster loved to carry a stuffed toy and take it to greet people with great exuberance. I'd trained him from puppyhood to do so. I was told that he was experiencing pain when he opened his jaw wide enough to drop the stuffed toy. Muscle relaxants were prescribed, and he seemed OK. I also experienced pain associated with TMJ, and it comes and goes. No big deal, right? Perhaps my Booster just needed a vacation! I'd planned months before to attend the North American Veterinary Conference (NAVC) in Orlando, Florida, following my return from Thailand. I invited Peggy and Tara to join Booster and me at the conference. We booked a wonderful "canine cruise" following the conference. An event organizer had arranged for canine specialists to conduct a series of lectures upon the ship. One of the lecturers was Dr. Aubrey Fine, who was on my BUCS thesis committee. We'd spoken often and exchanged many emails but never met in person. I counted the days until I could meet Dr. Fine and introduce him to Booster.

When it came time to fly to Orlando, Booster and I boarded the plane without circumstance. I *coincidentally* sat next to a gentleman who introduced himself as Dr. Frederic Gaschen, a canine gastrointestinal specialist at Louisiana State University (LSU). I mentioned Booster's TMJ during our conversation. When we landed in Orlando, I went to the luggage belt to grab my suitcase. I almost never check luggage, but I *coincidentally* did this trip. The veterinarian specialist walked over to claim his luggage and asked if he could examine Booster for me and check out his sore jaw. He looked into my Booster's throat, smelled his ears, and palpitated his head. He found a small lump on Booster's head behind his right eye. It was NOT noticeable before the flight. He suggested I get it checked out and referred me to a specialty clinic in nearby Maitland, Florida. I took a taxi to the resort where we were staying. I was met by Peggy's warm embrace. My Booster ran to play with Tara. We laughed as the dogs frolicked, play-bowed, and ran in circles. I gave Booster his stuffed toy, and he and Tara played tug-of-war. When the ritual ended, Booster opened his mouth to drop the toy and screamed in pain. He jumped in the air and ran as though a 240-volt electric cord had touched his tongue. We both panicked and worry overtook the moment. I had to do something immediately.

After locating the clinic that Dr. Gaschen had recommended, I made an appointment for the next day. That afternoon, he picked up one of Tara's toys and refused to drop it. He knew pain would follow if he opened his mouth wide enough to release it. I had to pry his mouth open to remove the toy and again he screamed horribly. I prayed he wouldn't think that I was the cause of the pain. I kept Booster away from all objects he would "automatically" pick up to greet me with. It was a learned behavior so entrenched that, even though it ultimately led to intense pain, he did it anyway. He was virtually pain-free until he opened his mouth wide. I was in such emotional pain I couldn't open my mouth either. It was awful!

Peggy and Tara went with us to the clinic the following day. The specialists at Maitland Veterinary Specialists determined with a CAT scan and MRI that the bump Dr. Gaschen had found was a tumor. It'd eaten through Booster's skull like a water balloon bursting through a saltine cracker. The seasoned oncologist suspected it was cancerous and likely squamous cell carcinoma. That form of cancer usually presents in the digits (toes and fingers) but was also occasionally found in the sinus cavity. The aggressive cancer had started in the skull's lining, feasted on the bone, and broken through. If pathology confirmed the diagnosis, Booster had just three weeks to live, each day promising more excruciating pain.

It was suggested that we give Booster a cake and ice cream party before putting him down. I wanted Booster to have some ice cream right then and there! Peggy drove me to get a pint of vanilla ice cream. It was surreal. It was worse than awful. I was traveling with the two souls I'd learned to love more than life itself. My Booster was ultimately diagnosed as terminal, and Peggy had to go along for the ride. She was rudely slapped with a reminder of her tenuous mortality on the way to our fabulous, forget-all cruise.

The emotional pain that day would sink the strongest battleship the world has ever known. My Peggy was terminally ill from cancer, just like my Booster! She had to listen to all the horrid details.

"The tumor is impinging on a nerve near the brain. The pain is likely great, and you must decide soon for Booster's best interest," I was told.

God, I didn't want Peggy to relive her own diagnosis and likely mortality. I was out of my mind with sorrow and resentment. *Why? Why? Why? MHP, why?* I was almost ready to put my Booster down when I **coincidentally** received an email from an angel located in what many in the US referred to as "enemy territory."

My Cuban friend Rodrigo sent me an email from Havana. "Davis, we Cubans are fighters. Fight for Booster. He fought for you." Cuba is known for medicine and education, coupled with discipline. He was an intellectual and wouldn't steer me wrong.

Fuck me! WTF was I supposed to do? I remembered my brother's words long ago, "What are you going to do with the dog?" Now, I really had to answer that exact question, post-haste. I wasn't capable of handling this, despite therapy and meds. I buckled and fell into a chair. My Booster ran to my side, licking my hand. *Oh, please put ME down, not my Booster. I give up. I absolutely give the fuck up*, I thought. My Booster always wanted to live, whereas I often did not. He cherished life, and I oftentimes resented it.

Peggy sat beside me as I entered a hypnotic trance. She hugged me, squeezed me, and said, "Take Booster home and take time to think." I made a reservation later that day for the last flight my Booster would ever take, the flight to hell, then suggested to Peggy to have a friend take my place so she could enjoy the cruise. With Peggy's conveyed strength and Rodrigo's fighting words, I somehow sullenly managed to board the plane later that day. As though he was on autopilot, Booster walked straight into the bulkhead seat he knew to find. He was an experienced traveler, not knowing what he was about to experience.

MY BOOSTER!

I'd been lied to. I'd been right all along. Life sucked and was NOT worth living. I was taking the second to last flight with my Booster. On the final and ultimate flight, he would leave this world. I would be lying if I didn't consider booking tickets for both flights myself. How could I possibly survive without my Booster and why in the hell would I want to? *Fuck. Fuck it all. Fuck life!!*

I arrived home and greeted my pack of canine lovers. My Booster was welcomed home in full regalia. The other pack members walked up and licked his mouth . . . a sign of respect and submission for the pack leader. Booster upheld his role, though his role in life was suddenly tenuous. I wondered how the pack would adjust to life without *our* Booster. After hugging him for the better part of an hour, I gave him multiple treats. Worrying about his weight was no longer an issue. It was the weight upon my shoulders that bore upon reality. I wasn't sure I could handle it, but I owed it to my other "family" members to try. After all, I'd once shunned and rejected Booster, yet he'd stood by me through thick and thin. He had unequivocally saved me from myself. I couldn't abandon my Booster. Perhaps, selfishly, I knew I couldn't live without him.

I thought about human parents presented with a child that's diagnosed with a terminal illness. *How in the hell do they do it? Where do they get the strength? What is their booster?* I wondered. I didn't get it then and I still don't. I guess it comes from the necessity of providing for the rest of the pack, if there is one.

After gathering any objects Booster could pick up, I tried to watch television. I might as well have tried to climb Mount Everest backwards. I inevitably ended up driving to the Louisiana State University (LSU) veterinary hospital. The trip was a complete waste of time, as the veterinary clinic didn't have a neurologist on staff. The internist said that it was most likely not squamous cell carcinoma, as that form of cancer is rarely found in the sinus cavity.

Coincidentally, at that moment her pager went off and the oncology department at Maitland Veterinary Specialists conveyed my Booster's pathology. He indeed had a squamous cell carcinoma tumor. I shook my head, hugged Booster, and knew I needed to get in touch with the specialist right away. It was indeed life or death, *perhaps* only for my Booster.

When I returned to my cabin, I sat at my desk, gazing intently at my computer. I utilized the BUCS research skills I'd acquired years before. I researched squamous cell carcinoma, trials, and treatments. At the computer-illiterate age of fifty-plus, I had barely known how to operate a computer before going to university. I searched the internet like there was no tomorrow, for there might not be a tomorrow. One after the other, I read scientific papers published in PubMed and interpreted statistical data. Strength from only MHP knows where, overcame me. I ran my fingers across my laptop like a treasure finder panning for gold. I resolutely read everything I could find regarding squamous cell carcinoma. There were conventional and alternative treatments available. I called around the world asking questions. I remained at my desk for the next two days . . . only abandoning ship long enough to feed my canine family. I then composed a list of the ten most likely treatments that could help Booster, conventional and unconventional. These options were like gold to me, but were they fool's gold? Were they real?

I assembled ten packets of desperation. Each packet contained a copy of Booster's MRI and CT scans, along with photos of him surrounded by Cuban children in a classroom and HIV-infected orphans in Thailand. I enclosed a note: "My Booster has done so much for the humans in this world, and he would like to participate in your research for the betterment of mankind. Can you help him? Can he participate in your trial?"

I then helped Booster get into my truck. Together, we went to FedEx and sent out the Hail Mary pass of all passes. I cried profusely on the way as Booster's head, containing the enemy within, lay on my lap. The recurring throbbing in my leg dissipated with the weight of Booster's head compressing it. We both had enemies within! I shouldn't have been driving that day. It was selfish of me, and I regret having done so. My Higher Power somehow enabled me to make the trip. I returned home and tried to think about a life without my Booster. Try as I might, I wasn't able to do so.

The pain was so acute that I didn't even try to drink to numb it. I hurt in the past due to my misconceived perception of love. This time I was hurt by REAL love. This pain was exceptional and exponential; I was numb to the bone, to the quick of my existence. I didn't eat, didn't watch television, and certainly never listened to the radio. Music was the worst, as it always revolved around love, despair, and torment, or so it seemed.

Three days after mailing the packets, the phone rang. I did NOT want to answer it. Surprisingly, I didn't answer it and say, "Whoever you are, fuck off." The melodic voice of an angel was on the line. At that moment, I knew this was a conversation of divine intervention of a Higher Power unbeknownst to me. "Hello, this is Dr. Elizabeth Pluhar calling from the University of Minnesota. I want to help Booster!" (Booster . . . not your dog . . . Booster!) The angel strummed her harp of hope and said, "I want to take a piece of Booster's tumor and make a vaccine to fight his cancer. We've had success with other forms of cancer, but we've never worked with squamous cell before. I will be available in three weeks." Reality dictated that Booster didn't have three weeks to live.

My entire being rode the instantaneous roller coaster of life. I cried in that lady's ears with reckless abandon. I was at the bottom of a bottomless pit, catapulted to the highest altitude of heaven, only to bungee jump downward without a rope. I explained, "My Booster doesn't have three weeks to live. He's in acute pain, and so am I."

The phone conversation came to a close, the window of life slammed shut. By this time, Booster had instilled within me a sense in a Higher Power greater than myself. There were no **coincidences**, right? I sat in my chair, clutching Booster like there was no tomorrow because there *was no tomorrow*.

Somehow, my subconscious called upon my BUCS veterinary lessons. I immediately picked up the phone and placed a call to heaven. A University of Minnesota operator answered the phone and connected me with "our" angel. "Dr. Pluhar here. How may I help you?" chimed the voice of optimism. "Dr. Pluhar, it's Booster's human calling you back. Might it be possible to send you a piece of the offending tumor to try to develop the vaccine?" I implored.

"I'm thinking that radiation therapy (RT) will shrink the tumor and might provide relief in the short run. I think, based upon my BUCS education, that irradiated tissue will be useless with respect to vaccine development. We need to excise a sample of the affected tissue prior to radiation. Is that correct?"

"That would work, Mr. Hawn," came the angel's response. My mind's gears accelerated rapidly, oiled by love, and accompanying desperation. At that moment, spirituality, trust, love, and all that is good in life melded, fused. I told Dr. Pluhar to expect a sample shortly. Once I'd calmed down as necessity dictated, I called Maitland Veterinary Specialists. I asked to speak to the oncologist, Dr. Lurie.

"Dr. Lurie, this is Davis Hawn and 'we' need your help. I've been on the internet for days looking for salvation. I've learned of several promising therapies not yet proven. Would you help us, please?" I asked.

Dr. Lurie, being the gentleman that he was, said in words I will never forget, "I will help you in any way possible, but you must do something quickly." I meekly asked,

"Would you be willing to excise a piece of the tumor prior to commencing radiation to shrink it?" Dr. Lurie replied,

"I'm board-certified in surgery, so I can certainly do that for you."

Wow, another **coincidence!** I made an appointment with *that* angel and then called the *other* angel back. "Dr. Pluhar, "I'm flying to Florida tomorrow to meet with Booster's radiologist, Dr. Lurie. He'll excise a piece of Booster's tumor and send it to you and keep an extra sample just in case. I'll temporarily move to Florida so that my Booster can receive radiation therapy for a month." My BUCS computer research skills provided a research rainbow of opportunity for Booster, bound for the Rainbow Bridge. I took him to the airport the next day for a flight that was never to be. It was "another" flight for Booster after he'd flown his "last" flight. We landed in Orlando, drove to Maitland, and entered the office of opportunity.

Dr. Lurie smiled and spoke in a soothing British accent. He prescribed a radiation therapy (RT) plan comprised of 18 daily treatments. I signed off on the disclosure form that included the prospect of blindness in the right eye, which was located within the field of radiation. I rented a condo for a month and drove my beloved Booster forty-five minutes to and from treatment every day. Within five treatments, my Booster no longer screamed in pain when he opened his mouth to release the prized toy he so loved to bequeath to any human who came within his personal parameter.

Dr. Lurie explained that the cancer cells were responding well to the radiation treatments. I, too, was responding to the radiation treatments; as went my Booster, so went the realm of emotions of Davis. I demonstrated to Dr. Lurie how Booster runs to my truck, grabs the tug rope attached to the door handle, and proudly opens it to bring me water or medicine. The dog that a week before couldn't smile without excruciating pain was once again tugging open a door, this time to the future. I was momentarily frozen in an environment of gratitude and free of pain from the love of another. My Booster, and my Peggy, were OK, "just for today," and I strived to live in the moment.

I decided to take Booster to Disney World to celebrate life, *just for today!* We rode a few rides together, but most of the time, Booster entertained children that ran to greet him. Both Booster and the children were oblivious to the black ink line on Booster's shaved head. It was the landing site for atomic weaponry once employed to destroy thousands of lives, yet today utilized to save one. The

children aimed their bubble guns at Booster, and he jumped up and intercepted the incoming bubble bombs better than the finest Star Wars defense shield ever designed.

While watching Booster, I happened to catch a glimpse of an artist doing caricatures. I instantaneously knew I wanted to immortalize that day and my Booster. We met the kind man and commissioned a drawing. The resulting caricature was unflattering of me, but Booster looked great. It summed up our relationship in real time. Booster was happy, as he got to play with children he loved while I steadily wondered if he'd ever be able to do so again.

After eighteen doses of daily radiation, with weekends off, Booster and I returned to the cabin. He was himself again and playfully wrestling with his pack as though nothing deleterious had happened. I lay in the sun with Booster like never before. I held him like there was no tomorrow because I knew tomorrow was now a luxury for Booster. During the six-week radiation regimen, he started to lose fur on his head. The radiation shrank the tumor, but Booster's radiant good looks were different now. He indeed looked like a cancer survivor, a hero, yet oblivious to his outward appearance. Unlike humans, who might lose face when their outside appearance changes, Booster retained his confidence. He was a martyr and a role model. I later told my Peggy that if Booster could do it, so could she!

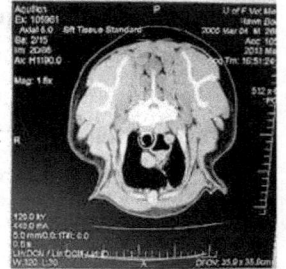

After two weeks of recuperation, Booster and I flew to the University Florida, Gainesville. We were back on yet another flight that was never to be. This time we were flying to have his skull cut open to scoop out the remnants of the aggressive tumor. Dr. Lurie arranged for us to meet Dr. Nicholas Bacon, a noted neurosurgeon from England. Dr. Bacon agreed to operate to remove whatever was left of the tumor. I left Booster in Dr. Bacon's learned hands and dejectedly returned to my hollow condo.

I couldn't handle being without Booster. He was in a cage fighting for his life. I had to go do *something*, so I went to see a movie on the college campus. It was entitled, *The Last Flight of Petr Ginz*. The words "last flight" forced me to go see the movie. By this time, I was more than aware **coincidence** was a code word that MHP used to tell me I was on track in life, partnered with my Booster.

I entered the screening room and saw distinguished, well-dressed older people . . . meaning people my age and beyond. The film told an emotionally devastating story about a young boy named Petr (Peter) who lived in Prague. He

MY BOOSTER!

was imprisoned by the Nazis during the Holocaust. Petr was amazingly talented, and by the age of sixteen, he'd circulated a newspaper in the prison camp and painted over sixty oil paintings. One of his paintings of the moon was eerily a mirror image of the first photos of the moon taken by astronauts decades later. Peter had a bunk mate by the name of Sydney who helped his father shoe the horses for the Nazi soldiers. One day, a Nazi soldier came to take both boys to the gas chamber. Sydney's father intervened and explained that his son was the only one who knew how to help shoe the horses. Sydney's life was spared, but young Peter, whose imagination took him to the moon, which he painted so beautifully, went on his "last flight" and died an early death in a Nazi gas chamber.

Peter's prison camp writings were later found when his prison camp was liberated. They ended up in an attic in Holland and were the basis for the movie documenting his life. At the film's conclusion, an elderly gentleman was on the stage. His name was Sydney Taussig. He was Peter's bunk mate decades before, a Holocaust survivor. I surveyed the audience, and there were few souls under the age of thirty in the audience of higher education! Mr. Taussig had tenuously held on to the possibility of living another day, one day at a time, just like Booster.

I drove back to my sterile condo knowing that Booster was also on his *last flight* in life. I started beating myself up—yes, damn it, again—because I was such a wimp! *After listening to Mr. Taussig's story, how dare I think that the life of a dog had import by way of comparison?* I'd been selfish to think in such terms. I was an older man who'd escaped potential death of my own making due to poor choices in life. Mr. Taussig had escaped death from events he had no control over. Far more devastating was Petr's death as a young man. "Like a Candle in the Wind," his life ended prematurely. My mind was on sensory overload. I was starting to care about others again.

I didn't know what to think or how to think. The world was evil and wasn't supposed to work like this. Why was this happening? Surely there's a big letdown to come, lurking just around the corner. I received periodic updates on Booster's condition from Dr. Bacons' staff. Two days later, the phone rang, and I just knew it was going to be "THAT" call. "Mr. Hawn, Dr. Bacon said you can come pick Booster up in the morning." I froze. I didn't know what to say. I was on sensory overload once again. My Higher-Power-instilled circuit breaker snapped before I shorted out.

An hour later, I pulled myself together and called the *Gainesville Sun* newspaper. I told them, "I want to report a miracle." The University of Florida coordinated a visit with a *Gainesville Sun* reporter. We'd all be present to visit my Booster when he emerged from the recovery room. More like a drone than a human, I entered the University of Gainesville Veterinary facility. A university official and the newspaper reporter greeted me.

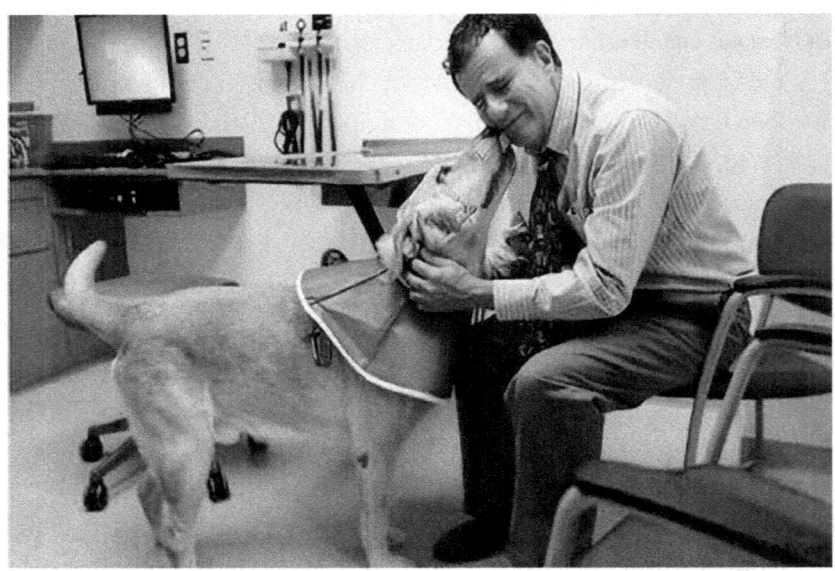

Shortly thereafter, I was brought into a room. I sat in a chair and waited. Suddenly, Dr. Bacon walked in with Booster, who wore a cone around his shaved, stitched head. I cried and cried some more. I slid out of my chair onto floor and Booster walked over and kissed me in the face. He was worried about "ME." The photographer's camera flashed! I looked up from the floor and searched for Dr. Bacon's eyes, speechless. With Herculean effort, I mouthed the words "thank you" with trembling lips. My body was like butter melted in the sun.

Dr. Bacon explained, "You may get six months, perhaps another year," as Booster licked the tears from my eyes.

MY BOOSTER!

He had stitches across his forehead and no fur on the right side of his face. He looked like a Frankenstein creation. I kept looking at Booster and he kept smiling all the while. I'd learned so much from him and knew he had more to teach me. He and Bonnie were miraculous mentors.

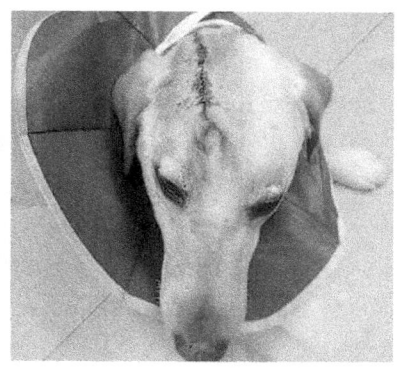

The day Booster was discharged from the University of Florida veterinary hospital, I received a call from Bonnie. "How's Booster, and how are *you*, Davis?" I told Bonnie that I didn't know how to answer that question, saying, "I'm numb, and my Booster is seemingly pain-free and still 'Booster.'" I kept looking for personality changes due to the brain

operation, but I didn't find any. Dr. Lurie and Dr. Bacon had pulled off an amazing feat and saved the life of a dog that had come within weeks of certain, painful death.

A few days later, my Booster and I flew home. I was worried that an airline employee might think he had some form of disease. I asked the oncologist to write a letter on official letterhead explaining Booster's medical condition. When we got home, we were greeted with hugs and kisses from joyous hounds that knew no bounds. I was happy in the moment. WE were happy in the moment. Life was good in the moment. Then it happened! The phone rang.

"Hello Davis, this is Liz Pluhar." She explained that Booster's squamous cell carcinoma cancer cells had grown prolifically within the confines of the "Petri dish of promise."

"Please tell me you have good news," I beseeched.

"I sure will she extolled exuberantly! The cells have grown prolifically, it looks promising.

"How do we proceed from here," I asked.

"Let's let Booster, and his immune system, recuperate from the surgery. A month from now, we'll send a dose of the vaccine every two weeks for a total of six doses."

"Dr. Pluhar, no words exist that can adequately express my sincere appreciation," You've impacted two lives, not just one. We thank you."

Yet another ray of hope illuminated the dark clouds of despair. How was it possible that such magnitudes of mind were working to save the life of my Booster? It was divine. I never thought mankind had it within itself to project such a vista of panoramic rainbows upon a backdrop of hopelessness and despair. My dedication to my studies at BUCS hadn't been a waste of time and money, as predicted by my soothsayer brother. In fact, over the years, I learned to run ideas by my brother. If he thought they were folly, I proceeded full throttle forward. The money invested, along with the hours of research enlightened enablement, seemingly culminated in a coordinated effort to save the life of a dog so deserving. It was as though My Higher Power became a general contractor, a conductor of the finest instruments known to man, to orchestrate my Booster's salvation. I was simply a pawn, moving across the chess board of life.

I spent every moment with Booster. My heart ticked away the seconds I had left to share with the most precious commodity life had to offer. Reality dictated that we didn't have long to go, and I wanted to be there for Booster as he'd always been there for me. I so loved watching him pick up stuffed toys, leading the other family members in a game of follow the leader. He ran around the couch with his loyal subjects in tow, only to stop and run in the opposite direction. Sometimes, the magnanimous ruler would intentionally get caught to provoke the inevitable tug-of-war that ensued. More often than not, the stuffed creature lost its life. The stuffing went flying, often half a toy in one mouth and the remainder in another.

I threw tennis balls into the pond and joyously watched Booster swim out and triumphantly retrieve them. Best of all, he was able to open his mouth to drop the ball. It had hurt me so much to watch him the month before. I'll never forget how my Booster picked something up and suddenly panicked. It'd been horrible, terrible to watch. The fear of pain was arguably as bad as the pain itself, I postulated. I'd rather have been the subject of such fate than subjecting my Booster to it. Perhaps I'd deserved what life had doled out, but my Booster certainly didn't.

The vaccine that Dr. Pluhar developed helped cure my Booster's cancer. It was a miracle of all miracles. A year later, Dr. Pluhar explained in an email that due to the resounding success of the vaccine therapy, the federal government had granted approval for its use in human trials.

I wondered if Booster's response to the vaccine helped win the government's approval. So, I asked Dr. Pluhar, "May I assume that this is the therapy that saved Booster's life and it may help humans in the near future?"

She answered my question with three capital letters . . . Y . . . E . . . S!

Many years later, I went to the local supermarket. As I was shopping, I noticed a lady staring at me. Not being God's gift to women, it was an uncanny feeling. I was under surveillance for some unknown reason. *Perhaps my zipper was down*, I mused to myself. After a good fifteen minutes, my stalker shouted, "BOOSTER!"

I almost fell over!

She pushed her shopping cart next to mine and said matter-of-factly, My husband's the veterinarian that saved your puppy's life when he ingested rat poison years ago. There was something special about that puppy and I've never forgotten him.

With a smile on my face, I told her, "If you take that cell phone in your hand and do an internet search for *Davis Hawn Booster*, you'll get over 10 pages of stories around the world."

I then went on to explain that "When Booster was eight years old, he was diagnosed with squamous cell carcinoma (SCC) cancer and given just three weeks to live. A cancerous tumor had eaten through his skull cap and impinged on a nerve." At that moment, she started to tear up and get emotional. "I'm surprised that upsets you so much, especially being the wife of a veterinarian. I'm sure you know that one in four dogs will get cancer in its lifetime, one in two after age ten."

"No, you don't understand, Dave. My husband is currently battling SCC." she said with tears forming in her eyes.

Yet another amazing **coincidence**, I silently thought. Guess who had tears in his eyes at that point! Like a pseudo-Paul Harvey I conveyed *the* *rest of the story!* I explained how Dr. Pluhar had taken a piece of Booster's tumor and made the first in the world SSC vaccine for a dog and it'd cured his cancer in conjunction with RT. I then told her that the University of Minnesota later got federal approval for human trials based on the success with the dogs. Lastly, I shared that I'd asked Dr. Pluhar if my Booster's experience contributed to getting human trial approval. She told me, point blank, "Oh yes," and said that it's referred to today as immunotherapy.

At that point, the lady became even more emotional and began crying. What's wrong, I queried. When she regained her composure, she tearfully explained, "Dave my husband recently received immunotherapy treatment for his squamous cell carcinoma."

Coincidence upon **coincidence** became the norm for me with Booster in my life. When I heard that, I was in shock, absolute shock. Booster may well have contributed to saving the life of the veterinarian who had saved his life years before. Seems once again that what goes around comes around, at least in a perfect world. That's the way my Booster saw the world as he devoted his life to bettering the lives of others. He saw the world better with one eye than most did with two. He became the world's *booster*!

MY BOOSTER!

Shortly after his recovery, Booster attended a canine conference with his son Alanon.

CHAPTER 15
PERU FOR US TWO

Booster's cancer became my cancer. I was absolutely devastated by my Booster's cancer diagnosis. Now both of my best friends, my Booster and Peggy, had the dreaded disease that would surely take them from me at any moment. My fragile world of recovery succumbed to an earthquake hitherto never experienced on the Richter scale. I was learning to live life on life's terms, but this was entirely out of the box. Suddenly, I just wanted to get away with my Booster. I needed a welcomed respite from life on life's terms, so I booked a ticket to Peru and made a reservation at a guest house owned by a man who loved dogs. Why Peru? Why not?

When we arrived in Lima, Peru, Booster was inspected by the airport veterinarian, who looked at Booster's Frankenstein-like head encased in stitches. The vet looked up at me as if to say, WTF? I couldn't blame him, as Booster looked like he'd escaped the morgue in the midst of an autopsy. I looked up at the man with tears in my eyes and explained Booster's cancer and the potential miracle cure. The Peruvian gentleman looked at me empathetically and stamped the necessary papers, and we were home free ... or so I thought.

After talking a taxi driver into transporting a dog in his taxi, we arrived at the guest house. We soon learned that I'd booked the wrong date and there was no room in the inn until the following day. I panicked, absolutely freakin panicked. We were in a foreign country with no place to stay, but I remembered that most

Hilton properties were pet friendly. I asked if there was a Hilton in Lima. The guest house manager informed me that indeed there was. I called the Hilton in the beautiful tourist district of Miraflores, explained my dilemma, and my hope to sleep in a room as opposed to the street simply because I had my service dog Booster. The young lady at the end of the phone instantly reassured me they would welcome me and my Booster. I was awestruck. I couldn't speak. A meteorite of amazement struck my vocal cords.

"Sir, are you there?" enquired the sweet voice.

"Yes, I'm here. I'm just surprised and so grateful," I explained. I spoke no Spanish at the time, but *coincidentally,* she was fluent in English. The gist of the conversation was that she understood the service dog concept, and Booster and I were welcome to stay at the Hilton. How in the hell a desk clerk in a foreign country knew of such, I will never know. Perhaps it was the excellence of the Hilton training program in action. After hailing a taxi and educating the driver, we arrived at the Hilton. We were greeted with enthusiasm, not greeted as a spectacle by those with spectacles!

I asked to speak to the person who'd answered my phone inquiry. A young lady shyly approached me. I explained my amazement at her knowledge of the service dog concept and asked her to please call the manager so I could express my gratitude. When the manager arrived, I did my best to explain my heartfelt feelings. I asked if they had a public relations department. Later that day, I sat down with a PR representative, who truly "got it." She arranged for me to meet a lady newspaper reporter who spoke little English. With the help of her translating friend, I tearfully explained what the Hilton open door meant for me accompanied by my service dog Booster.

Later that night, the Hilton concierge arranged for us to get tickets to see the play *Annie*. I was so excited. When we attempted to enter the venue, we were stopped. "*Lo siento señor, no se le permite entrar al teatro con un perro,*" bellowed the beckoning voice. ("I'm sorry, sir, you are not allowed to enter the theater with a dog."). I was devastated and pissed! I didn't know whether to scream or cry. On the one hand, we were treated like royalty and on the other, like second-class citizens. It was as though we were set up for a letdown. The ultimate irony was that they had a dog as a performer, nestled in disabled President Roosevelt's arms! Looking back, I should have done whatever it took, including jail, to accentuate the disgusting irony! The problem would have been: what would have become of my Booster? Sometimes, you must draw the line, though you wish you didn't need to. It was all very disappointing, yet I retained my composure, as BUCS and Booster had taught me to do over the years.

In days gone by, I would have fought my way in. They would have had to perform a different play, Irving Berlin's *Annie Get Your Gun*, the fictionalized story of a female sharpshooter. Such circumstances afforded an opportunity to enlighten the unenlightened and educate the ignorant, knowing that ignorance isn't an ugly word. I reflected upon the interview I'd done that morning in which I opened up and shared intimate details of my life. I was now more grateful than ever that I'd done so.

The following day, the newspaper story appeared in the largest newspaper in Lima. It included myriad photos of my Booster in action. Once again, a reporter found merit in my life's journey with my Booster by my side. It was validation of the highest magnitude. Yeah, I tearfully overreacted emotionally, but was it really overreacting?

After I read the last line in the newspaper story, I was totally stoked. It referenced Peruvian Awareness Law 29830 that states *assistance dogs can enter all public and private places, including means of transportation.* I took the newspaper in hand and walked to a local movie theater. When I entered the theater, the security guard tried to stop us, but we quickly sidestepped him. I bought candy and popcorn and proceeded into the screening room. A theater employee came running in, proclaiming dogs weren't permitted in the theater.

"So, you sell me popcorn, then want to kick me out?" I asked. I showed him our newspaper story, and he took it to his manager, who confronted me shortly thereafter. The manager wanted to eject me from the theater. I politely asked him to please call the police so they could document the discrimination and violation of the law. The manager forthright handed me my newspaper and left. I had no idea what was going to transpire next, but with Booster by my side and my newspaper in hand, I wasn't afraid. Booster had an angel upon his shoulders time and time again. The movie was in Spanish, and I had no idea what was being said. I thought, *I won the battle but lost the war!* After the movie, armed with the newspaper, we visited a local Chili's restaurant and met no resistance.

MY BOOSTER!

I researched the law with the help of loving Peruvians, who apologized for the problems I faced while visiting their city. It turns out that the law was passed for guide dog access, without provisions for assistance dogs. Often, guide dogs are permitted access before more inclusive assistance dog legislation is passed. The disability of blindness is most apparent and often evokes more sympathy, understanding, and willingness to adapt.

Later in the day, I was contacted by a lovely lady who explained that she had a blog site that promoted Lima. I explained that my respect for the city had plummeted as I was coldly rejected the night before, unable to see a play closed to a person with a disability. She empathetically published my story on her blog site. To reveal to the world your damaged soul, especially as a person who clammed up for a long time, was not easy. Her blog site was called *LimaEasy*. For me, it was NOT so easy! When I read our story on the blog site, I was amazed at the amount of time she'd invested writing the seven-page story! It was all there in detail.

Later, I was invited to tour a veterinary school while visiting the city. The director was an affable and courteous gentleman. He arranged for Booster to be seen by one of the few canine optical specialists in the country who **coincidentally** practiced at the veterinary school in Lima. I explained that I'd been putting drops into Booster's dry eye five times a day as a result of the RT. He examined Booster and explained that the eye had died as a result of the radiation therapy he'd received. He also explained that when it's dry, it's painful, and he suggested the eye be removed. "Dogs do great with just one eye," he assured me. Sadly, Booster would need another transformative surgery.

I experienced far more good than bad in Lima, and grateful that Booster and I were able to leave a footprint in yet another society other than our own. It was such an honor to be able to share one's soul and passion and have them respond empathetically. My experiences in Lima were part of a larger healing process taking place as a direct result of my blessed Booster's presence in my life.

CHAPTER 16
TICKED OFF

When I returned home, I arranged for my veterinarian in Arkansas to remove Booster's dead eye. He assured me it was a relatively easy procedure, and all went well. I no longer had to put lubricant drops into Booster's eye five times a day. I was sure he'd feel more comfortable. The Peruvian veterinarian was correct, as it never seemed to make a difference to Booster. He was the same Booster, positive and energetic as ever.

I continued working on my mobile home park and life marched forward with my canine family. Eventually, I bought some land on a mountaintop in Arkansas and built a large threestory log home. I soon learned that the ever-present chiggers and ticks on the property had voracious appetites. They were like little tanks and carried potentially deadly diseases affecting animals and humans alike.

While walking my pack down trails, I noticed Booster's deteriorating hips were hurting him as evidenced by his limping. I thought it might be time for another stem cell shot into the hip, as I knew the benefits of stem cell implantation weren't permanent. I called Medi-Vet America and arranged for Booster to get another round of stem cell therapy. The following week, we drove to a clinic in our home state of Mississippi. I invited the press to meet us. When they arrived, I explained how my service dog Booster was going to be forced into retirement due to hip dysplasia. I further explained that he was going to get a second round of stem cell therapy to improve mobility and relieve pain in an effort to extend his working life. Booster showed off his skills as the cameras started to snap photos and take videos.

Booster demonstrated opening my truck door and going inside to get a water bottle. I'd whispered into his ear, "I know it hurts." One of the reporters heard my empathetic words and quoted them in an article in *USA Today* and included video footage. The astute, empathetic reporter understood my relationship with Booster was indeed special. Booster and I both experienced pain in our daily lives and rituals. We each knew when the other was in pain. I'm sure that's a hard concept to grasp for many, but it's very true. There's nothing my Booster wouldn't do for me, and nothing I wouldn't do for my Booster. Our relationship was purely symbiotic. We are all animals, sentient beings, capable of love and nurturing.

After the demonstration, Booster had adipose-derived stem cells injected into his dysplastic hips to hopefully reconstruct affected tissue. Miracles always happened in my Booster's **"no-coincidence** life," so I summarily expected that the procedure would help as it had before. The procedure went well, and we went home that same day.

A few weeks later, Booster and his canine family members jumped into our truck, and we headed out to our mountaintop refuge in Arkansas. About a week later, I greeted Booster with my usual, newfound *joie de vivre*. He was sick. He wagged his tail but couldn't stand up. My heart stopped, and I panicked. I called my Arkansas veterinarian, and he saw us right away. He gave Booster a shot. My Booster rallied for a day, then returned to the same abyss of helplessness. He was sinking fast.

I returned to my veterinarian, and he referred me to an emergency clinic in Springfield, Missouri. The veterinarians at the emergency clinic referred me to the University of Missouri Veterinary Teaching Hospital (MIZZOU). I immediately called the university and informed them we were coming. Hours later, we arrived at the teaching hospital on the University of Missouri's campus. Volunteer staff members helped lift Booster's limp body onto a cart.

We wheeled Booster into the waiting room. He walked in circles and later started head-butting his cage. He had encephalitis; his brain was swollen. As Dr. Melissa Carpentier examined Booster, I explained he was

MY BOOSTER!

a world traveler and exposed to potential toxins from around the world, thus complicating any potential diagnosis. Dr. Carpentier explained that she would take immediate steps to try to help Booster. She ordered antibiotics and tests of all kinds. Of course, it had to be a holiday weekend, right? It was Memorial Day, and test results would be delayed. Dr. Carpentier prescribed everything known to man, not knowing what we were up against.

That evening, I went to an empty hotel room and cried my eyes out. It was doubtful that Booster would survive the night. I called my brother, who softly suggested I "let him go." My brother shared his opinion Booster was tired, had suffered enough, and I needed to let him go.

I resolutely explained, "I love my Booster with all my heart, and I, of all people, don't want to cause him pain and suffering. The specialists haven't even determined what's wrong yet, and I won't prematurely give up on my best friend. I wouldn't tell 'your' doctor to cease treating 'you' without even knowing what was wrong with you . . . and you're a lot older than Booster!"

I'd learned to speak up and not be so fearful of confrontation, but only when it came to advocating for my Booster. It took years before I incorporated that inner strength into my personal life. Booster taught me how to fight for things that mattered most in life. I also thought about all the times I had taken my brother's advice and done the opposite, which proved to be the right decision!

I reminded my brother about the time our father was gravely ill. My father had pneumonia and knocked on death's door. His newly acquired internist at the time suggested we let him go. My father had signed a "do not resuscitate" order. I explained to the internist that my father didn't mean to let him die if he had a cold! I found a pulmonologist who said with proper meds, my father would likely survive. After the battle of medical hierarchy was consummated, the pulmonologist took over and my father lived for many years with a quality of life better than he had previously.

The following morning, I called Medi-Vet America and asked them if there had ever been a case in which stem cell therapy had failed. "Have you ever had a dog that contracted an infection, or had a serious adverse reaction, as a result of stem cell implantation procedures?" I asked. The company's medical staff talked to me directly. They were empathetic and honest. They researched their data bank and explained that this was a total abnormality most likely not associated with the procedure. From the intonation of their voices, I trusted them. I called Dr. Carpentier and explained what I had learned from MediVet's staff. Then, I sent her photos of rat droppings I'd found inside my home, where I stored dog food. I explained I'd researched on the internet and found that dogs can get diseases from ingesting rat droppings. Some of the symptoms of the associated diseases mimicked those exhibited by Booster.

After patiently listening, she thanked me for the input. After all, my Booster was no ordinary dog. He'd traveled the world to exotic countries that have diseases rarely, if ever, seen in the US. She explained Booster wasn't any better, BUT he wasn't any worse.

I then shared with her I'd reached out to another veterinarian who'd once saved Booster's life when he had just three weeks to live due to squamous cell carcinoma. After explaining that Dr. Pluhar had developed the first custommade vaccine in the world to treat squamous cell carcinoma on Booster's behalf, I asked Dr. Carpentier if she would be willing to confer with Dr. Pluhar. **Coincidentally**, it turned out that Dr. Pluhar taught Dr. Carpentier when she was a veterinary student at the University of Minnesota! Wanna guess my response upon hearing those words? You're damn right! I cried and knew MHP was at work in my life. The **coincidence** factor was totally erased, no longer a possibility. So many thoughts bombarded my filled-to-capacity brain.

I visited Booster later that day and relished the touch of his warm fur. While hugging him tightly, I whispered into his ear, "I love you." My heart was ablaze. I was all alone in another state and in a state of despair. *What in the hell is going on and why?* Even worse was the fact that no answers would be forthcoming since Booster's calamity transpired on a holiday weekend. Some holiday!

Miraculously, Booster fought as he always did. He had Rocky Mountain Spotted Fever (RMSF) from a tick bite. Days later, Dr. Carpentier called me and said I could come visit Booster that afternoon. She said she thought, perhaps maybe, he was a little better. I went to the hospital, and Booster

MY BOOSTER!

recognized me immediately. His tongue lashed my face with undeniable love and appreciation. Somehow, he knew I was fighting along with him, ever-present by his side. I instantly knew he was better. I knew Booster as he knew me. We were indeed symbiotic. We were one. Later on, my upset became anger when I thought about how the flea and tick prevention medicine I relied on to protect my Booster failed and jeopardized his life. I called the "major U.S. manufacturer" that made the defective product and explained, "Your tick prevention medicine failed, and my dog almost died as a result. I think the least you can do is cover his medical bills *if* he survives." In typical corporate denial, I received a call a few days later, "Our product doesn't warranty protection from RMSF." It was a sorry and fuck off response. "Hey asshole, if your product did the ONE THING it was designed to do, prevent tick bites, contracting RMSF and other tick born illnesses wouldn't be possible!" Within a week's time, Booster, who'd once again come within hours of death, was going home. I subsequently learned that Dr. Carpentier had put her own dog down the day she saved Booster's life. She later confided that she wasn't sure Booster was going to make it. In my heart of hearts, I knew that saving Booster's life somehow provided solace to the doctor who had to say goodbye to her own canine best friend. I'd be lying if I didn't say that I shed tears for Dr. Carpentier. I knew that unique pain. The love glue is super glue. The Rainbow Bridge extracts a high emotional toll. Surprisingly, a few weeks later, a MIZZOU public relations representative contacted me about doing a story about Booster's experience at the University Veterinary Hospital. It would appear on Mizzou's Veterinary Health Center web page. I was glad to oblige, as it was the least we could do for the institution that saved my Booster's life. My Booster would soon become their *Booster* too!

When we got home, the pack came running to see their exalted but exhausted leader. They ran around and Booster grabbed a stuffed toy and played tug-of-war. After a few minutes, I ended the play and made Booster relax. Booster was home and would live to see another day. I thought about how prolific the ticks were in Arkansas and in many parts of the country, and how many different diseases they carry. After every hike in the woods, I saw ticks on my canine kids and on my pant legs. Ticks had fallen off my dogs inside my home on occasion. The tick that almost killed Booster could have just as easily infected me and killed me. Many of the Arkansas locals had contracted "tick fever" while growing up. I learned it was excruciatingly painful. One man said it was like you had your head in a vise and someone was turning the screw more and more.

Many families choose not to treat their pets due to cost or ignorance. My country neighbors had several dogs with swollen ticks all over their bodies. "It's just a dog and they get ticks. I ain't pullin' no ticks off no dog," I was defiantly told when I suggested they should remove the ticks from their suffering dogs. It was incumbent on me to try to do *something* after witnessing the life-threatening suffering that accompanied something as simple as a tick bite.

As if by remote control, I picked up the phone, called my Arkansas veterinarian, and asked him if he'd be willing to do a newspaper story with me. I wanted to better canine and human lives. I pitched the idea that people need to know that by using tick and flea preventatives for their dogs, they are also protecting their family members lives. Dr. Mark Whitmore agreed to help deliver the message. I then called the *Harrison Daily News* newspaper in nearby Harrison, Arkansas. Two days later, we met a reporter, and the story ran shortly thereafter. If Booster's story prevented just one animal or person (child or adult) from contracting a potentially deadly disease, and experiencing excruciating pain, his ordeal served a higher purpose.

MY BOOSTER!

A dogged determination to live; service dog beats Rocky Mountain spotted fever.

By DAVID HOLSTED davidh@harrisondaily.com Jun 19, 2014

Davis Hawn (right) credits Dr. Mark Whitmore and the staff at Boone County Veterinary Clinic for saving Hawn's 10-year-old golden Labrador, Booster, from a case of Rocky Mountain spotted fever. Lee H. Dunlap/Staff

About a year later, we attended the Caribbean Animal Welfare Conference held in Trinidad and Tobago.

We had no problem getting a taxi ride to and from the conference. Booster and I met all kinds of interesting people, including a university professor from Costa Rica who invited us to lecture at the University of

Costa Rica. He gave me the name of a lady I should meet with to arrange the lecture, so Booster and I took a taxi to meet the lady, who was on the campus. She explained the students were on holiday, and she couldn't explain why we had been invited to lecture when there were no students present. She was embarrassed, and I just went along with the flow.

She then told us she had a contact in the school system in a little town called Manuel Antonio and we could visit the school children there. I asked her, "Are you sureeeee?" and she confidently reassured me it would happen. The next day, Booster and I took a two-hour taxi ride to the town. We stayed in a no-pets resort run by a German man who understood the service dog concept and allowed us to stay in his resort. In the morning, we took a taxi to an elementary school where we were welcomed by the elementary school teachers.

Booster did what he always did and won the hearts of adoring children. It was so hot, and we were both a bit overwhelmed. After we completed our demonstration, one teacher informed me we had yet another demonstration to perform for another age group. Booster was tired, and I knew his hips must be hurting. I explained my concerns and did a limited demonstration with the second group of children. Toward the end of the demonstration, Booster's hips were failing, and he slid to the ground to recuperate. I invited the children to pet him, and we left shortly thereafter.

The following day, we took a taxi to see the famed Manuel Antonio Nature Reserve & Wildlife Refuge. We drove up to the entrance to purchase a ticket, but they didn't want to let Booster go in with me. I explained the service dog concept and why I needed a dog. The man smiled and said, "Sir, you don't understand." Miraculously, I kept my mouth shut for a change. I listened and learned. "Sir, we have a lot of monkeys here. They are high in the trees and often get upset when seeing a foreign animal; they're territorial. I don't want the monkeys to hurt your dog." This was the most logical, reasonable explanation I'd ever heard in over ten years for denying Booster access.

He also said visitors must walk a long way to get to the beach. Neither of us was capable of trekking along, especially in the hot sun. The man then offered to let the taxi drive us in. It was a wonderful accommodation, and I thanked him profusely. We arrived at the beach shortly thereafter. Sure

MY BOOSTER!

enough, the monkeys overhead started chattering like a bunch of old ladies playing bingo. They were aroused at the sight of the canine intruder.

We quickly walked to the beach, which was void of overhead trees and excited monkeys. In the background, the monkeys continued to express their displeasure. I'd expected the monkeys to throw things at us, but we were on the open beach before they knew it. Booster made a few runs at the waves coming in and out. He scratched the sand and threw it rearward between his legs. Within twenty minutes, he was tired but happy. I summoned the taxi driver, and we returned to our hotel. The next morning, we took a long ride to the airport and flew home. When we entered the cabin, the pack came running to greet Booster. Just two days later, I awoke to find Booster on the living room floor. I instantly knew that if he wasn't by my side, there must be something wrong. I had a sinking feeling, just like the time I had awakened to look for Booster at 2 a.m. and found him listless on the kitchen floor when he had ingested rat poison. As I walked over to Booster, who wagged his loving tail and smiled the toothy grin I so adored, BOOM, it hit me!! Oh, MHP, it hit me so hard. My Booster's legs were paralyzed. His legs were like limp noodles, 100% useless and gimp. I burst into tears and held Booster tightly. He couldn't possibly understand what had happened to him. He was so helpless. I, too, had once been helpless, but not like this. It was devastatingly pitiful. My Booster lay on the floor, unable to move, stripped of dignity as he urinated and defecated in his necessarily prone position. I called my friend Chris to help me get Booster into the truck to go to the veterinarian 911.

I just knew this was "it." Even a cat only has nine lives. Booster survived cancer to die as paraplegic immersed in urine and feces? REALLY? Again, life was a cruel hoax. This was bad. I felt as though Booster was the showcase of pain and near-death experiences. I loved my Booster so much and I just could not understand why MHP had put him, and the mortal who loved him, through so much. We arrived at my veterinarian's office and carried Booster inside. Dr. Beacham and his assistant looked at Booster and then they looked at me. No, they looked *into* me. They damn well knew I was hurting beyond belief. Booster received a shot and my veterinarian, the prince of a man, told me not to give up on Booster.

Dr. Beacham suggested I contact Dr. Pluhar and Dr. Carpentier because they'd helped me in the past. I took his advice and called Dr. Carpentier. She told me to drive up to Missouri and she would see us right away. I called my friend Warren, and he accompanied me on the journey. Warren and I drove with my incapacitated Booster throughout the night. We rented a hotel room with a grass patio and an exterior door. We carried Booster outside, and I said, "Empty," the command to tell Booster to urinate and defecate. With absence of dignity, Booster urinated and defecated while lying on his side. I hurt for Booster as he knew he hadn't "emptied" where he should have. Booster always defecated by hoisting his rear end and tossing it into a bush. I'd never taught him to do it. It was cool because I didn't have to whip out the plastic bag when his feces dropped into the abyss of the flora at hand.

The next day, we drove to Dr. Carpentier's office. She worked for the University of Missouri (MIZZOU) but also was a partner in a private practice. We drove up to the front door of her clinic, and a young lady pulled a cart to greet us. We hoisted Booster's incapacitated body onto the cart and wheeled him in. Dr. Carpentier greeted us and examined Booster, then ordered an MRI. The test results evidenced a small contraction affecting the vertebrae in the neck, but nothing that would explain the quadriplegia Booster experienced. Dr. Carpentier softly suggested that it "might be that time." I so respected her opinion. After all, she'd saved Booster's life on the day she had to put her own beloved dog down. She was an unquestionable hero of immeasurable proportion.

I called my veterinarian, Dr. Beacham. He suggested I put Booster on a steroid regimen even though he'd received medicines contraindicated for steroids. I thanked Dr. Carpentier and sullenly drove Booster home. I don't think a word was spoken. Although Booster had no use of his limbs, I was

MY BOOSTER!

grateful that he wasn't in pain. When we got home, I constructed a nice penthouse for my Booster. If ever an individual deserved such specialty housing, it was my Booster. I built a 5x12 wire pen in my living room, installed an automatically refilling water bowl, lined the floor with impervious linoleum, and drilled a half-inch hole through my cabin's floor.

Booster had never let me down and there was nothing I wouldn't do for him. He'd saved my life, and I loved him more than life itself. I must say, Booster knew I would do whatever it takes. Doubt as you might, he had cheated death on so many occasions that he'd grown to know I would rescue him. He didn't equate it with codependency and the "rescue the wounded bird" phenomenon. Booster just knew I'd damn well be there for him, as I equally knew he'd be there for me. Most will say that this is an extreme example of anthropomorphism, but I resolutely tell you it is not!

One day, I put my Booster in my truck and drove to a local supply store. I bought a cart usually used to pull flowerpots around in a garden, and plastic tarps. Then, I drove through a Mickie D's drive-through on the way home and bought Booster two hamburgers, gave him some water, and we went home. The next morning, I built a ramp onto the side of my raised porch. I nailed a tarp onto the front of the cabin and extended it into the yard. Booster now had ingress and egress via a hand-pulled cart, and shade so he could lie in the yard.

I woke up every morning and hoisted Booster's body onto the green cart of salvation. I pulled him through the front door that he'd walked through for over a decade. I then pulled Booster through the fields he'd once proudly carried a carrot through as a puppy. I pulled my Booster's cart high and low, left and right, as though he was King of Carnival. He never once complained, never whimpered, nor rebelled. He was a prince in the truest form of the word. Oh, MHP, I so loved my Booster. How could he be so brave when I had been such a wimp in my life?

I'd listened to the Al-Anon mantra for years: God grant me the serenity to accept the things I cannot change, change the things I can, and the wisdom to know the difference. Booster embodied that which Al-Anon extolled. He accepted his fate and never gave up. In turn, I so respected Booster that I never gave up! I thought about a sticker that once adorned my mother's bathroom when she had terminal lung cancer: "Miracles are always happening." That sticker invigorated my mother to go forth in life in the face of adversity. I took the memory of that sticker and went forth in life with Booster.

Weeks later, I awoke to witness Booster using his front legs to drag his body across the floor to greet me as I walked toward his pen. I thought I was dreaming. "Hey my Booster, good morning," I said exuberantly. I opened the pen's door, and Booster pulled his body through the gate. I cried so FN hard, perhaps the hardest I'd ever cried in my life. I started to hyperventilate as I saw him struggle with his newly found independence, such as it was. I sat on the floor and Booster once again licked tears from my eyes.

Booster was so brave. He was a fighter who knew no bounds. He refused to contemplate giving up. I ran to the phone and called Dr. Beacham, Dr. Carpentier, and Dr. Pluhar. I told each one that "Booster has regained the use of his front limbs." All three doctors were amazed at Booster's progress. I asked if he might in turn regain the use of his rear limbs. "We just have to wait and see," they responded. Dr. Beacham told me he'd had a case in which a family could not afford an operation when their dog experienced paralysis. He'd given their dog steroids and the dog fully recovered. I instantly thought about my mother's sticker in her bathroom: "Miracles are always happening." Within a month, Booster regained the use of all of his limbs, though his gate was affected. We will never know what caused the paralysis. Booster refused to give up and leave me alone in the world. He knew I needed him; his job on earth was not yet complete.

CHAPTER 17
THE HEART AND SEOUL OF CLONING

While sharing Booster's life, I experienced a personal educational renaissance. BUCS was a catalyst for my educational enrichment. Dr. Bergin was the alchemist who provided just the right mix of stress and simultaneous stimulus to ignite the educational passion within. As I was conducting research for a genetics class at BUCS, I happened upon an article that pertained to cloning. I was instantly mesmerized by a topic I'd often heard contentiously discussed in the press. I'd gone to BUCS as an old fart, champing at the bit to learn. Like a dry sponge immersed in water for the first time, I absorbed as much as possible from all directions. I soon realized that cloning was unique in that it involves science, politics, and religion, all wrapped up in one controversial package.

The more I read about cloning, the more fascinated and motivated I became. I read about Korean professor Hwang Woo-Suk. With the intellect of Einstein and the exuberance of a child on Christmas morning, he published a research paper extolling his purported success in establishing a line of stem cells. When other scientists marveled at his work but failed in their efforts to replicate it, his findings were deemed fraudulent. He was also accused of pocketing money along the way, but that's not exactly a unique happening in high-dollar medical research and pharmaceutical sales. Some say he was genuine and altruistic, yet others claim he was self-promoting and usurious. While he purportedly dreamed of restoring mobility for the disabled and curing diseases that plagued mankind, he was certainly before his time in lacking respect for political correctness, having purchased eggs from one of his female graduate student to establish a line of stem cells and perhaps pursue cloning a human embryo.

Eventually, the once highly regarded professor plummeted to the ranks of the obscure as associates, students, and government officials distanced themselves from a man who personified human frailty. The Korean government brought charges against him in to save face as it succumbed to international pressure from the scientific community. When he was at his lowest ebb in life, he was given handouts on the streets. A paralyzed man gave him a donation and said, "I know one day your work will help me walk again."

I, too, had once plummeted in life, was weak, and gave up and almost took the easy way out. In Korean culture, suicide is an honorable choice. To this very day, I believe the dear professor didn't opt out because he wanted to better the lives of others. He suffered through humiliation of epic proportions and threats of jail time, and yet was bolstered by his thirst for knowledge and the selfless desire to help others. As I researched the man, I started to identify with him. I felt a connection with a kindred soul in Seoul that I'd never met . . . a soul who didn't know I existed.

One morning, I looked at Booster and just started crying. He struggled to get up and walked to my side. I leaned over to pet him, and he sideswiped my cheek in a collision course with love. I was covered with slobber that was soon joined by a tributary of tears. My rock was eroding; my Booster was aging. He'd survived potential heatstroke as a puppy abandoned in a truck, a potential attack by a pack of javelina hogs, rat poison, paralysis, RMSF, cancer, and his human's ineptness. Booster was a walking testimonial to the extraordinary potential of the canine–human bond flourishing under the divine tutelage of a Higher Power . . . and more! With such an undeniable, established track record, I thought he might experience another first. Booster was destined to become the first dog that would live forever. I strived to find the solution to overcoming death just in case he might succumb to the ultimate fate all other living beings are subjected to.

In the insanity of the moment, I fired off an email to the renowned Korean professor. As an overseas amoeba, a virtual nobody, I explained that my dog Booster once saved my life when I was drowning in a sea of despair. I further explained that I subsequently promised Booster I'd share him with the world whenever I traveled. I asked the professor to research

MY BOOSTER!

our names—Davis Hawn Booster—to see our stories around the world. Those stories were an affirmation of the promise I'd made to my beloved Booster years before. I proffered, "He's getting older, and I'm worried about my future without him. My Booster is a way of life, and I'm not sure I could handle life in a *Boosterless* vacuum."

I knew there'd never be another Booster, but I needed something to believe in, to fill the inevitable void to come. Cloning might replicate an animal's physical characteristics, but personality was not cloneable. I also expressed my devotion to education and the fact that I went back to school in my fifties to get a degree in Canine Life Sciences. My passion consumed me, as did his. I hit the send button on my computer, never expecting a reply.

Within days, I opened an email from one of the dear professor's gracious associates, Professor Taeyoung Shin. He explained that Professor Hwang was moved by my story and my relationship with Booster. The conversation quickly gravitated to the *soul* of cloning. He immediately vocalized a disclaimer, in effect assuring me that cloning is not a way to bring a dead animal back to life. I had no such naïve expectations; however, I'm sure there are some who might think along those lines. He could only assure me that the clone would look like the original dog in *most* respects.

Cloning an animal with spots doesn't always produce offspring with spots in the same locations. A cloned calico cat will not have the same-colored spots in the same place as its predecessor. This aberration is because the cloning process is impacted by residual DNA located in the mitochondria (the powerhouse of the cell). My Booster was a solid yellow Labrador retriever with a faint white patch on his chest, so I felt confident he was an ideal candidate for cloning regarding physical attributes. My cloned *Booster* would be identical in appearance, with the possible exception being the white chest patch many Labradors have.

I then asked Dr. Shin if cloned canines were as healthy as those naturally born. I'd heard that Dolly, the cloned sheep, died a premature death, which gave rise to the notion that cloned animals were unhealthy. In reality, Dolly died from a form of pneumonia commonly found in sheep. Dr. Shin explained that historically, some pups had been born smaller than normal but, over a year's time, grew to the same size as other littermates. In the early days of cloning, some pups had been born with abnormalities, but such occurrences are rare today.

In the long run, cloned canines have virtually the same life expectancy as those naturally born. Professor Hwang cloned the first dog in 2015 after a heated competition with Texas A&M. He named the dog Snuppy, an acronym for Seoul National University Puppy, and it lived to a ripe old age of twelve years. I'd never know if Booster's cancer was environmental or hereditary. If he'd fallen prey to cancer at an early age, I would have concluded it was hereditary and I would not have considered him a candidate for cloning. At age eight, it was more likely that the environment played a role. Reality dictates that one in four dogs will die from cancer. After age ten, one in every two dogs dies from the dreaded disease.

The real concern was that Booster had crappy hips. Hip dysplasia is common in Labrador retrievers. I'd once attended a veterinary conference where a speaker stated that perhaps only 10% of Labradors have excellent hips. The genetics guru advocated only breeding Labradors with excellent hips to others with excellent hips. The guru spoke ill about the "backyard breeders" that indiscriminately bred dogs.

I was certainly *not* a genetic guru nor a veterinarian, but I certainly *was* a BUCS graduate trained under Bonnie, who taught me to be objective and to think "outside of the box." I raised my hand and was called upon to speak. "Excuse me, are you suggesting that we breed 10% of a population to itself? That suggests to me that we are eliminating 90% of the gene pool. Will we still have a Labrador retriever? Thank God for the backyard breeder in light of such circumstance," I exclaimed. As a man who'd lived a two-decade life of submission I stood up and bucked the established norm, risking confrontation. I'd been empowered by the love of a dog and a university founded by one of the few humans I held in high esteem. I'd acquired self-confidence and self-worth emanating from a dog I once shunned and resented. It all started with Booster.

The geneticist paused to reflect. The gist of his response was, "Well, everything in moderation."

MY BOOSTER!

"Well, where do you draw the line?" I queried. I wanted to dive in deeper but elected to avoid potential confrontation. I had to draw my own line in that respect.

When confronted with canine-related issues, I learned to stand my ground. I once strived to attend an Assistance Dog International (ADI) conference. I applied to attend with my service dog, but I was rejected because Booster was "intact." I attended the conference without Booster. When I was called upon to speak, I stood up and grabbed the bull by the horns, or rather, the dog by the balls! I explained that my service dog had been barred from the conference because he had testicles, like most males in this room. I further proffered that I learned about dogs in a canine–human perspective, having studied under the tutelage of the finest canine authorities, at the only university in the world dedicated to canine studies (BUCS). We don't neuter human males, though I think we often should!

I went on to explain that the latest research evidences the fact that neutered canines suffer an increased incidence rate of torn cruciate ligaments due to a lack of sufficient amounts of testosterone in the neutered male dog. They also experience higher cancer incidence rates, except for testicular cancer, which is easily eradicated by castration at time of diagnosis. Spaying and neutering are one of the greatest hot-button topics one can discuss.

At yet another conference, I proffered the same proclamation. The conference was sponsored by a pet insurance company that limited policy benefits if a dog wasn't neutered by one year of age. I offered a hypothetical of a family who paid their pet insurance premiums monthly as required. I then presented the scenario of a dog in the family's fenced backyard and a drunk driver who crashed through the fence and injured the innocent dog. The family's beloved dog was taken to a vet's office and needed an operation. The family was so grateful that they had pet health insurance. But the veterinarian opened the one-year-old dog's legs and saw that he had testicles, so the pet insurer wouldn't cover the cost of the surgery because the dog was intact. The family couldn't afford to pay for the expensive operation; hence, the dog lost its life because it hadn't been neutered by the age of one. Human ignorance being force-fed to paying customers.

I spoke to one of the company's pompous executives at a veterinary conference. I explained that neutering a dog is not healthy for reasons previously alluded to. Additionally, I explained that in Latin culture, castration was often not acceptable. It was not macho. I asked why his insurance company would sentence a dog to death because of the decision of its human family. "Why do you execute an innocent canine due to the decision of a human?" The arrogant man justifies the company's policy by saying that unneutered dogs more often exhibit aggression and chase cars, etc.

At another veterinary conference, I was approached by two women. "Why is your boy intact?" they asked me. "Because I want the best for my dog. It's unhealthy to neuter a young dog and by adulthood it doesn't alleviate aggression as the testosterone is already in the body." I profoundly stated. "Unneutered dog's cause neutered dogs to become aggressive in their presence," they told me. I looked at the complaining humans, smiled and shared, "Don't blame me for your boy's aggression. I'm not going to enhance my Booster's likelihood of contracting cancer or tearing a cruciate ligament because your dog may be insufficiently trained or restrained and was subjected to castration." The decision to spay or neuter is a personal decision, and I don't condemn people for it, but I don't want to be condemned for *not* doing it. The problem is irresponsible humans not irresponsible animals. In some countries, it's illegal to spay or neuter an animal. In Germany and Scandinavia, it's considered mutilation and illegal. Human responsibility is the key to successful canine partnership.

I was, and still am, a canine advocate. I put the welfare of an animal before my own. When considering whether to clone Booster, I was conflicted. I certainly didn't want to bring a dog into the world to suffer from extreme hip dysplasia. I'd learned at BUCS about a procedure called juvenile pubic symphysiodesis (JPS), a simple surgical procedure, optimally performed at twelve weeks, that would likely ensure a puppy would have better hips at an adult age. A special evaluative test called a Penn HIP study had determined that Booster's hips were worse than 70% of all other Labradors tested. I thought it would be amazingly valuable to have JPS surgery performed on Booster's genetic duplicate to potentially eradicate hip dysplasia while helping to determine the efficacy of the procedure.

At BUCS, I learned that additional weight adversely impacts a dog's hips and read a Purina study that showed obese dogs die two years sooner than those whose weight is kept within acceptable parameters. Remember, everything at BUCS is taught in the canine–human context. Does anyone think obese humans are healthier than those who are slim and trim and exercise regularly? I've fought obesity all my life. Obese humans often have obese children and obese dogs. Genetic factors are often cited for the causation of obesity; fact or fiction, I can't judge. I was painfully guilty of over-feeding Booster to where he weighed 105 pounds instead of a proper 87 pounds! I learned at BUCS to mend my ways for Booster's betterment. Over time, Booster slimmed down to a healthy 87 pounds, but the damage to his already genetically inferior hips had manifested.

Much to his credit, Dr. Shin spent myriad hours on the phone answering my often-provocative questions. He marveled at my layman's knowledge of canine topics. I later learned that he, like Dr. Bergin, was a professor. He was patient, kind, and thoughtful. I opened up to him and explained the importance of cloning Booster. My family and friends were worried about how I would handle Booster's ultimate demise, or *if* I would be able to do so. They knew there was always the option to "opt out." What they didn't know was that I'd made Booster a promise years before to never consider such an option.

I prodded Dr. Shin for information and wanted to learn anything caninerelated. I didn't have the required $100,000 fee to clone a dog. My doctor would have doubled the strength of my psych meds if I'd even considered spending that kind of money on cloning a dog! I was after a unique education that I valued more than ever because of Booster, Bonnie, and BUCS's influence upon my once-worthless life. I was developing confidence and self-worth that came with education—I was living to learn and learning to live! I lamented the fact that such a renaissance transpired so late in life yet felt so grateful that I'd experienced it. So many souls are lost in the turbulent sea of life and never come ashore to discover fruitful bounty.

My conversation with Taeyoung became a foundation for mutual respect. We talked on many occasions. The fact that he was willing to share his busy life with an ultimate stranger was testimony to the man. He felt my exuberance for living and knew it emanated from Booster. One day, I told him I was fond of Asia and would soon go to Thailand. I asked him if it might be possible to visit Professor Hwang's laboratory, SOOAM Biotech. Within days, Taeyoung called me and explained Professor Hwang had extended an invitation for me to tour the cloning facility in Seoul, South Korea.

I celebrated within my heart of hearts that the lauded, yet chastised Professor Hwang felt my pain. Within weeks, I was on a plane, my soul bound for Seoul! With earthquake-like emotional tremors, I'd ventured into foreign territories, personal and international. Would I be student enough to be accepted by such a profound research center? Would they consider cloning Booster? I didn't have the money necessary to clone a dog. I'd emptied my personal coffers months before to have Booster's cells preserved and shipped to Korea. It was a pipe dream kept alive by an initial investment. Surely, I was setting myself up for hurt and personal devastation of nuclear proportion. I'd never be able to afford to clone Booster.

Just as I started questioning what I'd done, I landed in Seoul. Like a puppy emerging from a protective womb, or a butterfly from a cocoon, I emerged from the airport in Korea. I sheepishly looked around and saw a distinguished-looking man holding a sign: Davis Hawn Booster. I walked up and shook the man's hand. He was a SOOAM Biotech employee sent to welcome me. I subsequently followed him, like the puppy I was, to a black Mercedes as polished as his demeanor. He welcomed me like a long-lost family member. I instantly felt at home. I wished Booster had been with me at the time to help process my emotional overload.

Booster was responsible for yet another amazing life journey. I was experiencing an opportunity of a lifetime, at an advanced age, in a new culture. I was treated as somewhat of an intellectual equal because of a special dog and a special university. It was all quite surreal, to say the least. How'd this happen? I was the luckiest human on earth because My Higher Power had introduced a unique canine soul, the Al-Anon program, and

MY BOOSTER!

BUCS. The empowering combination had introduced me to spirituality and instilled faith. Without restored faith in my fellow man, I never would have been able to experience such a magical moment; never, no way.

Eventually, my Korean host pulled into the driveway of my hotel. He looked at me and queried, "How'd you choose this hotel?" I told him I'd gotten a good internet deal. He accepted my explanation with a smile on his face. I checked in and went up to my room. There was a Jacuzzi in the middle of the room. I'd booked the hotel because the warm water of a Jacuzzi often helped soothe my leg, which was still problematic at times. Mounted on the wall across from the bed were two computers with large, wall-mounted screens. *Different!* I thought. I later came to find that it was a "love hotel" where young Korean love birds spread their wings and spawn under Cupid's watchful eye!

I returned to the lobby, and my host whisked me away to a Korean barbeque meal garnished with all the side dishes like kimchee and only they knew what else! I devoured the unknown as my senses weren't focused on taste but thought. Like a cold front meeting a heat wave, emotional lightning struck. I missed Booster, was lonely, fascinated, learning, and wished Bonnie was by my side to relish the sight and nurture me. But, alas, I was on my own, fending for myself, and that took on an import all its own. I enjoyed the meal and company, then soon returned to my hotel.

In the morning, my host arrived with the black Mercedes to take me to SOOAM Biotech. When we arrived at the facility, I walked in and suddenly froze. I looked up at an electronic billboard billowing welcome. In neon lights, it read, "Welcome to SOOAM Biotech, Mr. Davis Hawn." I was welcomed like royalty and treated as such. I was given a general tour of the facility and told that I was invited to witness the cloning process the following day. After a wonderful Korean dinner with the professor, a staff member drove me back to the hotel. I was too exhausted to use the Jacuzzi. It had to wait for another day.

The following morning, the black Mercedes returned to pick me up. I enjoyed a warm conversation in route to the biotech. When we arrived, I kicked off my shoes and dawned hygienic plastic sandals like I'd done the day before. I soon became an integral part of an entourage that included research intern students from Paris. We entered an elevator to ascend the throne of scientific research. As we exited the elevator, a radio sounded. "There are two members of the press here to do a story about the American who is cloning his dog."

I'd reached out to the press the day before via telephone to propose doing a newspaper story. I explained my love for a dog that'd saved my life, my love for my university, and my newfound appreciation for the Korean scientist who bestowed such a great honor. SOOAM's staff didn't think a member of the press would cover the story. Professor Hwang had shunned interviews, and I perceived there might have been a certain animosity with the press. On that fateful day, a SOOAM employee approached me and said, "Mr. Davis, two newspapers want to cover the story. What are we going to do?" I replied, "Great, please tell them both to come!" My ability to convey to others Booster's importance in my life grew exponentially over time. *Coincidently*, the two newspapers sent their reporters to SOOAM at the same time! When they arrived, I reassured my hosts that I could handle the situation. They trusted me and deferred to my judgment.

With reporters in tow, our entourage entered the laboratory. I looked into a microscope and witnessed a needle extracting DNA from a dog's cell and subsequently implanting donor DNA. A radio then sounded that the delivery had arrived. Moments later, a man with a hand cart sauntered in with a metal jug that looked something like a milk jug from the 1950s. They explained that it contained Booster's cells I'd shipped from the US. It ***coincidentally*** arrived at the same time I had. I should have been wearing a diaper because I almost pooped on myself in disbelief. In tears, I reached out to simultaneously touch Booster and my future Booster clone-to-be, both encapsulated in the silver jug of promise. It was a hard concept to grasp. I

MY BOOSTER!

lost it emotionally, and the reporters' cameras caught it. I trembled while tears flowed; I was emotionally naked among strangers in a foreign country. A warm and comforting hand soon found its way to my shoulder. It was just a hand, but it radiated warmth. It belonged to Professor Hwang. I was "touched" beyond belief. It added to the profundity of tears and the gravity of the moment in which I'd landed.

Professor Hwang disappeared shortly thereafter, soon to reappear behind a glass wall in an operating room. He implanted embryonic cells into the uterus of a surrogate dog while speaking into a microphone, explaining his actions. I, too, spoke into a microphone. I asked the professor questions, and he answered them. It was such a rich experience that I felt undeserving. As I met various staff members, I was ushered into a room to be interviewed by the two Korean reporters assigned to

cover my story. They asked insightful and compassionate questions that caused my voice to crack. I often had to stop and regain my composure. I was thinking of Booster the entire time. *He should be here*, I thought, *and he needs to be with me always. I don't need to clone him, as he will live forever. He always cheats death.* With Booster in my life, all things were possible. Hercules had his hair, and I had Booster! I couldn't fathom a life without him. It simply wasn't an option.

While touring Asia the week before, I'd found a painting of several dogs in a country scene. Three similar-looking puppies were sitting in a wicker basket in a field. I had the artist paint "SOOAM" on the side of the basket. I had it framed in Seoul and delivered to SOOAM. It *coincidentally* arrived the day of the interview.

The reporter left after he completed the interview. When he learned I was about to present a gift to the professor, he returned to get a photo of me presenting *Booster's* gift to Professor Hwang. It appeared in full color on the *front page* of the *Korea Herald* newspaper. A story featuring President Obama was found on page 6! I whimsically thought, *Purebred Labrador page one, selfproclaimed mutt page six!*

President Obama: page 6
My Booster's clones: front page
A few days later, I checked out of my hotel. The front desk clerk told me he'd read the newspaper stories. I asked him to call a taxi. He explained that the bus around the corner went directly to the airport. He insisted on accompanying me to the bus stop at 5 a.m. to make sure I caught the correct bus to the airport. While walking, he went into a coffee shop and bought me a cup of coffee. As the bus approached, he put a small envelope in my hand. It had a dog sticker on the front. I tucked it into my computer bag and forgot about it. Days later, I found it in my bag and opened it.

The envelope contained a note written to Booster in Korean. I sent it to my friends at SOOAM and asked them to please translate it for me. Upon its return in English, I concluded it was composed by My Higher Power, delivered by a Korean courier angel. I started to cry and shake as I read each word in slow motion. The more I read, the more emotional I got. I simply couldn't fathom that a total stranger had taken time out of his young life to create such a beautiful, loving, inspirational letter.

MY BOOSTER!

Young folks simply don't do that in today's world, or do they? To this day, I re-read the letter and cry crocodile tears. One of my goals in life is to meet the young author again one day, hug him, look into his eyes, and simply say, "Thank you." I also want to meet the parents who reared such an amazing young man. I had that letter duplicated and framed twice. One copy adorns a wall in my home. The *cloned* copy is prominently displayed in the front office of BUCS. Both bear the same irrefutable introductory proclamation:

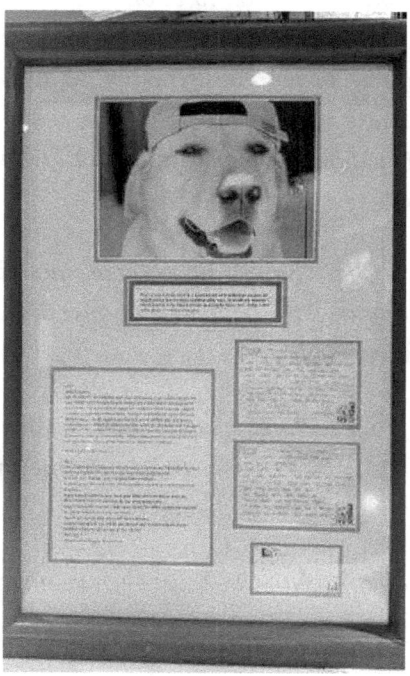

The canine–human bond is a powerful tsunami of energy capable of transforming the world in unfathomable ways. In evidence thereof is the following note from a human to a dog he never met, living 7,000 miles away in a distant country.

Hello Booster!!

I'm not sure if I can write this right after greeting you but . . . I really want to tell you . . . Thank You!!! It might be very sudden, but I heard that it was because of you that Mr. Hawn was able to regain his strength and live a new life. That he was able to open up to others again . . . that you supported him during his most difficult hours . . . At the beginning I only saw you as another case but without knowing it I was moved so much that I even wrote you this letter, and in Korean to boot. ^^ It's because I'm a Korean . . . The fact that you were able to move a complete stranger you've never met living in a country far far away . . . that's very awesome. If you were a person, I think you would be a celebrity . . . what I want to tell you is:

I don't know what "Squamous cell carcinoma" is exactly but I know that you are suffering because of it . . . and that you don't have much time left.

But still . . . Your feelings, your thoughts, your memories . . . Everything you felt while living, all the thoughts you had and all the memories together.

If you keep all of this in your heart even death won't be able to scare you . . .

The fact that I can't do anything for you really saddens me.

Even knowing that you can't read I write to you this letter, hoping that you will be able to understand it with your heart . . .

Even if you're gone your prints will remain Booster!

I will be hoping that you will be reincarnated and reunited with Mr. Hawn.

MY BOOSTER!

I will be waiting for good news in the internet. 2014/11/10

Your fan from Jong-ro, South Korea

Once again, I reflected upon the fact that Booster taught me there are no **coincidences** in life. To this day, I marvel upon the fact that I'd unwittingly checked into a love hotel . . . and consequently found love! It was meant to be. My life continued to change exponentially. Most importantly, I learned that love wasn't just a concept conjured to inflict pain upon the soul. In its purest form, it's energy of unquestionable positivity, the likes of which will preserve mankind. Months later, I spoke with Taeyoung. He explained that Professor Hwang and his devoted family of employees had been moved by my experience. They'd read the *angel's* letter to my Booster and wanted to help me realize my dream of cloning my life partner. After a few months of sentimental exchanges, SOOAM made me a special offer they'd never done for anyone before. They made cloning my Booster possible. Yes, damn it, more tears! Koreans, I swear! They sure knew how to make a grown man cry . . . repeatedly! They gave me the greatest gift the world had to offer me. I'd won the lottery of human empathy and was incapable of feeling, thinking, and utilizing my senses. I sat on the couch and rocked back and forth like a metronome, arms grasping my sides, oblivious to the outside world. It seemingly took hours for me to break the hypnotic trance. I felt tired.

No, exhausted. I wasn't sure what had happened or why.

After a lot of *Seoul* searching, I realized the news was overwhelmingly beautiful. Like a rainbow after a hurricane, I eventually beamed with pride. I'd lived through a storm and others had found something redeeming within my once sorry-ass self! I was no longer emotionally bankrupt; I'd found self-worth. The offer to clone Booster was far more than just an offer to clone a dog. It was restorative. I then remembered the young Korean's letter of love. I'd been the recipient of the ole *one-two* knockout punch. While I didn't feel worthy, I did feel tons of gratitude, even more so as time marched on. When the reality sank in that Booster was going to be cloned, I called everyone I knew, and even some I didn't know! On cloud nine, I exuberantly shared the Korean love storie(s).

"What are you going to do with a dog?" my brother had asked years before. That day I answered his question with resolve, "I'm going to clone him!"

As expected, he replied, "What a foolish waste of money."

Others told me they'd have mortgaged their home to clone a dog or cat they'd loved dearly. By far, most people were overwhelmingly positive. The consensus was, "Hey, it's your money. You worked for it. Enjoy it." When considering whether to clone my Booster, I read about a couple who'd cloned their dog. They said they'd saved up money for a new Land Rover, but later spent it on cloning their beloved dog. They further explained they decided to spend their money on something they'd appreciate rather than depreciate. Those words resonate today with perfect clarity. I wholeheartedly concur!

Months later, I attended a party for my niece, who was going to get married shortly. I presented her with enlarged, framed photographs of her childhood and sang Harry Belafonte's song, "Turn Around" to her as the guests looked on. I'd practiced singing the song a hundred times at home and while traveling the world. Now, I risked being a fool, hoping that I could share love the way Booster had taught me to—unconditionally and without regard to oneself. Luckily, it went over well. My niece had tears in her eyes, and the guests clapped. It warmed my heart.

I'd mentioned to a few of the guests that I was cloning my dog and they voiced fascination. One elderly man sat me down to explain that he once had a dog in his life he surely would have cloned. I shared with one lady that I'd kept one of Booster's pups and named him Al-Anon and he accompanied me to Al-Anon meetings. I mused I call him "Al" in public so as not to embarrass him. She laughed and shared that she attended Adult Children of Alcoholics meetings. It was a warm exchange that we mutually valued. We lauded the program's ability to help the lives of those who'd been affected by the ravages of other's addiction.

The following day I received a phone call from my sister, "I can't believe what you did at the party!"

"What'd I do?" I implored.

"You told people you were cloning your dog. Do you know how embarrassing that is?"

I replied, "Hey, I study dogs and train them to help others. Cloning is a unique educational opportunity, and it may well provide stability in my life when Booster passes.

"You also talked about the Al-anon program, and that's supposed to be secret and private," she said.

I replied, "The Al-anon program is all about helping people too. Twelve-step programs save lives. Everyone could benefit from a twelve-step program of some kind. What individuals *share in meetings* is confidential, but the program is very well known around the world. You should consider working for the Chinese government, help censor the internet, and control access to reality." My explanation fell on deaf ears.

My sister and her husband are wonderful people. They are bankers, very conservative, and successfully raised an extraordinary pack. I frankly find it weird that people can work around something as valueless as money, but I never condemned them for it. I didn't even do it in 2008, when millions lost their homes due to banking irregularities. As a taxpayer, I'd bailed out the bank scoundrels. Only a dog, my Booster, rescued ME and bailed ME out! Given the opportunity to work with dogs, sharing unconditional love and helping the disabled, versus working with money and greedy banks, seems to me to be a no-brainer. After all, according to the Apostle Paul, the love of money is purportedly the root of all evil. The canine–human bond is the embodiment of unconditional love, time tested, and most often revered. It needs to be cloned!

I later received a call from my beloved sister. She apologized for trying to tell me what I could and couldn't say. I laughed to myself, thinking, *our parents are surely looking down from heaven, saying, "Clone the dog, but don't clone our children!"* For the record, I love my sister dearly. I credit Booster's unconditional love for furthering my familial unconditional love. I once again applied what I learned at BUCS by looking at things in a canine–human context. My Booster taught me to celebrate life with song and playful pack interaction.

A few dog aficionados criticized me for spending *my* money to clone a dog when that money could feed *their* interest . . . shelter dogs. You know what came next? Humans, including my sister, then asked, "Why are you spending *your* money on dogs when there are starving children in this world?" Then select humans accused me of playing God! I felt compelled to postulate that I so loved the unique creature that God created that I simply wanted another one . . . a photocopy. I wasn't tampering one iota with the DNA that God assembled and put into my life in the form of the dog who became my Booster!

When a dog *does its business,* other dogs sniff it because it contains information; it's the canine version of doing research or reading a book. Humans stick their noses into other people's *business*, often to condemn or push their own agendas! Dogs usually move on when not provoked. Humans stop to provoke, comment, judge, and then publish on the web with social media. Collateral damage often takes the form of bullying, sometimes resulting in death. No wonder we turn to dogs to help solve human issues.

While eagerly awaiting news regarding the day the cloning would commence, I learned of a book that chronicled the history of cloning from stem (cell) to stern. I found it to be rather negative, honest or not. The book's revelations fascinated me. I knew people would likely have a negative opinion about cloning after reading it. I found it to be less than objective, and frankly, quite biased. Booster taught me that there are no **coincidences** in life, so I reasoned that finding and reading the book were meant to be. It was like a warning salvo of the ballistic battle to come. Once again, I was going to have to educate an ignorant populace that would espouse theories about a clone when they'd never shared their life with one. I was not to be dissuaded. Such humans wasted time barking up the wrong tree!

On a whim, I emailed Taeyoung asking him if he would consider sharing his expertise with BUCS students. He philanthropically agreed to lecture at the university free of charge. I later learned that he'd boarded a bus from his hometown in Wisconsin, bound for the Chicago airport. He took time off from work and traveled all the way to California to enrich the minds of aspiring students. I'd arranged to mail a copy of the cloning book to all interested BUCS students. When Taeyoung arrived at BUCS, negativity abounded based upon conclusions drawn from the information presented in the book.

The students graciously listened and then asked questions over a two-day period. The mood changed as Taeyoung presented current, factual information regarding cloning and DNA replication. He didn't advocate cloning, but rather remained neutral and asked for opinions. Just before he left campus, the students asked if they could take a picture with him, then presented him with a BUCS parka and profusely thanked him for coming and sharing. I'd experienced Korean love and dedication in Seoul. For the BUCS students, it was Korean "takeout," as they had the opportunity to feast upon the intellectualism of a Korean and the education that ensued.

Days came and went. What seemed like an eternity *was* an eternity! Virtually every day, I awoke awaiting news Booster had been cloned. I often fired off emails, asking for updates, imploring, "Has the cloning begun?" I always got polite replies, but never a positive response. One day, over a year later, I got the news! "Mr. Hawn, we have commenced cloning Booster." I froze right then and there. I stared at the email on the computer screen. *Really? Really? Really?* I asked myself. Like an expectant father, I beamed with pride and looked forward to the new family member and next phase of my life. Did you hear that? I LOOKED FORWARD TO THE NEXT PHASE OF MY LIFE! My Higher Power had answered my beckoning call once again. My life changed at that moment and change it rapidly did! The ramifications of what I'd done suddenly set in. I started to analyze my actions and bombarded myself with introspection. I'd have to go to Korea to work with the clone and leave Booster behind. How could I possibly devote myself to Booster in his waning days while necessarily showering the cloned pup with attention and education during the socialization period, the first twelve to fourteen weeks of his life? Would I be a traitor? I had a self-imposed requisite to train the clone-to-be as the finest service dog on the planet. I was suddenly torn, and rightfully so, as I had roughly sixty-three days to figure it out. It would be a moral gestation period coinciding with that of the cloned pup. I concentrated on preserving my mental well-being, as I had learned in Al-Anon. For the immediate moment, I focused on myself, not the clone. It proved to be the longest sixty-three days of my life.

I'd lived a life filled with an abundance of apprehension, never filled with anticipation! There'd never been the possibility of a rainbow after the storm; only a new storm to come. This was new to me. Rather than dwell on the inevitable evil and certain relapse into destructive depression, I was denied that option. I was going to have to live life on life's terms. I needed to make *big boy* decisions previously stunted by the lack of options in a codependent relationship. As I'd learned from attending Al-Anon meetings, "If you let go of the past, it will let go of you." I'd worked hard and focused on putting the past in the rearview mirror but had lost track of the windshield. Truthfully, I never thought in my wildest dreams that I'd live long enough to look *forward*, much less be *able* to or *want* to! It was the dawning of a new day and a new dude. I woke up hugging Booster and smiling. I played with all my canine family members with renewed vigor and reinforced exuberance, and I pet dogs and cats I met in public as never before. Rather than a guy who hated those who found happiness in greeting Booster as a pup, I became *one of those*. My balance sheet of life had changed. Whereas I once valued economy of words, I now started to exhibit diarrhea of the mouth. I no longer cried while battling depression. My newfangled emotions presented as tears due to a formerly elusive concept called happiness. I wanted to run away and join the circus. I'd learned to juggle my emotions!

Thus, I decided to fly to Korea to witness the birth of the cloned pup. Days passed like images on slowly shuffled cards in the early days of animated cartoons. One day out of the blue(s) I received an email with a rather unique photo attached. "Mr. Hawn, we have detected a fetal heartbeat in one of the surrogates. We will be monitoring progress 24/7 and give you periodic updates. Congratulations!" I visited my Mecca of emotions. I pinched myself to confirm the reality of the moment. It was more than a clone; it was confirmation of karma.

MY BOOSTER!

My Booster had blazed a path in the world doing good for others. He was a people pleaser and loved interaction.

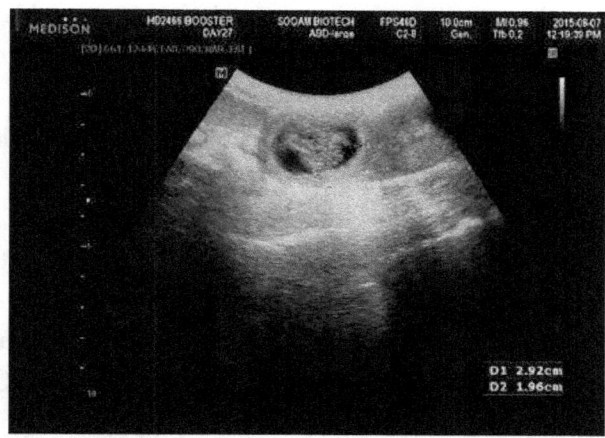

I was his favorite human, and as such, I believed he wanted me to be happy and continue his work in the human world, which needed a *booster*! I'd once held him back from the human interaction he loved. Over time, I could not contain his love for others. His personality overshadowed my shadowy past, and I changed. I, too, became a people pleaser; I loved to give and felt guilty receiving.

The SOOAM family had made me a unique offer, worked around the clock to fulfill it, kept their commitment, and used a plethora of accumulated knowledge to make a dream come true. It was monumental for me in a special way. Absolute strangers made an incredible promise and kept it. It was a novelty, as my addicts rarely did such.

In my "former" life, promises were made and never kept. "I'll never drink again, I'll never pick up that pipe again, I'll never get violent again . . ." cajoled the ones I'd faithfully trusted, commencing at a formative age. My father wantonly promised change in the morning and morphed into unabashed, repetitive behavior later the same day. Those I later forged relationships with, my addicts, followed that precedent. I was accustomed to being lied to, let down, and being left wallowing in pain. If I questioned, "Are you sure?" the response was, "What, you don't trust me? Why am I with you then?" I remember driving to the bank and covering my ATM card when withdrawing what little money I had. Immediately, with the intensity of a sonic boom, "What the fuck, you gotta hide your PIN code from *me*?" I immediately responded subserviently, "Sorry. it was force of habit . . . it's 2345!" The following month I received my bank statement and found withdrawals made in the middle of the night with my ATM card.

Eventually, the day came to hug Booster and board the plane again for Korea's heart and Seoul. With trepidation, Booster and I jumped into my truck, and friends drove us to the airport. The day was sunny, but I experienced squalls of internal emotion. Booster looked into my eyes as though we were going to the park when, in reality, I wasn't coming back anytime soon. I was dying inside as the clone was about to be born. I hurt inside as I had long before. My Booster of inspiration became the source of my downtrodden spirits. I was beating myself up. Learned behavior is hard to unlearn. That's why most service dog training facilities start with puppies rather than grown dogs. I learned at BUCS that it takes at least thirty correct repetitions of a positively, properly taught task to undo the damage of one wrongfully instilled. I had thousands of wrongfully instilled lessons I needed to unlearn, and not enough time to accomplish it.

My BUCS lessons helped quell the internal uprising of my emotional battlefield. I appropriately applied the psychology I'd been taught to apply to dogs in the canine schoolroom to *myself*. I told myself over and over that Booster would want this for me, I needed it, and the world needed a *booster*. I thought about others' condemnation for seeking to clone Booster, but I mentally reviewed my Al-Anon teachings. "What other people think about me is none of my business."

The veterinary and research staff at SOOAM is one of the finest in the world. Their cloned pups are customarily brought into the world by cesarean section to lessen the risk associated with birth. In fact, some breeds can't give birth naturally. Man invaded the sanctity of the canine world through artificial selection and engineered breeding often to the detriment of the species. SOOAM's clones were valued at $100,000, a culmination of huge investments, economic and emotional, that warranted additional safeguards to ensure the newborn puppy's problem-free birth. I made an ad hominem appeal to the fine folks at SOOAM to allow Booster's clone to be born naturally. Bonnie taught me it was beneficial for a puppy to experience early neurological stimulation in the form of natural stress experienced during the birthing process. Many assistance dog associations and breeders introduced stressful stimuli to prepare a puppy for the stress to come in the human world. I wished I'd undergone such training when I was just a pup! When breeding assistance dogs, you select high-performing dogs, hoping their progeny will have the same aptitude. The follow-up training of the newborn pups in a controlled environment is even more critical. It's the proper mixture of attention to nature versus nurture that ensures the greatest chance to train the best assistance dog. In the 1970s, the United States military designed the Bio Sensor Program, colloquially known as the Super Dog Program. Puppies were subjected to sensory stimulation, both physical and environmental, hoping to enhance the military dogs' ability to handle war time stress. To this day, many breeders abide by the principals of the program and continue to implement it.

I dutifully arrived in Seoul the day before the clone's birth. The familiar black Benz arrived, and the previously befriended SOOAM employee took me to my hotel. This time I'd forgone the love hotel in favor of an extended-stay hotel near SOOAM. After all, I wasn't *looking* for love. I'd come to welcome it at birth. I'd formerly asked the SOOAM staff for permission to work with the cloned pup at the research center as I needed to work with the pup fifteen minutes twice a day. As it would be a pain in the ass for a stranger to be lurking while intense research was being conducted at SOOAM, I didn't know what to expect in the form of a reply. Professor Hwang respected my love for Booster and my desire to further my education and graciously granted access. I decided to incorporate the biosensor program into the cloned puppy's service dog training regimen.

The next morning, I was picked up by a SOOAM researcher who was my in-house go-to person and new friend. "Mr. Hawn, we have some news for you," he said. "There's been a development." My heart imploded. I just knew my Booster-to-be had been stillborn. In presuming the worst, I automatically reverted to my old behavior like a dog that had undergone many repetitions of positive training to change an unwanted behavior but relapsed. You can change a previously learned behavior, but you can't erase it. Therefore, many assistance dog training schools prefer to start with puppies to eliminate the possibility of relapse into a former behavior that could be problematic for the assistance dog's disabled partner. A dog taught not to chase the cats he once hunted, might do it again spotting a "cat burglar" stealing his food! In my case, I instantly relapsed into a tsunami of negative thinking. It's often said in treatment centers that relapse is part of recovery. While I had always considered that concept a great excuse, I suddenly had to revisit that interpretation. Just as I "knew" (wrongfully surmised) that Booster had been hit by a car as a pup, I just knew the cloned pup must have died during the birthing process. In a nanosecond, life instantly sucked once again!

"Mr. Hawn, remember when we sent you a copy of the sonogram that showed the fetal heartbeat?"

They're letting me down slowly; how thoughtful they are, I mused, unamused! "We are embarrassed. We should have taken a follow-up, second sonogram."

I relived the Cuban Missile Crisis and waited for the bomb and subsequent explosion.

"We didn't see the *other* fetal heartbeat," he explained.

Like the emotional ritual it was, I lost it. The "for certain" dead puppy was, in fact, two healthy puppies! The surrogate had gone into labor a day early, so I missed the birthing process, but I was relieved. I still don't know why I was granted such duality of greatness. Why two? With negativity, I wondered if one was destined to die in the future, so My Higher Power was covering all bases. My mental state of mind still wasn't what it should have been.

I entered SOOAM that morning surrounded by a plethora of well-wishers. As before, I was directed to the rack where I swapped my shoes for sanitized slippers. I was escorted up to the floor that housed all the cloned dogs and their pups. One glass stall had a poster featuring an American flag and the birth date. ARE YOU READY FOR THIS? ARE YOU READDDYYY FOR THIS? The pups were born on arguably the most emotionally charged day in American history! They were born on 9/11. Before I could digest the significance, I was beckoned into the sterile stall. I approached the surrogate mom at floor level, from a slight distance, and spoke with her calmly. She was a large dog and cared for her sons like a mother should. I read her body language as I had learned to do at BUCS.

MY BOOSTER!

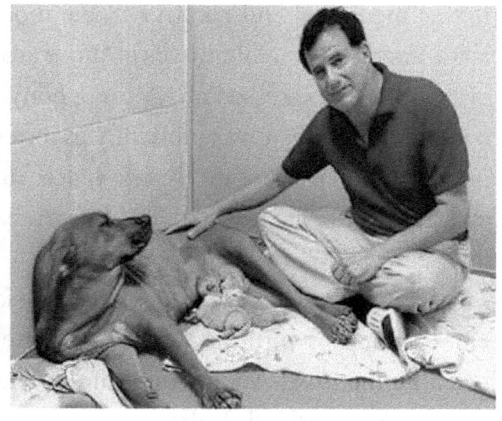

Once I felt acceptance, I moved closer, sat beside her, petted her, and let her know she'd done a great job. She was tired, but patient and accepting . . . far more than I would have been as a grumpy old man having given birth just hours before! I then reached out and simultaneously petted her and her offspring. It was a family within my SOOAM family. I was sitting on cloud nine. It was as though 86-proof Imodium had cured my diarrhea of the mouth. I was verbally bankrupt; absolutely speechless. I was floating on a cloud in another world. The Koreans spoke perfect English, but I didn't hear them. I was introduced to uncanny stress, and I was . . . happy! REALLY? I HAD LEARNED TO HANDLE STRESS AND BE HAPPY? (OMHP). I'd done my best to hide my weird-ass emotions from family and friends in the past.

I struggled to do so in the accompaniment of the Korean staff members. It was hard, damn hard. I needed my Booster, then and there.

Much of what happened that day is a blur. I remember speaking with researchers and interviewing the clones' caretakers at great length. When the facility was about to close for the day, I asked the exhausted staff if I could see the clones once again before leaving SOOAM. Rather than balk, they smiled genuine smiles oozing the milk of kindness I came to know as SOOAM. With the clones nestled in the bosom of my chest, I equated the helplessness of the newborn pups and their need for their mother, with my life and my need for Booster. At that moment, I realized both puppies had Booster's signature white patch on their chests. I suddenly derived Herculean strength from the frailest of creatures. I was mystically enveloped in serenity I couldn't immediately explain. It was divine in nature, calming, and reassuring.

I later surmised that I'd not only cloned Booster but also my belief in the tailor-made curative qualities he bestowed upon my battered psyche.

It was medicinal and curative in the moment. Spirits boosted, I gingerly arose and looked into the eyes of those around me. No words were needed; my emotions expressed all. A cacophony of shrill Asian dialect bestowed congratulations as I was jubilantly escorted to the exit gates of heaven. My interpretation of heaven? A safe place, surrounded by Boosters, releasing endorphins the likes of which I'd never experienced. I'd found heaven in my Seoul.

Prior to embarking upon my *Seoul's* journey, I'd decided to attend the cloned puppy's birth and then take time to go away and reflect before teaching them. Al-Anon taught me to take care of myself. I knew I'd be on sensory overload. I planned to return to SOOAM roughly two weeks later to teach the clones, giving fifteen-to-thirty-minute lessons twice daily until they were old enough to bring home to the US.

Before leaving Seoul, I reviewed the biosensor protocol with the clones' caretakers, and they agreed to work with the clones accordingly in my absence. I handed them a tape recorder and asked them to play my recorded voice and environmental noises to the pups several times a day, commencing at age two and a half weeks. Puppies are born deaf and begin to hear around three weeks of age. Knowing that puppies are born with a fully functional ability to smell, I'd brought sweaty T-shirts to be placed with the puppies so that they could smell my body odor at an early age. They could learn my body smell, which differed from that of the Asian staff. I also provided special baby food and fish oils for enhanced brain development.

During WWII dogs were trained to "sniff out the enemy." Second-generation Japanese Americans volunteered to be tracked by the sniffing dogs, donated by pet owners from across the country. Dogs could be trained to smell and alert to the scent of a human based upon perspiration. The scent given off by a human is determined by diet. You can often smell an alcoholic's perspiration, or perhaps that of a person who's eaten a lot of garlic. Americans had a wheat-based diet whereas Asians had a rice-based diet. The problem was that the second-generation Japanese Americans ate an "American" wheat-based diet so there was no discernable differentiation. The project failed.

MY BOOSTER!

I left Seoul a few days after the clone's birth. I was a mental mess and traveled throughout Asia with duality of purpose. I learned a lot about other cultures and even more about myself. I rode an elephant in Thailand and learned from the animal's trainer the harsh reality of training an elephant. I learned of the horrid pain the dancing bears in India endured to learn to dance . . . to dance! I cried my ass off when I learned of Chinese bear bile farming. Bears were kept for decades in small cages, squeezed like an orange in a juice press to extract their bile used for medicinal purposes . . . even though generic bear bile is readily available. I learned of cats being skinned with a blowtorch before being cooked. I visited a Vietnamese restaurant that served dog meat, though I would never partake! It was an educational pursuit. Perhaps it wasn't so bad, after all, to be overly emotional in a seemingly overly cruel world. I so adored Booster that I sought to obtain another copy, a clone. Others subjected animals to torture that defied belief, animals for which a gas chamber would have been far more benevolent.

While on my journey of introspection, I put a lot of thought into naming the clones. I wanted to somehow name them in honor of their father. Booster had stolen a toy from a pet store . . . he was a thief . . . a *booster*! I in turn *boosted* his skin cells and sent them to Korea for cloning. My brother and sister hadn't approved, so I got *busted* for it. Hence, I named the cloned pups Boosted and Busted! "What's in a name?" one might ask. In this case, it's legacy. An internet search of our names, Davis Hawn Booster, reveals stories around the world. The same stories pop up if you substitute the name Boosted or Busted; hence, the clones inherited their father's legacy upon birth. I envisioned a newspaper story, "Cloned pups get cloned legacy."

I worried, however, that the clones might not differentiate between the two similar-sounding names. If anyone could answer that question beyond reproach it was Bonnie. She quite literally wrote the book on canine behavior. I sent her an email inquiry, and she readily assured me they'd be able to do so. She also made a point of telling me that each was their own man; they might be clones but they were individuals in their own right. Hence, I resoundingly named Booster's clones Boosted and Busted. They quickly learned their respective names. The problem arose when I suddenly realized that I couldn't tell them apart. I was the one with the differentiation problem! Eventually, I put a large dot of red hair dye on Boosted's head. I wondered if parents of identical twins did the same thing!

While traveling in Thailand for two weeks, I constantly received written and photographic updates from the dedicated SOOAM employees in Seoul. Boosted and Busted were doing well. They were weighed daily and grew at the same rate. Their caretakers reported they didn't detect any notable differences in their personalities. I asked that Boosted and Busted be placed with other pups of similar size for a while each day to promote their socialization. I felt sad that they had no littermates to socially interact with. Puppies learn proper interaction from play. If they're too aggressive, they might get called on it by a returned bite. It's a learning curve. Observation of socialization between littermates is vital. The largest pup in a litter often becomes a bully, and the smallest pup gets picked on. This has the potential to affect their personality in the years to come. We might not choose them as assistance dog candidates because of this. We observe the "in-between" pups and make a selection.

On another tangent, ever notice how humans are often shy when it comes to our naked bodies, but dogs couldn't care less? Breastfeeding a baby in public is often shunned. What could be more natural? I'd always wanted to experience a nude beach and got the opportunity to do so years later when I visited Barcelona, Spain. One day, I took a bus to a nude beach, dropped my swim trunks, and planted my coconuts in the sand. I was soon bored. The letdown was more moving than letting my trunks down. I resolutely stood up, re-entered my trunks, and went to grab a drink or two or three at the beachside cantina. I ordered a pina colada, sat, and watched two Spanish guys throw breadcrumbs to the beach birds. The smallest bird timidly hopped to get a crumb, but its efforts were supplanted by a larger, more aggressive bird. Then suddenly, an even larger bird swooped in from nowhere, and the beach Battle of Normandy commenced once again.

Bemused, I watched the birds for over an hour. Something struck a chord within me, and I began to chuckle, then laugh overtly. Onlookers probably thought whatever drugs I must have previously ingested had hit their mark. I'd subconsciously employed my BUCS training and observed the interaction of the birds as though I was observing a litter of puppies. Astonishingly, the allure of going to a nude beach for the first time in my life lasted fifteen minutes at best. Watching birds chase breadcrumbs lasted over an hour. I laugh about that to this day. I reflected that my life's tears, which once emanated from depression, transformed into tears of wonderment and happiness due to Booster's intervention in my life.

Later, I returned to the *Seoul* of Korea filled with unbridled excitement. The day of arrival, I took the subway to SOOAM and walked up to the front door and pressed the buzzer. The young researcher who'd accompanied me from my hotel to SOOAM the day Boosted and Busted were born greeted me with a huge smile.

"Boosted and Busted have been waiting for you," he chimed in perfect English. He was a brilliant young man who was serving his military obligation by working for the research facility. He reminded me to take my shoes off and don the sanitary slippers. We walked up to the room containing all the cloned pups.

I looked over at Boosted and Busted; they had grown so much. I picked up one and then the other and held them for an equal period. I learned at BUCS that dogs have a sense of fairness. With two dogs in a room, treat each dog for giving you its paw. Stop treating one while continuing to treat the other and the dog that stopped receiving treats will stop offering its paw! I was very careful not to show favoritism. Each day I sang to the pups as the surely amused staff members looked on. I crooned like Frank Sinatra and bellowed like Elvis Presley. "I Can't Help Falling in Love with You" and "Love Me Tender" were my songs of choice! Seriously, I sang those songs to Boosted and Busted every day! I wanted to get them acclimated to varying tones of my voice and joked with the Korean staff that they didn't get paid enough to listen to all that!

I began wearing glasses and fake beards when working with the pups and occasionally walked menacingly, like a scarecrow with a bad posture. Many of the dogs started barking when I did that but Boosted and Busted never did. I explained to the Koreans how vital puppy socialization is. I tugged on Busted and Boosted's tails and ears and tickled their bellies. I spoke softly and loudly, but never loudly enough to cause fright as puppies experience fright, but more acutely at ages eight to eleven weeks. I had a toy cat that *mewed* and a clock that *ticked*. I played the tape recordings of doors slamming, people screaming, and musical concerts. When visitors appeared, I asked them to please hold the pups or play with them for a short period.

At six weeks, the pups were tugging open a swinging child gate blocking a door. They were taught to sit, stay, go on, off, leave it, and especially come. I'm sensitive about that command as I want my canine partners to stop what they are doing and come running when told to do so. It could be a matter of life or death, whether a poisonous snake or a car in the road. It became apparent early on that these pups had what it took to become service dogs. They looked into my eyes. They concentrated. Best of all, they seemed to love to learn. I was teaching them, and they were teaching me! The SOOAM staff members often visited the training room to witness my training sessions. I was happy they were interested. We ALL shared learning! It was like working in a Mensa factory!

I often worked barefooted, and the Koreans would say, "It's OK to wear slippers." Then I would say, "Shoe," and the six-week-old pups would run and get my slippers. I was aware that I was always on stage, and I wanted the staff to see service dog tasks being performed by mere puppies. In addition, I wanted Boosted and Busted to smell my feet as they delivered the slippers that entirely covered their young noses. As I taught Boosted and Busted to fetch my shoes (aka slippers), a SOOAM staff member taught me how NOT to do so! I had a favorite pair of slippers in the arrival room shoe locker. I'd dutifully worn them every day upon entering the facility. One day a staff member walked up and said, "Mr. Hawn, you're taking the slippers out of the wrong section of the locker. Those slippers came from the employee section and belong to Professor Hwang! He was looking for his slippers again today!" It's often been said that you can better understand a person if you walk in their shoes. I figured in that first weeks'

time I'd walked at least a mile in those shoes/ slippers. It instantly reminded me of a song that Joe South wrote in 1970, "Walk a Mile in My Shoes."

Professor Hwang was once held in such high regard that the pope might have paled in comparison! He fell from grace due to his research-related scandal yet somehow arose from the abyss to regain stature in life. Once a target for prosecution, he subsequently fortified his life with conviction of purpose. He, like I, had led a difficult life. I had indeed walked a mile in his shoes. What were the chances that I'd take slippers from the wrong section of a locker, and they'd belong to my benefactor? **Coincidence?** My Booster would have politely said, "Helllllllll no!" in English, or 팽숓 in Korean.

A lot of my time was spent teaching Boosted and Busted not to scream when I put them in a rolling doggie crate. They were going to be flown home inside of a plane and I didn't want them screaming. I started by placing them inside and then taking them out. After a week's time, they grew accustomed to their rolling homes. I then zipped the top closed for a moment. Eventually, the top stayed zipped, and the pups were content inside. I then started rolling them along the hallways so they would learn to accept motion and not fear it.

Boosted and Busted were going to be with me in a plane for over fourteen hours from Seoul to Dallas. They'd be at an age when a fear stage set in when it was time to fly them home. We never fly service dog puppies in a crate in the belly of a plane for that reason. They needed to be content in their crate for a long time. When I called the airline to book my ticket home, I was told that I couldn't travel with a puppy in a travel crate on a flight over eight hours in duration. I was stunned. They were too young to qualify as service dogs, and airlines usually don't fly service dogs in training. I was really getting stressed out. My last option was to consider them to be Emotional Support Animals (ESAs).

I'd always proclaimed ESAs were a potential liability. I sympathized with airlines that were mandated to fly them by law. What are they? They're simply someone's pet that they rely on due to a recognized emotional disability. A pit bull fighter's dog might have lost a vicious fight and been bummed out. With a note from a medical professional, he could bring that fighting dog aboard the plane, and the airlines would have to fly it. The dog fighter had no dog training experience with respect to public access. The dog had training, but only to kill and maim. What a hoax and safety issue! When the FAA had a public commentary period regarding potential changes to the ESA policy, I submitted my thoughts.

It suddenly dawned on me, that in my case Boosted and Busted were indeed emotionally supportive. The *red line in the sand* was about to shift. Not a day passed that I didn't think about Booster's eventual demise. Pets help their owners release endorphins. Puppies probably help release more than adult dogs! I called the airline and asked if there was any age specification for an ESA. I was told no. I then asked if one person can have two ESAs. The ticket agent said she didn't think so, but she would check. I explained that I'd flown with two service dogs before. She returned to the line after a lengthy hold and said that it would be OK if the medical professional stated in writing that I needed both puppies for emotional support reasons. I called my dog sitter back home. **Coincidentally**, she saw the same psychiatrist as I did, and her monthly appointment happened to be within days of my call. *Our* psychiatrist gladly wrote the required letter. *God bless the USA and the ESA!* I thought.

I booked tickets in the very last row of the plane across from the lavatory, then I went to a Korean hardware store and tried to explain that I needed Visqueen plastic sheeting. It took a while, but I got a roll of it. I then went to the grocery and tried to explain that I needed air freshener and NOT in aerosol form (since I was taking it on an aircraft). Try asking for pump spray air freshener as an English-speaking person in Korea. I thought about the television show and movie *Mission Impossible*. "Your mission, Mr. Hawn, is to explain to a Korean that you need air freshener and in a pump spray bottle." I clearly and succinctly asked for *pumpy airy fresh ner*. The Korean grocery clerk simply refused to understand. I thought I'd clearly enunciated my wishes in *Korenglish!* I got nowhere fast, but a thoughtful Korean shopper overheard my conversation and felt my frustration. She explained in Korean what I needed, and the problem was resolved then and there. For the record, if you ever need non-aerosol air freshener in Korea it's pronounced *bi eeolojol gong-gicheongjeongje*. I labeled the bottles "smell" in hopes that the airline security would understand what was in the bottle.

As the time to go home grew near, I became leerier of flying with puppies that would eliminate and defecate inside their crates in the plane. I sent a friend a ticket to Seoul to help me get the puppies home. If I was sleeping and a puppy pooped and smelled up the plane, they'd surely throw me out at 30,000 feet. I figured we could take turns sleeping so neither one would be too *pooped* to freshen the air as rapidly as possible if the used dog food bombs fell. I hoped other passengers might be sleeping and dreaming they were visiting a farm back home if the environmental odor took a turn for the worse. In addition, I purchased a third seat, hoping the others would remain empty. Often empty seats are strategically placed adjacent to service dog partners traveling with their service dogs.

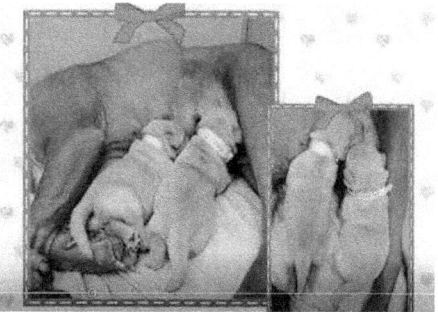

A few days before we were due to fly home a *Dateline NBC* crew flocked to the hallowed halls of SOOAM. One of the producers interviewed me, wanting one-sentence answers to difficult and sensitive questions. Try as I might, I could not provide one-line, succinct answers. It was no easy task to get Booster cloned. It was even more difficult to explain *why* I'd elected to do so given the construct of a single sentence. Perhaps that's why my footage never aired. The producers chose to air footage of an interview they'd conducted with a US military dog trainer who was at SOOAM at the same time I was. He explained that he's cloned one of the military's finest dogs, a Belgian Malinois. I had my two Booster pups, and he had his five military pups. When asked about his expectation concerning the cloned pup, the trainer said he thought it'd be like all the other pups. "Was it?"

queried the interviewer. The astounding reply was "Oh no, no . . . the cloned pup was more focused, more mature, and seemed to exhibit a previous life experience."

Finally, the big day arrived, and we'd soon be flying the (hopefully) friendly skies! SOOAM arranged a graduation party to mark the momentous occasion. All the employees joined us in a large conference room, and we watched a video presentation documenting Boosted and Busted's evolution from the day they entered this world. It was accompanied by heartwarming music that provided the last straw. My damn dam broke once again as my serenity was impacted by extreme global warming within the room. The *Dateline NBC* cameras arrived at the scene as Boosted and Busted were gingerly placed on my pounding chest, one by one, entering my heart. Somehow, I got it together long enough for a thank you speech that I made sure to deliver to Korean eyes that watched yet likely couldn't understand my *spoken* words of gratitude.

I explained to the SOOAM staff that Professor Hwang was known for telling his graduate students at Seoul National University he expected them to work Monday, Tuesday, Wednesday, Thursday, Friday, Friday, and Friday! I tearfully looked into each of the thirty sets of eyes around the room and said, "I want to thank you from the bottom of my heart for working Monday, Tuesday, Wednesday, Thursday, Friday, Friday, and Friday to clone my Booster and make this all possible."

The Koreans taught me far more than dog cloning. It was a life lesson and an undeniable honor. As an old dog, I learned new tricks that I would

MY BOOSTER!

carry forth in life and never forget. The ultimate crescendo popped up just as we were departing the building.

When the graduation party ended, Derek and I wheeled Boosted and Busted to the biotech's van. I was then given a parting, one-of-a-kind gift. Professor Hwang gave me a box containing a keepsake photo and samples of cosmetics he'd helped develop. I remember thinking what a class act the whole SOOAM experience had been. From giving me free rein of the biotech daily to train Boosted and Busted, to presenting me with cherished videos and gifts.

Once the clones had taken their seats, we departed. I honestly don't remember being driven to the airport that day. I only remember rolling Boosted and Busted in their *suitcases* surreptitiously into the unsuspecting flier lounge that most likely had never had a canine visitor. While my friend Derek watched my *Boosters-to-be*, I befriended the airline counter personnel. With swollen eyes, I visited the airline counter staff and shared Booster's legacy and why I felt Koreans had a special Seoul. I'd typed a multi-paged dossier of my Booster's history, culminating with the cloning. With empathetic understanding, we were allowed to board the plane first.

Upon entering the plane, I presented my Booster dossier to the flight attendants that greeted us. I found our three seats and quickly laid down the sheet of Visqueen. I rolled the puppy carriers in, and we sat down. As luck would NOT have it, the plane was full. The one seat left in our cluster of seats was occupied by a lady who smelled like spoiled Durian fruit, and yet *she* complained about sitting next to *dogs*. Boosted and Busted smelled far better; they'd been lightly sprayed with Ralph Lauren Polo Blue cologne.

I was lucky my fellow passengers were humans and not dogs. If the shoe was on the other paw, I might have been in trouble. The human sense of smell pales in comparison to that of a canine that can smell ten thousand to one hundred thousand times better. Scientists theorize a dog can smell a teaspoon of sugar in a million gallons of water, or a rotten apple among two million barrels. I wanted to be sure that if my fellow passengers had to smell anything emanating from my direction, it was apple blossoms blasted forth from the deodorizing spray I'd purchased for the special event. If I so much as farted, I didn't want Boosted and Busted to take the hit! I fart, I spray, I save the day! As always, I was acutely aware that my actions would affect the ability of others who would follow in our paw prints.

I opened the carriers, petted both Boosted and Busted, and gave them each a treat. They looked up at me with a look I knew too well. It was a look of adoration that instantly had me thinking about its origin. It was my Booster's smile and look of trust times two. I was instantly overwhelmed, overpowered, and mesmerized. I was going home with an entourage of love, both canine, and that of a friend who chose to help me with this seemingly impossible endeavor. Booster had taught me to recognize love and to not be afraid to use the word. I turned to my friend Derek and shared, "I couldn't have done this without you . . . my friend."

Once the flight was underway, a flight attendant approached us. With a smile she said "Mr. Hawn, we've all read your paper. We're here to help, but I must ask you a question." She then asked if she could pet the puppies. I suddenly knew everything was going to be alright. I put Boosted in my lap and her adoring hand petted his head. He immediately wagged his tail in recognition of the honor bestowed. I then explained that it was important for Busted to have the same opportunity due to fairness. I then put Busted in my lap and the process repeated itself. For the duration of the flight the flight attendants fawned over Boosted and Busted. I will never forget the flight attendants' graciousness.

An hour before landing, they insisted on moving us up to first class so we could deplane quicker. The flight attendants had one requisite; they insisted on carrying Boosted and Busted in their arms into the first-class cabin. Once seated, businessmen stopped what they were doing, enquired about the pups, and a couple asked to pet them. I cloned my Booster, for which I was subsequently chastised by family members, while others proclaimed I was guilty of playing God. I miraculously ended up in an aircraft descending from a heavenly visit! OMHP! (Oh, My Higher Power) OMB! (Oh, My Booster).

MY BOOSTER!

Clearing customs was another matter. I was worried, not for any good reason, but worry I did. As I approached the inspector, I meekly asked, "Have you ever seen $100,000 puppies? These are clones of a dog I love dearly," I explained.

"Got rabies certificates?" he asked.

With a somewhat shaking hand I gave him the Korean veterinary papers hoping no issues would arise.

The inspector looked into my eyes and said, "Enjoy your pups. Welcome home, sir." **Coincidentally**, he enthusiastically shared, "I train dogs."

I was awash with gratitude again in my life.

My friend looked at me and said, "In England, where I'm from, I don't think the Queen receives better treatment than the pups did this entire journey!"

We rolled the pups in their carriages to the car rental car counter in the Dallas airport. I'd rented a roomy minivan and drove to our hotel room to unwind. I took Busted and Boosted outside to romp freely in a grassy area not likely frequented by other pets or animals. Puppies are highly susceptible to canine parvovirus, which has about a 50% mortality rate and can be expensive to treat. Discovered in the seventies, the virus spread around the world within a few years. Parvo can live in the harshest of environments up to a year with no 100% sure way to eradicate it in contaminated soil.

How do you socialize an assistance dog puppy, critically important during the first twelve to fourteen weeks of age, while simultaneously protecting it from parvo? That's a judgment call, and you must use common sense. Far more dogs lose their lives due to lack of socialization than parvo. Unsocialized dogs often end up in shelters, unadoptable, subject to being euthanized. I had to risk exposing Boosted and Busted to parvo rather than setting them up for failure due to lack of socialization. This bodes true for all assistance dog puppies in training.

I put Boosted and Busted into the ceramic-tiled bathroom that night rather than their carriers. I wanted them to be able to stretch their young legs and not cry. In the morning, I had to drive to a store to buy bleach and ammonia to wash the floor. I wasn't happy I'd given them ill-fated freedom that resulted in a dirty floor and a delayed departure. I *was* happy, however, that I had encountered bathroom havoc rather than an aviation disaster! With the bathroom cleaner than it originally was, we departed for home, with Boosted and Busted in Derek's lap. He was an ideal au pair for the new babies. Home was wherever my Booster was. My thoughts accelerated in NASCAR-like fashion. Booster would soon be in my arms once again; though not soon enough.

I felt wracked with guilt for having been gone so long. Once again, I began to beat myself up. My bully of a psyche tormented me. I pulled over and took Boosted and sat him in my lap as I drove. I petted him as he, much to my surprise, fell asleep. After I looked over at Busted to acknowledge him, I looked at my smiling human friend, Derek, started to explain, and then realized he knew I needed comfort. He knew . . . he was my friend.

When we arrived home, I burst into tears and hugged Booster. I cradled him and looked deeply into his eyes, He looked over at Boosted and Busted and had a befuddled look upon his face. He cocked his head to the right, then to his left. He couldn't possibly understand the seemingly unexplainable connection he instantly felt. It was subtle but ever-present. I kept the clones at bay for a while, slowly introducing them to Booster and the pack. All went well. I was so alive inside; I experienced a festive Fourth of July explosion within *my Seoul.*

CHAPTER 18
CLONING: TRIALS AND TRIBULATIONS

The clones were an exact anatomical copy of Booster, who had horribly dysplastic hips. I knew I'd brought them into the world, and they would necessarily develop bad hips. Why would I do such a thing? One advantage to cloning is that you often know to a certain extent what you're getting... the good and the bad. I'd learned about JPS surgery at BUCS and knew it had to be done early as it loses efficacy with each successive week, so it was imperative to have the surgery right away. I'd called around the country for a clinic to perform the procedure and got responses from flat out, "We don't know what that is," to "We can't do it because you have a clone valued at $100,000, and our malpractice insurance won't cover us for that amount." I was also quoted figures up to $3,000 per dog. After exhaustive research, I spoke to the fine folks at the University of Missouri Veterinary Health Center (MIZZOU). I spoke to Dr. Torres, who specialized in small animal orthopedic surgery, with an interest in osteoarthritis and sports medicine. He was extremely knowledgeable and exuded confidence—he was unquestionably the doc for the job.

Within days, Derek and I, along with Boosted and Busted, set out for the University of Missouri Health Center. Upon arrival, we were handled with kid gloves. A smiling Dr. Torres beckoned us into an examination room. He was fascinated by my story and couldn't have been any nicer. He explained the surgery was minimally invasive and set the appointment for the next day. I was worried about Boosted and Busted undergoing anesthesia, but I worried more about their hips to come! The following day, all went according to plan. A day later, Boosted and Busted were released. I suggested we do a story to promote the procedure. They arranged for a photographer to take photos. The cost quoted for the procedures was incredibly reasonable, and I was floored when I saw that they'd given me a discount because the puppies were service dogs in training, or to be utilized as service dogs. It meant a lot to me.

My Booster (s).

Seeing double.

A trio of happiness..

Who am I? asked Boosted, looking into a mirror.

(Photos courtesy of Karen Clifford University of Missouri Veterinary Health Center, MIZZOU)

Booster enjoyed his progeny daily. They romped and played all the time as the clones vied for his attention. Often, the other canine kids would join in. A year later, I went to a festival held in a city park. I walked Boosted and Busted side by side. We met all kinds of people, young and old. To say that a dog is a social lubricant is a gross understatement. I'll never forget Busted walking up to a gentleman who stood out among the crowd. Many dogs might have been uncomfortable or barked at a man wearing a cap, carrying a large stick in hand. Busted remained calm. I'd

MY BOOSTER!

learned at BUCS to introduce "environmental triggers" at an early age and the training paid off. Suddenly, the man kneeled, love ensued, and he warmly received Busted's fervent kisses. I ascertained that the man was a homeless veteran who used the stick to help balance due to an injury sustained in battle years ago. Though Busted had a far easier time connecting with the man than I did, I learned the veteran had two things close to his heart . . . the US flag proudly worn on his chest and the unconditional love of a service dog.

My memory flashed back to my BUCS education. I'd learned how dogs were changing the lives of veterans around the world and lowering the suicide rate. This was a real-life experience that corroborated my classroom education. I reflected upon how much my BUCS education had impacted my daily life, and subsequently, the lives of many others. I instantly thought about the time my good friend Charles informed me he'd been to the VA hospital and was diagnosed with a liver ailment. He was a candidate for a liver transplant, but needed someone to be a caretaker should he be operated on and receive one. Booster and I accompanied Charles to the VA hospital in Houston, Texas, where they were to qualify him for the procedure.

We arrived at the hospital and checked into the VA Fisher House that provides free housing for visiting patients. and their families. Upon entering the room, the phone began to ring. Charles answered the call and immediately handed me the phone. "You got. a *dog* in the room?" queried the authoritarian-sounding voice.

I replied, "I have a service dog in the room, just like the one that appears in the brochures on your front desk!" I wasn't prepared for the conversation that ensued.

"That dog gotta go," the woman said dictatorially.

I responded politely, "No ma'am, the service dog don't gotta go!"

"Does he have his papers?" (This was nothing to do with vaccination records, which she would have been entitled to ask for.)

I almost lost it and said pointedly, "You want his high school diploma, GED, or college transcript?"

She hung up, thus avoiding a meltdown of nuclear proportion.

The following day, as a trio, we walked into the hospital. Charles was to underdo myriad tests. Some of the doctors smiled, yet one particular lady doctor of foreign origin looked dismayed and agitated. She obviously didn't like seeing a dog in the hospital. In some cultures, dogs are shunned. Later that day, when Charles finished a test, a nurse approached us and said that Charles had an appointment with the Chief of Staff. I presumed it was to verify he had a caretaker.

The first words out of the man's mouth were, "Gentleman, we're here to talk about the dog!"

"Wonderful," I replied, remembering my BUCS training to remain calm in the face of adversity or ignorance (ignorance not being a derogatory term). I explained, "Sir, you have a beautiful facility here. I have a master's degree in Canine Life Sciences with an emphasis on Service Dog Education. I attended the acclaimed Bergin University of Canine Studies. The university founded a program called Paws for Purple Hearts to help lower the suicide rate amongst our Veterans. As you're likely aware, more veterans die from suicide than battle, roughly one every hour. If you get your guys in body bags, there's not a lot you can do for them. Sir, we are on the same page to save lives."

The gentleman explained it was his job to inquire. I applauded him for his diligence, and we left the office. My Booster and I then went directly to the physical rehab unit, with Charles following sheepishly behind. Upon arriving at the unit, I asked if it might be possible for my Booster to do a therapy dog visit—he was certified by Therapy Dogs International—and demonstrate lifeenabling service dog tasks. The lady explained that they already had therapy dog organizations visiting, but if they were interested, they'd call me later.

Sure enough, around 5 p.m., the phone rang, and an invitation was extended to visit the staff the following day. "Could you and your dog Booster come around 12 p.m., during our lunch period?"

MY BOOSTER!

I pondered; *How does she know my Booster's name?* So, I asked her that very question.

"Sir, I did an internet search and found you on several pages around the world." "You credentialed me?" I asked in awe.

"You don't think I'm going to have just anyone walking in off the street talking to my staff, do you?"

How cool was that? Once again, education begets education . . . hard work and dedication reap rewards. I only had a master's degree, but my Booster earned his PhD—**Ph**enomenal **D**og. From "that dog gotta go" to "please visit our staff" still BOW-wows me to this day!

The following month, a neighbor invited Boosted and Busted to join the Scouts! They'd have been excellent Scouts; however, this was an invitation to join the Scouts for a meeting to demonstrate service dog tasks. They took turns demonstrating their skills, equally talented at performing their requested tasks. Booster would have been so proud to see his progeny performing up to his standards. The clones inherited the unique skill set required to be the finest service dogs, whether calmly offering emotional support or physically opening a refrigerator or truck door.

As the adage goes, you get what you pay for. Though that's not always true, it sure was in the case of cloning Booster. My brother chastised me for wasting a lot of money to clone a dog. As was always the case, that was the green light to go forward with the decision-making process. It was the litmus test I often used when making decisions. If he said "No," I heard "Go" once again! With every passing day, I gave thanks to My Higher Power for putting a *booster* in my life. I had recharged *my booster* by cloning my Booster!

Months later, I saw an advertisement on television. *Dateline NBC – The Clone Zone: Would you clone your dog?* was prominently displayed on the screen. I later tuned in and watched the somewhat skewed story. It included interviews with a cloning specialist and a couple from Britain who had cloned their beloved dog. The discussion that ensued questioned whether cloning took advantage of vulnerable pet owners' emotions, perhaps leading them to believe they could essentially get their deceased pet back. I'm sure none of the commentators had ever cloned a dog and probably had more experience with hogwash than dog cloning and the canine–human connection. The British couple explained they were initially a bit apprehensive but were very happy with the experience.

While at SOOAM, I befriended a Japanese gentleman who'd cloned his dog there. The Japanese government imposes a six-month quarantine on the importation of dogs into the country. Remarkably, the gentleman flew from Japan to Korea almost every weekend to play with his beloved cloned puppy. For the record, I've never met anyone disenchanted with the decision to clone a canine loved one.

In addition to cloning pets, SOOAM developed models for cloning puppies that will develop certain diseases like Alzheimer's and diabetes. As a direct result, researchers now have a valuable tool to search for preventive or curative medical treatments. There's a focus on cloning human organs for implantation as those organs, made from your own cells, shouldn't face rejection, or require the recipient to take a lifetime regimen of anti-rejection drugs. How would my sister feel about cloning if a family member received a life-saving, cloned organ transplant? I don't dare ask! She couldn't handle such an "environmental trigger."

Human and canine DNA are very similar, so dogs are often used in scientific experiments. I'm sure this understandably has PETA pissing! Humans today receive lymphoma treatment based on knowledge gained through studies conducted utilizing donated Golden retriever blood. In the US, Golden retrievers have a high lymphoma incident rate, often succumbing to this form of cancer commencing at eight years of age.

I personally find using animals to test for things like reactions to perfumes as unsupportable. When it comes to curing cancer, diabetes, Alzheimer's, and other dreaded diseases, it's cause for additional consideration. Booster participated in the *first in the world* clinical research of its type for treatment of his squamous cell carcinoma; humans benefited directly as a result. Research can be performed ethically and beneficially, though it is often regarded in a negative context with respect to animal participation. It isn't possible for anyone to love a dog more than I. While learning to love life due to the unconditional love of a dog, I learned to appreciate those things that preserve it. Ethical research is a tool for doing just that. Granted, the definition of "ethical" is a subject for another book! For the record, I'm quite the advocate for cloning, especially for a reasonable purpose. In my case, it was to avert inevitable depression and the possibility of cataclysmic consequences. I also needed what is commonly referred to as a *successor dog*, a new assistance dog when the current dog is too old to work or has passed away. Booster was an integral part of who I'd become. He was my evolutionary stimulus that transformed my life for the better, providing reassurance, direction, and purpose. Under his tutelage, I learned to live, and more importantly, desired to do so. Cloning Booster was essential for my well-being.

Cloning may not appeal to some, and I respect that. I often share my thoughts on the topic as I feel I'm coming from a defensive posture when, really, I should feel just the opposite. I'm proud of my decision and my subsequent life journey attests to that. A somewhat negative article appeared in *Psychology Today* and I just had to contribute to the online dialogue:

P SYCHOLOGY TODAY

CLONING REALITY
___

Submitted by Davis Hawn and Booster on August 2, 2016 – 4:57pm

I cloned my dog Booster who once saved my life. I promised to share him with the world. I got a Master's Degree in Canine Life Sciences from Bergin University of Canine Sciences located in California so I could do just that! Booster was cloned at SOOAM in Seoul, South Korea. I am plagued with depression and once almost opted out. Booster changed my life 180 degrees. Google: Davis Hawn Booster and see what a dog did for a man and others around the world. His clones Boosted and Busted embody his qualities: confidence, zero aggression, sensitivity, and a keen work ethic. Cloning allowed me to go forward in the world in the same way that Booster did. The personality match between a canine and human is everything! In reality, the clones evidence previous life experiences. The pups opened my truck door, found a water bottle, and delivered it to my hand HAVING NEVER BEEN TRAINED TO DO IT BEFORE! They had been trained to open a fridge. EVERYONE I've met has been happy with the results of cloning their pet. One said it was either going to be a new Land Rover, or a clone we invested in. The car would depreciate while the clones would appreciate more every passing day! Cloning is the best decision I have ever made. I wish all pet owners had the option. The naysayers are doing a great disservice to those who need the unique animal qualities that changed their lives. Karen nailed it. She got it right. Look, Booster was by my side for 12 years as my Service Dog. The clones started off with one year old maturity and inherited intelligence. If anyone wants to talk to an individual who cloned his dog . . . and wants an unbiased opinion . . . please email me.

Davis Hawn

PS At the very least preserve your pets' cells for future cloning if you have any interest at all in cloning.

My efforts to explain my cloning experience, predicated upon real-life experience versus ignorant conjecture, paid off.

I'M SO HAPPY FOR DAVIS,

MY BOOSTER!

Submitted by Karen on August 2, 2016 – 10:46pm

I'm so happy for Davis, Booster, Boosted and Busted for finding unconditional and boundless love. We should be documenting information like Davis' to enhance our understanding. I've saved all of Baby's toys and beds to see if her clone recognizes the scents. Love is energy which transcends physical boundaries. Who are we to impose limitations on things we don't completely understand? We can only observe, document and study for more awareness in the future. I'm so grateful for the science and technology which has opened doors and minds to new discoveries and possibilities.

Submitted by Jessica Pierce Ph.D. on August 2, 2016 5:18pm

David—Thanks for offering your personal experiences. Three cheers to Booster and his clones for making such a difference in your life.[4]

    Years later, I was interviewed by a local news reporter working for television station WLOX, Gulfport, Mississippi. He did a remarkable job and filmed Boosted and Busted in action, bringing me a bottle of water from the refrigerator. Amazingly, that day they both grabbed the bottle at the same time and brought it to me. It was a beautiful team effort, perfect for the story. The reporter later sent me a photo he'd taken with his cell phone in the front yard. I later had that turned into an oil painting when I was in Thailand years later (back cover).
    In 2016, when Boosted and Busted were about a year and a half old, I decided to attend the Western Veterinary Conference in Las Vegas. I called my buddy Warren, and he agreed to go with me to help. When I walked

---

[4] Davis Hawn, "All Dogs Go To Heaven," *Psychology Today* (February 2016), https:// www.psychologytoday.com/ie/blog/all-dogs-go-heaven/201602/cloning pets#comments_bottom. [link unpublished]

into the conference with Boosted and Busted, people saw the word CLONE on their service dog vests. Many thought it was the dog's name! Veterinarians and other attendees clamored to meet the clones and hear my story. I attended lecture after lecture, soaking up knowledge like a paper towel in a flood. Warren and I walked Boosted and Busted around the exhibition hall where vendors hawked their canine-related goods. I'm not sure who enjoyed the meandering more, us or the dogs!

One veterinary lecture was conducted by a canine orthopedic specialist, who put a radiograph up on the screen of a puppy with obviously bad hips. He then offered three treatment options: (1) monitor the hips, (2) put the puppy on hip meds, and (3) operate on the puppy right away. When he asked members of the audience which option they would recommend to their pet parents, almost all the veterinarians in attendance chose options one or two. My hand shot up instantly, almost hitting the ceiling, opting for option number three—to operate immediately. The specialist asked me why I would operate on the puppy.

I eagerly replied, "With minimally invasive JPS surgery, optimally performed at age twelve to fourteen weeks, the hips of the mature dog will have benefited tremendously. In fact, these two dogs seated beside me are clones of a dog who had exceptionally bad hips. Both clones had JPS surgery performed at the appropriate age. The radiographs of their hips look great. It's as though I took my older, original dog, put him in a time machine, returned him to puppyhood, and had JPS surgery performed. Then, like the movie *Back to the Future*, I brought him back to adulthood and had new radiographs made. The clones are anatomically the same dog as my original dog. Though there may have been some subtle environmental differences, overall, it's indisputable that the procedure benefited the clones."

Once I'd cultivated the audience's attention, I explained how difficult it was to find a facility capable of performing the procedure. I then closed by explaining that I wasn't a veterinarian, or even a vet tech, but held a master's degree in Canine Life Sciences from the acclaimed BUCS where I'd studied under the auspices of many renowned canine educators and researchers. At that moment, I was so incredibly proud of my BUCS education and Dr. Bergin, the university's founder, and originator of the service dog concept. I reached down and hugged Boosted and Busted.

MY BOOSTER!

The next morning, I called a local television station to see if they'd like to cover the story since there were thousands of people in town attending the conference who'd likely be interested. They agreed to send a reporter that afternoon. Sure enough, a young man contacted me and arrived with a camera in hand. It seemed a little cheesy to me, but I was grateful for the effort. That night, the story didn't air. I called the station the next morning and the station manager thought I was trying to perpetrate a scam. I explained that my life story was enshrined on the internet.

The manager explained matter-of-factly, "That's where most fraud takes place these days." **Coincidentally**, the station was an NBC affiliate.

I then asked him, "Aren't you an NBC affiliate?" He responded, "Yes."

"Would you trust an NBC executive producer?" I asked. "What are you getting at?"

"Call the office in New York City and ask for the lady producer of *Dateline NBC*. "She interviewed me at the biotech in Seoul; she'll vouch for my authenticity," I gleefully explained.

That afternoon, a "real" television film crew filmed us at the station. It was a wonderful, warm interview. When the story aired, it opened with a sign at the conference center and the anchor was *coincidentally* an enthusiastic Korean woman. I freaked out when I watched the story on the television as it included footage taken years before at SOOAM Biotech that had been filmed during the *Dateline* interview. How cool is that?[5]

---

[5] Gabby Hart, "Man Who Cloned Deceased Service Dog Shares His Story," *NBC News* (May 19, 2016). https://news3lv.com/news/local/man-who-cloned-deceased-service-dog-shares-his-story

Boosted, Busted, and I returned home a few days later. It was nice to get back to the pack! I shared the television video with friends and realized more than ever how my Booster, Boosted, Busted, and the canine kids had transformed my life. My passion for sharing canine medicine with the world was growing exponentially, powered by an ever-emerging sense of spirituality. Life settled down . . . until I was on a trip in Asia and received a phone call from an assistant deputy attorney for the county in which I lived in Mississippi.

A man's body was found decomposing in the woods on my property. A search warrant had been issued, and my home thoroughly searched. The lady who lived in my home and took care of my canine kids while I was away had a son recently released from prison. The thirty-something *Hannibal Lector look-alike*, with a face tattooed beyond recognition, had ordered drugs, and arranged to have them delivered to my home, which he had moved into unbeknownst to me. He'd just been released from prison,

MY BOOSTER!

so he didn't have a dime to his name. When the drugs arrived, he simply pulled out a shotgun and killed the drug dealer. He then drove the drug dealer's car to the rear of my 20-acre property and covered it with branches. Months later, his girlfriend ratted him out, and the detectives came looking for the body.

I'm not a gun advocate, but I do understand why people need them for selfprotection. I owned a small .410 shotgun to kill the poisonous snakes that were seemingly ever-present on my property, especially on the banks of the pond directly behind my cabin. The gun used to commit the murder was none other than my own. The freak of human flesh had found my shotgun under the stairs in a storage area. I was the lawful owner of the gun, so I was asked to present myself for an interview upon my return to the country. I was instantly pissed off because I'd been pissed on.

Even though I'd done nothing wrong, the fears and trepidations of the past instantly cascaded upon my psyche. How could I possibly testify against *Hannibal*? I started shaking and rocking. I hadn't done that in a long time. The fear was ingrained. I didn't have Boosted or Busted with me, so had to fend for myself without a drop of canine medicine. I knew I'd be asked to testify at the monster's trial, and I felt obligated to do so. But how? I went walking and found the closest bar and downed a few drinks rapid-fire.

When I returned to the States, I immediately contacted the assistant attorney. I agreed to meet the following day, and I took Boosted with me. When I walked into an office comprised of smiling faces, and Boosted joyfully trotted in beside me, I was instantly put at ease, if just for the moment. While I was being interviewed, I relentlessly hugged Boosted. I must have looked like a school kid hugging a teddy bear! The murder weapon was found between my bed's box spring and mattress. I was asked if I slept with my gun there, and I explained that I really don't like guns and would never do so. *Hannibal* had been sleeping in my bed, making love to my shotgun. *OMG*, I thought. I threw away the mattress and box spring and slept in another room for months.

I told the assistant attorney that I would testify at the trial though I suffered from PTSD, and that it was kicking my ass once again. She totally got it, being the empathetic soul that she was. I then asked if I'd be permitted to have my service dog, Boosted, by my side when I testified as I knew *Hannibal* would be staring at me. I wasn't sure I'd hold up in court, but I was far more likely to with Boosted by my side.

She explained that they'd never had a dog accompany a witness inside of the courtroom, so she'd have to defer to the judge. A few days later, she called me and explained that the judge agreed to my service dog's presence at the trial. Yes, you damn well guessed it . . . tears were a-flowing. I had gratitude for the assistant attorney and the judge, who understood my needs and granted the accommodation.

I later entered the courtroom and took the stand. Boosted calmly lay at my feet. I answered both counsels' questions to the best of my ability while being mesmerized by *Hannibal's* tattooed face. Pure evil was focused on me. I was numb as I constantly petted Boosted for comfort and support. He licked my hand as if to say he knew I was stressed out. I knew he would lick my emotional wounds unconditionally until the psychological infection healed. Before long, the ordeal was over, and I was allowed to step down. I exited the courtroom and was greeted in the street by a dog-loving attorney who came to see the dog at the trial. A warm conversation ensued, and then I walked with Boosted to a bench and sat calmly for about an hour before attempting to drive home.

The following morning, I read the newspaper story sharing what had transpired at the trial. Turns out, it was the first time an assistance dog had accompanied a witness in a courtroom in the history of the State of Mississippi. I thought, *Booster would be so proud.* In that moment of reflection, I was hurting. Boosted got up and walked across the room and sat on my feet. I was an emotional train wreck.

MY BOOSTER!

As if that wasn't enough, the trial ended up being a mistrial because a detective testified about what *Hannibal's* girlfriend had shared with him. She originally agreed to testify but later changed her mind. Nobody had informed the detective. That meant I would have to go through the whole ordeal again! I was in Arkansas when I received a call, saying I was needed to testify the following week. I hired a doggy nanny to take care of my dog pack. Boosted and I later boarded a plane to Mississippi to testify once again. Turned out the trial was postponed because the docket was full. We jetted back to Arkansas and rejoined our pack, issue not resolved. The trial was scheduled once again for a later date. Luckily, *Hannibal* connected the dots . . . like those tattooed teardrops below his eyes. He eventually agreed to a plea bargain. I was spared.

Somehow, I kept my cool throughout the whole ordeal. I'd been taught by a dog, the Al-Anon program, and BUCS. I'd learned to interpret life's signals and live life on life's terms, good and bad. In addition, I had learned how to live in the now, let go of the past, and not obsess about the future. In other words, I learned to live like a dog! My life had indeed been *boosted* to heights never envisioned possible. I wondered if it could go any higher. Like an addict crashing, I dreaded coming back down. I was high on life. DID YOU HEAR THAT? I WAS HIGH ON LIFE!

Months later, I decided to visit my dear friend Peggy. I needed inspiration, and she was one of the most inspirational people I knew. Peggy graciously invited me to her home, though I knew she was almost bed ridden. She'd previously undergone chemo treatments and lost the battle of the hair, but not the war. Recently, she'd lost her mobility, and I knew I needed to see her while I still could.

I'd raised one of Booster's pups named Savior, who became my *savior* in the absence of his father. Funny how life works. I never knew that I'd named him so appropriately when he was just a pure white bundle of energy bounding through the cabin. Savior had a knack at an early age for learning commands and tasks easily. He was as loving as Booster and wooed people in his own special way. He was far clingier than Booster but that was exactly what I needed at that point in time. Peggy had visited my home when Savior was just a pup. She looked at me and said, "Dave, he's a keeper." With such encouragement, I did indeed keep him. I took Savior with me to visit Peggy.

I'd lost Booster, and I was losing Peggy. I was desperate to visit her. *Am I being selfish?* I wondered, needing her when she was facing mortality. I reassured myself that knowing my Peggy as I did, she'd want to be there for me. After second, third, and fourth guessing myself, I decided to see Peggy and then visit friends in Mexico City. I booked a round-trip ticket from New Orleans to Mexico City on United Airlines. United at the time allowed customers to jump off and return at a later date on a round-trip ticket.

United's ticketing routed me through McAllen, Texas, where Savior and I jumped off to visit Peggy. I'll never forget lying beside Peggy on her bed as we laughed and carried on like a bunch of school kids (which, of course, we were). All the while, Savior was on the bed beside us along with Peggy's canine benefactor, Tera. We were all enmeshed with one another, humans and canines alike. It was nothing short of glorious. It was just what I needed at the exact moment in time.

After a few days, Savior and I returned to the McAllen International Airport to catch our flight to Mexico City. United had booked us on a partner airline, Mexico's Aeromar Airlines. We went to the ticket counter and the Aeromar ticket agent refused to issue my ticket. "We only fly small dogs in a box, sir."

"But you must fly service dogs," I replied. "It's the law. Please call your home office in Mexico City," I implored. The ticket agent made the call, but the home office specifically instructed her not to allow me to board with my service dog. Savior looked up at me, and I looked at him. I knew to remain calm as to scream would make me the bad guy and justify the airline's refusal to fly a dangerous man, aka *un hombre peligroso*.

I thought about my Booster, who'd limped in pain to champion access rights and to visit children equally in pain. I had to think clearly and with conviction of purpose as I couldn't let Booster down, nor others who would follow in my footsteps, treated similarly by an airline violating established law. So, I took a deep breath and composed myself as best I could, then I called the McAllen sheriff's department and explained the

MY BOOSTER!

situation. They dispatched an officer, who did his utmost best to explain the law to the airline representatives, to no avail. He made a clear, concise report. While he sympathized with our plight, he couldn't force the Aeromar assholes to fly us.

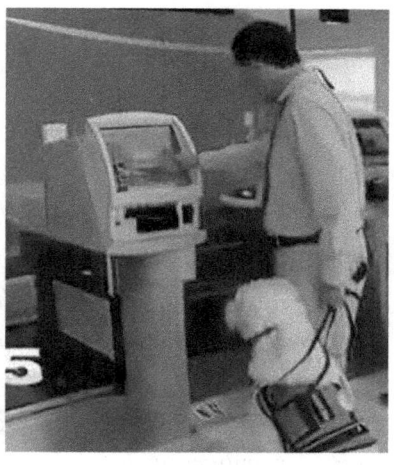

I then called a local television station. Within thirty minutes, a reporter and cameraman arrived to conduct an interview. *Coincidentally*, his station had called him just before he was about to do a story elsewhere. He explained my story sounded more intriguing, so they'd packed up and headed my way. I adamantly explained, "My service dog, my Savior, is not going to be put in a crate, in the belly of a plane in 100-degree temperature . . . not gonna happen!"

The airport was closing at the conclusion of the interview, but I was able to obtain a rental car at the last minute. I returned to a warm Peggy embrace as she gleefully explained my story had flashed across the television screen, "Stay tuned at 5 p.m. Man refused access with service dog at the McAllen airport!"

Within a few hours, Peggy's phone rang. It was a United Airlines representative, apologizing for the actions of their partner, Aeromar Airlines. The United representative arranged to put us on a United Airlines flight the next morning. She also volunteered to pay for my rental car and my money lost on the night's hotel room in Mexico City. It was a nice accommodation for failing to accommodate! UNITED we stand!

DAVIS HAWN

UNITED

August 17, 2015

Dear Mr. Hawn,

Allow me to apologize for my delayed response and the inconvenience you experienced while traveling with Aeromar Airlines flight 0799 on 30JUL2015. Your request and receipts for reimbursement were received. As discussed in my telephone conversations with you, enclosed is a check for $259.42 USD; representing reimbursement of the rental car ($56.86 USD) and hotel expense ($159.85 USD) in McAllen, TX; and $42.71 USD for the hotel in Mexico City on the night of 30JUL2015. A $50.00 refund representing one entry to the United Club has been processed to your visa card ending in xxxx. Please allow seven to ten business days for the refund process to be completed. Please be assured United Airlines has forwarded your complaint to Aeromar Airlines, as according to the US Department of Transportation part 382, the operating carrier is required to handle disability related complaints involving their flights. Your patience and your business are greatly appreciated. We look forward to having you aboard United/United Express flights in the future.

Sincerely,
Corporate Customer Care

The next morning, I returned to the airport and boarded the United flight without incident. Upon arrival in Mexico City, I was unexpectedly met by an Aeromar manager who greeted me and took my suitcase in hand. He took me to an airport eatery, where we talked. He explained that there was a legal issue with entering Mexico with a dog on an airplane. I explained it wasn't my first rodeo, and I'd flown into Mexico with my service dog many times previously. I felt sure he was the man who answered the call in Mexico City that resulted in Aeromar's refusal to fly us in violation of the law. I explained that Aeromar had discriminated against the disabled in violation of the law, and I expected an apology. Rather than an apology, I was subjected to a misrepresentation of the truth.

The next day on the McAllen television news, the anchorman quoted an Aeromar official who said, "We are sorry for the incident, but Mr. Hawn didn't have the necessary paperwork." That demeaning misrepresentation motivated me to seek legal resolution. It ended up costing Aeromar a lot of money and years of aggravation. For the record, it was the *exact* same paperwork that United used to fly me into Mexico City the following day. I knew the requirements. From Cuba to Thailand, to Mexico to the Bahamas and beyond . . . I was well versed with respect to international travel with a dog, whether service dog or pet. I was ready for the fight. *Every dog has his day . . . and Savior will eventually have his!*

As a man who'd flown to many countries in the world (and Mexico many times), I was offended that Aeromar didn't acknowledge their mistake and own up to it. I was demeaned to the extent that I was shaking mad. I had been made to look like a novice who didn't know his ass from a hole in the ground. When we got home, a local television station interviewed us. I was asked, "Is it fair to say that they picked on the wrong guy?" Without a moment's hesitation, I excitedly extorted, "Oh no, they picked on the right guy!" I had my Booster in my heart, my BUCS education in my head, and my Savior by my side. This was a battle that was meant to be.

I ultimately filed a twenty-page complaint with the United States Department of Transportation (DOT) explaining Aeromar's transgressions. I later had to deal with a New York City lawyer hired by Aeromar. That lawyer referred to my *comfort dog*. I explained that I wasn't sure what a comfort dog was, but my *service dog* was trained and notoriously dressed as such. If my dog was a comfort dog, the New York lawyer was a Girl Scout!

The issue took over a year to resolve. At one point, the lawyer produced Aeromar's manual explaining the requirements for a dog to be recognized by the airline as a service dog. It referred to special requirements that absolutely violated ADA and DOT requirements. It bolstered my case that the airline was ignorant regarding service dogs, as was the New York attorney. They were a perfect match. Further, Aeromar later published on its website that:

> Service animal.
>
> *If you have a service animal, such as a guide dog, you can travel with it. If your animal requires traveling to your next service, remember that you can not occupy a seat, even if unoccupied, or obstruct the movement of other passengers or their comfort. If traveling with a guide dog will be assigned a seat in the hall.*
>
> *If traveling on an international flight note that most countries implement strict policies regarding the arrival of foreign wildlife, take all precautions to avoid mishaps and misunderstandings in customs. Some measures include a passport attesting to the animal as a service animal and an official primer applied vaccines.*

MY BOOSTER!

> *Service animals* other than guide dogs, such as emotional support, they can not travel in the cabin with you, unless it *is proven with medical documentation (letter from the treating psychologist or psychiatrist)* that it is essential that you travel with them. Not have the necessary documentation will be treated as a pet and must travel in the baggage compartment, assuming the cost for transportation of the pet and meet the necessary requirements. (http://www.aeromar.com.mx/politicas/pasajeros-particulares/) (link unpublished).

The website stated, "A service dog may not sit in a seat, and **YOU MUST REMAIN ON THE FLOOR.**" A preschooler could have done a far better job of writing . . . and yet Aeromar Airlines was responsible for thousands of air passengers' lives on a daily basis! Halloween was less scary! I explained to the DOT that this evidenced Aeromar's complete lack of understanding of the topic of assistance dogs, guide dogs, and ESAs, and it's caused problems for the disabled. Service dogs do NOT need a letter to travel aboard an airplane and it is illegal to ask for one. ESAs do.

The legal volley seemed to never end. I wrote many lengthy letters in response to questions posed and corrected erroneous legal questions and responses filed by the New York lawyer. I'm not sure where he got his education, but it was no match for my BUCS education regarding assistance dogs. The lawyer had to have cost Aeromar a pretty peso. I relished the fact that his incompetence would certainly lose the case for the discriminatory airline and run up their bill! It seemed that with each new communiqué, the lawyer made his client's case even worse.

The lawyer questioned whether Savior was identified as a service dog. I explained the law to the lawyer, with a copy sent to the DOT:

The Department does indeed provide a means for an airline to identify a Service Dog. In 68 Federal Register page 2487524876 the DOT states:

Carriers shall accept as evidence that an animal is a service animal identifiers such as identification cards, (My service dog had this) other written documentation, (Shown to officer and Aeromar staff as stated in sheriff report) presence of harnesses, (my service dog had this) tags (my service dog had this) or the credible verbal assurances of a qualified individual with a disability using the animal (Federal Register, DOT). (Both I and an officer of the law gave myriad assurances).

I met every suggested DOT qualifier. I had the officer's report and the television footage to corroborate it. Everything was documented, as I had been taught to do by renowned BUCS instructors. Both Savior and I acted in a calm, professional manner, beyond reproach. In my response to the DOT, I explained Aeromar discriminated against a minority class called the disabled by not allowing me to board their plane. In Aeromar's apology, I was blamed due to "lack of proper paperwork." Their lawyer also blamed me for calling the police/TV/press to document the airline's discriminatory practice. They also commented that I should have, or could have, boarded a United flight out of McAllen. It suggested to me that as a disabled man who relies on a service dog, I wasn't good enough to fly on Aeromar's plane. The fact that they wanted to pawn me off on another airline was unconscionable and unacceptable.

"Rather than manufacture excuses for discriminating against the disabled," I asked, "wouldn't it be proper for Aeromar to acknowledge its mistake and simply apologize? Is that too much to ask for?

"I will be traveling the same route in the near future. I will be the same man and have the same service dog of the same appearance. Will I be allowed to board an Aeromar flight like non-minority members?"

Interestingly, the McAllen sheriff who wrote the incident report quoted Aeromar officials as saying that they don't fly large Labrador

MY BOOSTER!

service dogs. I was in Thailand when the DOT informed me they were going to close the case because it was an issue regarding the weight of the large dog. I demanded to see that flight's cargo/weight manifest—there was no way my dog's weight would have prevented the plane from taking off!

So, I explained to the DOT that if one airline can refuse to board a service dog or guide dog due to the subjective term large, then that should be the same for all airlines. Then I demanded that they send that determination out to ALL airlines immediately! Could you imagine how many blind or disabled passengers would be stranded, nationally and internationally, if that edict prevailed? It was a ludicrous decision. I explained I was good at getting press releases out and suggested that they Google me and my dog, Booster. The powers that be had a "reconsideration," and after two years, the issue was finally resolved. Despite the efforts of Aeromar's legal beagle, the United States DOT cited Aeromar for two violations of the law!

US Department of Transportation   GENERAL COUNSEL   **1200 New Jersey Ave. S.E. Washington, DC 20590**

Office of the Secretary of Transportation

INVESTIGATION SUMMARY SHEET

Complaint/Issue: Carrier refused to transport service dog

Applicable Section of 14 CFR Part 382:   382.117(a)(d)(e)

Section Summary:

(a) As a carrier, you must permit a service animal to accompany a passenger with a disability.

(d) As evidence that an animal is a service animal, carrier must accept identification cards, other written documentation, presence of harnesses, tags, or the credible verbal assurances of a qualified individual with a disability using the animal.

(e) If a passenger seeks to travel with an animal that is used as an emotional support or psychiatric service animal, you are not required to accept the animal for transportation in the cabin unless the passenger provides you current documentation on the letterhead of a licensed mental health professional.

Rule Violated? Yes

For the reasons stated above, we find that Aeromar violated section 382.117 in this instance for failing to allow Mr. Hawn's service animal on his originally scheduled flight. If we decide to seek enforcement action against Aeromar with respect to this issue, this complaint will be among those considered, which may lead to the issuance of a cease and desist order and to the assessment of civil penalties.

MY BOOSTER!

Applicable Section of 14 CFR Part 382:	382.41
Section Summary:	382.41 As a carrier, you must provide the following information, on request, to qualified individuals with a disability or persons making inquiries on their behalf concerning the accessibility of the aircraft expected to make a particular flight. The information you provide must be specific to the aircraft you expect to use for the flight unless it is unfeasible for you to do so (e.g., because unpredictable circumstances such as weather or a mechanical problem require substitution of another aircraft that could affect the location or availability of an accommodation). The required information is: Any aircraft-related, service-related or other limitations on the ability to accommodate passengers with a disability.
Rule Violated?	Yes

In this instance Aeromar violated section 382.41 when it failed to provide accurate information to Mr. Hawn regarding its service animal policy. If we decide to seek enforcement action against the airline with respect to this issue, this complaint will be among those considered, which may lead to the issuance of a cease and desist order and to the assessment of civil penalties.

Trusting Aeromar to do the right thing was like asking the same of one's angry ex! Hence, after the decision was rendered, I booked a ticket on the same itinerary. I wanted to be sure Aeromar would no longer discriminate against the disabled opting to utilize service dogs. Unfortunately, my Peggy had passed away and was unable to share the David versus Goliath story. Savior and I returned to the Aeromar ticket counter where we'd been rejected before. This time we were treated cordially. The ticket agent was the same one who had previously denied our boarding. She explained she had only been doing her job as directed. I told her I understood completely, as I had been there when she called the home office that day at my request.

My Booster's unconditional love was the impetus for my emergence from my selfexiling cocoon. I think back to my mother's tutelage of how a caterpillar becomes a butterfly. Booster transformed my mother's life lesson into life-enabling reality. As a Booster and BUCS graduate, I was able to stand up for myself and for those not capable of doing so. One of Bonnie's greatest wishes was that her students would go forth and change the world, utilizing the canine–human bond to do so. I'd kept my promise to Booster, made years ago, to share him with the world. It suddenly dawned on me that fulfilling that promise simultaneously fulfilled Bonnie's wish. I realized that I had a life-sustaining passion to travel internationally to promote the canine–human bond, coupled with the education to do so. While traveling, I always remembered to pack my bags with gratitude as Booster had taught me.

One day, I awoke and drank my usual one cup of coffee. Being the wonderful laxative that it is, I subsequently used the "facilities." I happened to witness what appeared to be blood in the bowl and consequently made an appointment to see a proctologist. It turned out to be a simple hemorrhoid that I'd somehow offended, but the doctor ordered a PSA test for prostate cancer to be on the safe side. I'd had one years before and had a biopsy taken. It all turned out OK. This time my PSA was a 7, resulting in a 25% chance of having prostate cancer. I had to undergo another biopsy. After the procedure, I went home in pain and crashed early, with Boosted and Busted at the foot of my bed.

MY BOOSTER!

The following morning, I awoke and went downstairs. Boosted and Busted usually rush to the front door to go outside and bless the yard with yellow rain. Busted ran outside as usual, but Boosted remained inside, rubbing against my leg. I looked down, and he had a small book in his mouth! I had a lot of books in a waist-high bedroom bookcase. Boosted had *coincidentally* grabbed a Bible! In awe, I slowly slunk to the floor and hugged him. Then I hugged him some more . . . then hugged him again! I prayed I'd be OK so I could continue caring for my canine family.

It took over a week to get the pathology report, but it turned out I was OK. Years later, I was at a communal breakfast table at my hotel in Bangkok, Thailand, when I overheard a man telling someone that he'd had a radical prostate removal years before. I interjected and asked him how he'd discovered his cancer. He said he'd had a routine PSA test. I asked him if he remembered his score, and he said, "Yes, it was 7!" Another **coincidence!** I almost fainted. Oh, how I wished I'd had Boosted or Busted by my side to hold on to.

CHAPTER 19
LOVE THY NEIGHBOR: MEXICO

As the new year of 2015 unremarkably unfolded, I relished playing with my canine kids more than ever. I was enjoying life on life's terms. It was as though I had landed on the moon. "One small step for me; one giant leap for my life!" One day, I read an article promoting a Humane Society of the United States conference to be held in nearby New Orleans. I emailed my friend Les, a past HSUS president, and he arranged for me to attend the conference in March.

When the conference date arrived, I took Booster and was immediately surrounded by fellow animal lovers. To the delight of all, he carried his stuffed Mickey Mouse in his mouth and approached passerby after passerby. He was a master at public relations, having perfected the art form. I thought back to his trip to the nursing home in Truth or Consequences, New Mexico, when he never missed greeting a single resident.

Booster suddenly pulled me to an exceedingly attractive lady whose English was slightly better than my Spanish, which was nonexistent! We relied on a cell phone translation app to communicate. She genteelly introduced herself as Doctora Claudia Edwards, DVM. She explained she worked for the Humane Society International (HSI) in Mexico. She was also the Director of the Veterinary School of Mexico at the Universidad Nacional Autonoma de Mexico (UNAM), located in Mexico City. I shared my Booster's story, and we became instant friends. We were two peas in a pod, sharing the vine for the love of animals. Our friendship remains to this day, a bond of the finest glue.

Within weeks of our "Booster-coordinated meeting," I proposed bringing Booster to Mexico City to explain the value of service dogs in society. The service dog concept was relatively new to most of Latin

America. Dr. Edwards was so enthusiastic that I excitedly hugged Booster when I read her response to my emailed suggestion. Within weeks, Dr. Edwards arranged for Booster and me to lecture at the University of Mexico Veterinary School under the auspices of the Humane Society International (HSI). She had beautiful promotional posters prominently displayed across the UNAM campus announcing my presentation entitled, "Changing the World Through Canine-Human Bonding."

This was a unique opportunity to share Booster and discuss canine-related topics with veterinary students, professors, and the dog-loving public. It was a canine trifecta of sorts. I envisioned sharing my passion in Mexico, just like I'd been doing for years elsewhere in the world. If we were well received at the lecture, it would bode well for the potential to help the Mexican disabled community get an assistance dog access law passed.

Though I'd found acceptance in the Bahamas and Cuba years before, I was still nervous about public speaking in yet another foreign country. I relied once again upon Booster to help *boost* my confidence as only he knew how. I'd *never* faced rejection, ridicule, or scorn with my Booster beside me. In fact, I'd always found acceptance and seemed able to do no wrong. The strength and self-esteem I derived from our partnership was simply unfathomable. My life's transformation from suicidal to embracing a passion to share Booster and better the lives of others could only be explained as a miracle.

I immediately got to work chronicling my life's story, resolutely deciding to construct a freeway to my soul; the only toll to be paid was my own. It was as if I went to the gambling table of life and doubled down with every ounce of my being. I wrote day and night, clutching Booster so often I thought his hair would fall out! I had to get it *right*. There would be no second chance. If I screwed it up, if I came across as insincere, I would never em*bark* upon such an emotional expedition again.

When I'd just about completed scribing my thoughts to paper, panic set in. Crazy as it sounds, it suddenly dawned on me that I was going to a country where my words could not be understood, even if I did my best to convey their heartfelt meaning. I immediately called Dr. Edwards and explained my dilemma. She calmly suggested that I try to relax and that her boss, Anton, was bilingual and would surely help. I wondered if this lady was an angel posing as a human. I caught myself rocking back and forth. With the strength of Job, I got up, walked to a window, opened it, and inhaled deeply repeatedly. Booster got up, walked to the window, and lay upon my feet.

Days passed quickly and before long, it was time to meet our new friend Claudia in Mexico City. My friend Chris once again opted to be our chauffeur and drove us to the New Orleans airport. I presented my passport and Booster's paperwork to the airline counter person. Soon, we were seated in the bulkhead of the plane headed to Mexico City. It was *one small step for man, one giant leap for my Booster!* Upon our arrival, we waited to be last off, as usual. The flight attendant started complimenting Booster. Flight attendants often extolled that Booster was better behaved than many children. Before deplaning, Booster insisted on taking a pic with the flight attendant, who willingly obliged.

We walked into the Mexico City airport with paperwork in hand, ready to present to the Mexican immigration officials. I took Booster to the official animal inspection department. The kind lady stamped his paperwork. I then passed through human immigration. I'd arranged to stay at a pet-friendly hotel. Getting a taxi was easy and upon our arrival at the hotel, we were greeted by the gracious manager. Once we were settled in, I fed and walked Booster. Around the corner from the hotel was a wonderful boulevard with lots of "pre-utilized" plants with canine smells that Booster savored. His olfactory system (smell processing) percolated vigorously. He was so happy. It was such a delight to watch.

After grabbing some grub and a margarita, we made our way back to the room. I called Dr. Edwards, who excitedly answered the call. "Señor Davis, I welcome you and Booster to Mexico . . . bienvenido (welcome). How was your flight?" I explained everything was great. My Booster and I were so happy to be there. Dr. Edwards then explained that in addition to my lecturing at UNAM, she'd arranged a plethora of interviews. I was simply ecstatic. I hugged Booster, sat on the floor, and resolutely petted his stomach for what seemed like an eternity.

The following day, Dr. Edwards introduced me to Anton, who graciously offered to translate my presentation. He also put it onto a

MY BOOSTER!

memory stick, which he later gave to the UNAM projectionist. Dr. Edwards then explained that she'd arranged for us to visit organizations dedicated to helping children who had various disabilities.

The following morning, she greeted Booster and me with a huge smile and an all-encompassing hug. We then jumped into her car and drove to meet representatives of two organizations. The first organization, Fundación un Angel te Cuida, was founded to support children suffering from chronic and degenerative illnesses. The second organization, Fundación Casa Alianza Mexico, provided care for children ages twelve to eighteen who were victims of violence, abuse, sexual exploitation, or human trafficking.

Upon our arrival at the first location, several smiling individuals met us and beckoned us inside. Booster grabbed his stuffed Clifford dog and walked right in as though he owned the place; in fact, within minutes, he did! All the children and adults were looking at the one-eyed Labrador walk around and greet the youngsters of all ages. I instantly felt overwhelmed, but I owed it to the children to maintain my composure.

Booster demonstrated opening a refrigerator door. Then I asked a young man to please take off his shoes. I then told Booster, "Shoes please," and he ran across the room and brought me one of the boy's shoes. Next, I told Booster, "Other shoe please," and he ran and fetched the other shoe without a moment's hesitation. The youngsters went crazy as they watched Booster do what he did best . . . reach into the depths of the human soul. The kids were bonding with Booster.

I then decided to liven things up a little. I'd learned at Camp Gone to the Dogs years before how to train a dog to roll over and play dead after saying *BANG* while pointing your finger like a gun. You start the dog positioned on his back and then work backward. I looked Booster and asked excitedly, "Ready?

Ready?" That always synchronized his energy level with mine. I then pointed my *gun* and said, "*BANG!*" Booster performed better than John Wayne ever did! The kids went wild, and I took my audience hostage. The kids and their parents were no longer concentrating on their life's challenges, even if for the moment.

I noticed a young blind boy in the back of the room. His mother was by his side, explaining to him what Booster was doing. I looked at Booster and said, "Sit please." I always followed his commands with the word *please,* as though I were speaking to a human. Then I asked the boy's mother if her son would like to pet Booster. She repeated my request to her young son, who seemed very hesitant. With the encouragement of his 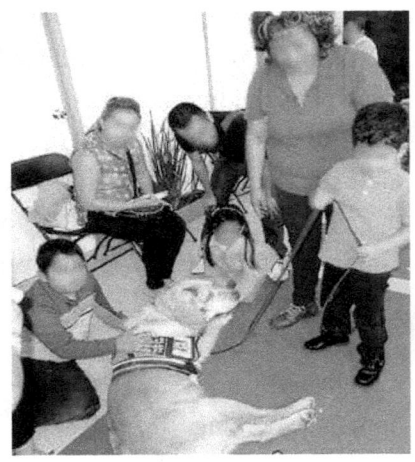 mother and peers in the room, he cautiously walked forward. My softly spoken words of encouragement in English were calmly translated into Spanish.

As the boy approached, his hand rose into the air of darkness, bravely searching to pet my Booster. After several failed attempts, Booster raised his head to meet the boy's hand. The boy quickly jerked his hand back. Booster remained calm, and the boy's hand returned less reluctantly the second time. This process was repeated several times until the two souls connected; unity and trust prevailed.

Suddenly, I saw another young man eagerly asking *his* mom if he could also pet Booster. Soon, the boy was seated on the floor, giving Booster a bear hug. He squeezed so hard that I thought Booster would pop like a piñata. His mother then leaned over and whispered into my ear, "Señor, my son just lost the eyesight in his right eye due to cancer, just like your dog. He's bonding with your dog." They saw eye to eye.

I almost lost it as I was not prepared in any way, shape, or form to handle the emotion of the moment. I sat on the floor with the brave boy, and we both held Booster. Little did anyone know I, too, needed comfort and reassurance. I truly believed Booster had no limit when it came to elevating the emotions of countless individuals at the same time. Further, he relished the opportunity to do so. He was especially fond of children and had an uncanny ability to relate to them.

MY BOOSTER!

At the conclusion of the presentation, I told the children Booster was a professionally trained dog. I explained that most dogs are very loving, but some are not. Some have been taught to fight and can bite. I told them to please be careful around dogs they didn't know. After the presentation was over, my hosts kindly offered me something to drink and pointed to snacks on a table. I'd been so busy and talked so much that I never noticed the table. I gratefully downed some punch and grabbed a potato chip.

As I drew the potato chip to my mouth, I froze. I couldn't move, couldn't process the moment. I had started to rock a little when an empathetic hand touched me on the shoulder. Tears flowed. I held up the potato chip with a shaking hand for all in the room to witness. It was in the shape of a heart! **Coincidence?** There ain't no way! My Higher Power put in as much overtime as I did. Soon, the adults in the room cuddled by my side, just as the children had done with Booster moments before. Love begets love, especially unconditional canine love. After we all exchanged hugs, we left the room, perhaps a little changed for life. The brave young souls that day taught us courage, and Booster taught a young man to trust. We all loved. Love exemplified by a potato chip provided by a power greater than ourselves.

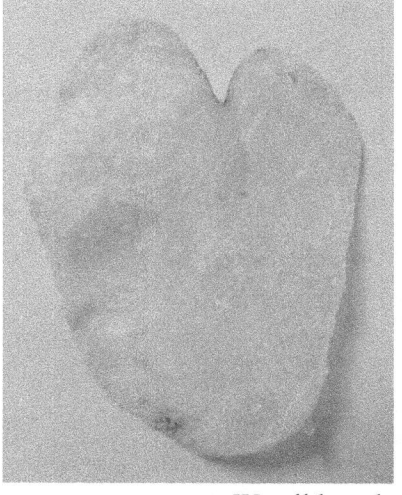

A couple of days later, two newspaper stories appeared chronicling our visit. "Therapy Dogs should be allowed everywhere: activist," one story read. The other story read, "Davis Hawn with his dog Booster urges not to close the doors to service animals." I was grateful for the coverage and interest expressed. It was such a wonderful tribute to Booster, who seemed to be able to charm reporters with his uniqueness. I wished he'd been able to teach *me* to be so charming. For Booster, it came naturally. *For me, it's likely to never manifest itself*, I sullenly thought. Truthfully, I think I was jealous.

The following day, we visited la Fundación Mosaico Down, a facility for autistic children. While waiting for admission, I reflected on how I'd studied autism at BUCS. I'd learned that some autistic children perimeter-check an environment, looking to escape. Some would escape their home and end up in a neighbor's home or yard. Many service dogs are trained to alert the family when the child leaves a certain area. Some are trained to softly herd the child away from an exit or grab them in the buttocks, preventing them from leaving.

A polite, "Hola, Señor Davis," suddenly interrupted my thoughts. Booster, Dr. Edwards, and I walked with the facility's director into a huge room filled with autistic children. Some of the children were quietly seated, yet others were running around aimlessly. When Booster walked in with his stuffed toy, it was as though a UFO had landed. In retrospect, my Booster *was* a UFO to these children who'd never had a 100-pound dog visit them. None of the children came running to greet the alien being. When Booster wagged his tail, they ran away. Amazingly, Booster didn't synchronize his energy level with theirs, run to play with them, or join in. I watched as he sat, lay down, and remained stoic. It was a waiting game of wait-and-see.

After a while, the children ventured a little closer to the calm dog. Eventually, most of the children were seated on the floor around Booster, who basked in the well-deserved affection. The dog who'd proactively greeted every nursing home patient in Ajo, Arizona, did the opposite this day. How did he know to engage one group and yet refrain from approaching another group, irrespective of the energy level in the room? I marveled at Booster's uncanny abilities. I still hadn't learned all the intricacies that comprised my Booster. Whereas I was hampered by my inability to communicate due to a language barrier, Booster found no such impediment.

MY BOOSTER!

A few days later, a story appeared in a local newspaper. It alluded to our visiting the children that I referred to as "special" … because they were indeed special. As I was reading the article, I was amazed at how the reporter absolutely "got it." I think it takes an extraordinary person to convey sensitivity in such a special manner.

Dr. Edwards and I later discussed the events that had transpired over the past few days. We were both so proud that canines were an integral part of the human world. She exuded confidence that Mexican society was holding canines in higher esteem. I told her I had come to lecture to help educate Mexican society as to the true canine potential. She instantly said, "Yes, I know. And you will have the opportunity to do so on Mexican television tomorrow, Davis."

My head bent at a 45-degree angle like a bewildered puppy. She smiled, as she knew I'd be so happy, and I certainly was. This lady was indeed amazing! She worked for UNAM and HSUS and yet still had time to arrange amazing things and accompany me. I was dumbfounded, simply dumbfounded. We went out to dinner, after which Dr. Edwards drove me back to my hotel. Booster was on the back seat, snoozing and snoring.

The next afternoon, I'd secured permission from the hotel manager to film Booster's interview in the hotel's front lobby. I expressed my gratitude, to which he replied, "*De nada*" (you're welcome). Within hours, a very professionallooking television crew arrived. I soon found myself sitting under a microphone dangling from above and began by explaining my life story and how Booster saved and changed my life. I wasn't sure whether the crew understood my words, but they were amazed when Booster started performing!

I asked Booster to open a drawer and bring an item, find my shoes, remove my socks, etc. The cameraman couldn't believe that a dog could open a car door and get a medical kit, so outside we went. I hired a taxi to sit empty in the driveway. To the amazement of all, my one-eyed Booster ran to the taxi on cue, opened the door, grabbed a shaving kit/medical bag, and brought it to me. We were then asked to walk down the city boulevard as they filmed us. The conclusion of the interview was an array of smiles and pats on the head for my Booster!

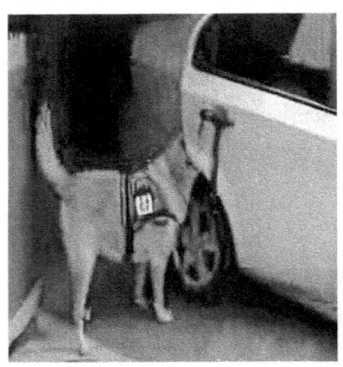

The next day, the story aired. It was quite a lengthy piece set to music. If I'd have paid for such a production, it would have cost thousands of dollars. It was such an honor and tribute to Booster, who'd once again *boosted* the awareness of how canines can help their human partners. It was another country, another language, yet Booster never failed to convey his message. I was quite humbled that the television station found merit in our journey and spent their valuable resources to share it with viewers. It bode well for the possibility of national acceptance of the service dog concept. They sure seemed to "get it" in Mexico City!

That night, I searched online for a karaoke bar and located one near our hotel.

I walked into the bar with Booster and quickly grabbed a table. Hell, yeah, I was a bit nervous because I walked in with a 100-pound dog, who drew a lot of attention. Within minutes, the server beckoned me. "Cerveza, señor?" (Beer, sir?), while two attractive Mexican ladies asked to pet Booster. They were exceedingly friendly, as were the other patrons. We had a great time that night, even though Booster was the only one who got a belly rub!

The following day, I practiced delivering my lecture. I didn't know what to expect as I'd never lectured before a university audience. The audience was indeed special as it was composed of veterinary students, professionals, and welleducated individuals who had all expressed an interest in animal welfare. I had to be at my best, focused and composed. That was a feat I could never have accomplished years before. It took years of learning under Booster's tutelage to acquire that ability.

I didn't sleep well that night, even though Booster was beside me with his head on my chest. Suddenly, the phone rang. It was the fateful wake-up call, beckoning me to start my day. I got dressed, fed Booster, then we

MY BOOSTER!

took the elevator down to the lobby so I could grab a bite to eat. When I finished, we approached the elevator to go back up to the room. I dropped Booster's leash. Before I had a chance to pick it up, the elevator door opened, and I instructed Booster to *go in.* As he entered the elevator, the door closed, and half his leash was trapped in the door. *No big deal,* I thought. *I'll pick it up when the elevator door opens.*

Suddenly, as the elevator ascended, the leash was being pulled toward the door with Booster being pulled by the neck. It happened so suddenly. **Coincidentally**, the leather leash I'd used was quite old and dry. When Booster's head was at the door, the leash snapped. Had it not broken, Booster's neck would have been deeply cut, at best, or more likely broken. My heart stopped. When the door opened, I struggled to regain my composure as best I could and stumbled out of the elevator. We later walked to the front desk and explained what had happened. The next morning, the man behind the counter called me to the desk and handed me the half of a leash found in the elevator shaft, under the elevator. My body started shaking. I struggled to drink some orange juice and couldn't eat, even though I knew we had a long day ahead of us. I was tempted to find some vodka to make a screwdriver cocktail, but those days were long behind me. All I needed was some down time with Booster when my nerves frayed, and my body betrayed me. Within a few minutes, Dr. Edwards walked in, smiling brightly as the morning sun. She had a pleasant persona that instantly put one at ease. With Booster and Dr. Edwards by my side, I knew things would be OK.

When we arrived at the UNAM, I saw myriad "Booster" posters adorning the walls. When I entered the auditorium, I looked out at an audience who'd taken time out of their lives to come to hear what we had to say and demonstrate. It was heartwarming and gave me a boost of confidence. Before long, Dr. Edwards was beckoning me onto the stage. I walked up and thanked Dr. Edwards, looked down at Booster, and said, "Y gracias Booster tambien" (And thank you, Booster, too) very succinctly. Then I began my seventy-eight slide PowerPoint lecture. As I spoke imperfect Spanish, which I jokingly referred to as *Spanglish*, my words were written in Spanish on the slides to be sure the audience understood what I was saying.

I shared intimate details about my life, then explained that dogs help humans in many ways, both physically and psychologically. I referred to it as non-addictive, holistic, canine medicine and further explained that more US soldiers die from suicide than battle. When I presented a slide demonstrating how canines help soldiers with damaged limbs or psyches, the slide's photos spoke for themselves. My second to last slide showed pictures of Booster's travels, domestically and internationally. It was quite a testimony to the work ethic of a dog that traveled the world trying to make it a better place in which to live. I looked at my Booster and softly said, "See, I told you I'd share you with the world!"

MY BOOSTER!

I then stated, "If Booster could speak, he would thank:

"All the human beings who allowed us to share the canine–human bond . . . "All the universities and organizations that teach the importance of dogs in the human world . . .

"All the human beings who dedicated their lives to promoting canine health that saved his life . . .

"All the corporations who have compassion for animals . . .

"All the children and adults from around the world who loved him, as he unconditionally loved them."

My last slide gave thanks for humans who study so hard to become veterinarians. After all, I was at the finest veterinary school in Mexico and congratulations were due!

For the most part, my lecture kept the audience's attention for about an hour. Booster, however, was sound asleep at my feet. I woke him up, and he demonstrated his skills, to the amazement of all. Upon our conclusion, attendees from all walks of life approached us. It was heartwarming to witness the genuine interest they expressed. One particularly aristocratic-looking lady approached me, and before long, we were engrossed in canine-related conversation. Enriqueta (Queta) was well versed in dog training and human training as well. She was a retired UNAM professor of psychology.

I momentarily flashed back to that day in the BUCS classroom when we listened to the child psychologist and were instructed to use his methodology while working with dogs later in the day. I instantly knew this lady would become a good friend. Before parting, she introduced me to her husband, Antonio, a distinguished-looking gentleman, and attorney. We exchanged contact information and made a mutual promise to get together for a meal sometime in the days to come.

The next day, Dr. Edwards introduced me to the director of UNAM K9 Search and Rescue (SAR) dog teams. He was gracious enough to give me a tour of his training facility located on the university grounds. I met a few of his trainers and learned that they were all volunteers. The director was the only person paid to train and work with SAR dogs. Mexico had a history of devastating earthquakes in the past and was likely to experience more. The UNAM SAR dog teams practiced relentlessly, never knowing if or when they would be needed. The team's devotion to their dogs and SAR work was uncanny.

Before leaving the facility, I asked the director if his team might be interested in learning to train service dogs for the disabled. He seemed interested, and had all the requisites, including a devoted team and a wonderful facility. My mind was awash with the possibility of forming collaboration between BUCS and UNAM. I thought it might be fruitful for one of the team members to attend the BUCS six-week summer training seminar.

After what seemed like an eternity, it was almost time to return home to the US. I decided to sponsor a dinner at a local restaurant and invited Dr. Edwards and her other half Paco, the SAR dog director, Enriqueta and her husband Antonio, and members of the press who had written such wonderful stories about my Booster. I picked an upscale seafood restaurant, and because I wanted to conclude my adventure with yet another adventure, I also invited Booster to come along. Dogs aren't allowed in finer restaurants in most countries. Hell, it's often ruff-ruff to get them as service dogs into restaurants in the US! It was going to be interesting.

I arrived at the restaurant half an hour early. I walked into the restaurant with Booster in full regalia by my side. His bright orange vest featured a patch, "Perro de Servicio" (service dog). The greeter at the door was stunned and said, "Uno momento por favor" (one minute, please).

I thought, *That was a lot better than "get the hell out of here with that dog, señor!"*

Within minutes, the manager greeted me and explained that they didn't allow dogs inside.

I explained I was disabled, and that Booster was a professionally trained dog with a $50,000 education. I then explained that he would behave better than I, especially if I drank a few of the house special margaritas!

The manager laughed and said, "Follow me, señor." Follow him we did, and we were seated at a nice corner table on the veranda.

When my invited company showed up, I was asked to explain how I got Booster inside. I explained it was a combo platter of trust and Mexican hospitality; the manager trusted me and was very hospitable. I also explained that at BUCS, we were trained to always enter a public venue as though we owned the place, exhibiting confident body language. If you look insecure, you will more likely be questioned. I found this to be the case in my travels everywhere I went with Booster. The server offered to bring Booster some water, and I joked, "no gracias el preferiria una cerveza" (no, thank you, he would prefer a beer!) We all laughed. For the record, we never feed or water a service dog in a restaurant.

The server shared the story with the other employees, who came by to greet us. It was a great opportunity to explain that they were fortunate to have two eyes, two legs, etc. I further reminded them that not everyone was that blessed. I explained the service dog concept and then looked around. There were few other patrons, so I nonchalantly stood up and walked across the room and kicked my shoes off and walked back to the table and sat down. The staff must have thought the cervezas had won the battle! I looked down at Booster and nonchalantly said, "Shoes please." Without a moment's hesitation, Booster calmly rose, walked over, grabbed a shoe, and brought it to me. I then said, "Other shoe please." Within seconds, my other shoe was in my hand, albeit a bit spit polished. I knew at that moment they would never forget me at that restaurant. I also knew if I ever returned to Mexico City in the future, this would be my restaurant of choice, though I'd want to enter other restaurants as well to spread the service dog concept and polish my entrance skills at the same time!

I was quite impressed with Mexico, at least Mexico City. It had its problems like any other major city, but it was the home of the prestigious UNAM. I often wondered how the UNAM SAR team volunteers kept motivated. It'd been roughly thirty years since the famous 1985 8.0 magnitude earthquake that killed and injured tens of thousands of Mexican citizens. Due to the catastrophic event, the government hired *an* individual to establish a SAR dog foundation. Over the years, the Mexican SAR dog foundation grew under the director's leadership. A plot of ground on UNAM's campus was dedicated, and a building was erected on the site. For the next thirty years, the dedicated volunteer trainers lived at home with their dogs and trained them at the facility. They never got a call for help, yet never became demoralized. Kudos!

When I returned home, I learned that the Mexico City mayor, Dr. Mancera, had signed a proposed amendment to an existing law that mandated that dogs entering public venues must be muzzled. That negated much of the value of a service dog trained to bring objects to a disabled person in a public venue. I don't think the amendment ever took hold, but it was certainly a step in a *pawsitive* direction! I'd previously arranged for the mayor's assistant to bring a copy of a letter to the mayor asking that he consider proposing an assistance dog access law. While I doubt the letter, or my appearances, had anything to do with the mayor's proposal, the timing was kind of cool!

Upon hearing the news, I immediately composed a thank-you letter to Dr. Mancera. I'd read that he was European-educated and, thus, I guessed, very forward-thinking. I would have loved to have met the man, but never had the opportunity to do so. Later in the trip, I attended an outdoor disability-related event and saw him on stage, so I walked up and handed my thank-you letter to his assistant.

MY BOOSTER!

Months after I returned home, I contacted the SAR dog director and Enriqueta. I had an idea I thought would be beneficial for Mexico, its citizens, and the canine population as well. I envisioned the UNAM SAR dog team members training service dogs. The team members would be motivated by working with the disabled community. They already had a building and land on the UNAM campus, with a potentially unlimited number of college student volunteers. The scenario seemed perfect indeed. I gave a UNAM SAR dog team member a scholarship to attend the BUCS summer service dog training seminar. The SAR dog director suggested a particular team member who was also a private dog trainer. He then arranged for us to meet.

I decided to fly back to Mexico City roughly six months later to meet the SAR team member and director and discuss my idea with Dr. Edwards, Enriqueta, her husband, and others. I also had an ulterior motive. The US DOT had issued the two sanctions against Aeromar Airlines, and I wanted to see if the airline had learned its lesson. I booked a reservation using the same itinerary as before, and once again planned to visit my friend Peggy in McAllen, Texas. I notified the Aeromar reservation agent that I'd be flying with my service dog and had all the papers arranged to do so. I decided to take Savior along so it would be the exact same scenario . . . the same "Large Labrador service dog."

When I arrived at the McAllen airport and approached the ticket counter, my reception was markedly different this time. The lady behind the counter was the same one who'd denied my boarding the plane with Savior the year before. She recognized me instantly and apologized for the previous indiscretion. I told her it wasn't her fault and explained that the airline had been sanctioned for violating the law. Within fifteen minutes, we boarded the plane and were treated like royalty.

I'd arranged for everyone to meet at my previously conquered restaurant. Dr. Edwards had a member of the press join us. I spent a lot of time at the dinner table discussing the value of service dogs in society. Though SAR dogs and guide dogs were known in Mexican society, the service dog concept was relatively new. I discussed the possibility of giving the SAR dog team member a personally funded scholarship to attend the BUCS summer training seminar. I thought it was an opportunity of a lifetime for a Mexican dog trainer to attend BUCS and work beside Dr. Bergin. The team member said he was interested. I decided to let the offer sink in and then wait to see if he followed up.

Dr. Edwards then mentioned there was an organization run by a couple of Mexican women who trained service dogs. She further elaborated that she would get more information so I could arrange to visit them if I wanted to do so. She also told me that there was a guide dog school in Mexico City. I knew I would have to visit both venues to get a feel for the way working dogs were trained in Mexico. Before the week was out, I did indeed visit the service dog group run privately by two women. It was more like an animal rescue facility with many rescued or abused animals, some of which were dogs with an unknown past being trained. It was interesting. The women were wonderful, yet it underscored the need for a professional training facility. That is all I can say. To their credit, the women did their best training the stray dogs using a methodology introduced by a Spanish organization called Bocalan Madrid.

After the dinner, Savior made his debut at the karaoke bar that Booster and I had frequented the year before. We walked in, sat down, and history repeated itself. I remember thinking that it was often easier to get a service dog into a public venue in Mexico City, where no access laws existed, than it was to enter similar venues in the US, even though there were access laws on the books. Those laws existed, in great part, because Dr. Bergin fought before Congress to get them passed into legislation. When it was my turn to sing, I walked up onto the stage and explained that my dog Savior "es mi perro de servicio y me ayuda a vivir una vida mejor" (Savior is my service dog and he helps me live a better life). I then attempted to sing a lovely Spanish song entitled "Tu Primers Vez" (Your First Time), written by famous Mexican singer José José, who wrote songs mostly about love and loneliness. **Coincidentally**, he often spoke of his struggles with relationships and alcoholism. It was a beautiful song about a young man about to make love to his girlfriend, who was a virgin; hence, it was *her first time*. The following day, I awoke with renewed vigor. I'd truly enjoyed the dinner the night before as well as the company of the Mexicans in the bar who accepted me as the foreigner and, more importantly, my Savior. While I was sad that I was leaving, I missed my

MY BOOSTER!

pack back home. I had a lot to think about and wondered, *Can I recreate what I'd done in the Bahamas in Mexico?* I wanted to help the Mexican people get an access law for the disabled. The potential was certainly there. I just had to summon the energy and conviction to make it happen. On the plane ride home, I wondered if the SAR dog director would really help get a Mexican service dog training program started. I envisioned the Booster Center having an alliance with BUCS. It was my newly emerging dream.

Many stories appeared in Mexican newspapers. The reporters had indeed done their job, and I appreciated their thoughtfulness and thoroughness. I was so proud, not of me, but rather for my Booster and, in turn, his son, Savior. It was abundantly clear to me that canines do, in fact, have a deeply entrenched work ethic. They enjoy working.

It doesn't take much effort to reap great results from minimal input. A pat on the head and eye to eye contact extolling praise is all it takes. Of course, a treat or two helps augment the dedication!

Once home, I continued to stay in touch with my ever-expanding group of dog-loving Mexican friends. Later, I got an email from Enriqueta, notifying me of an upcoming assistance dog conference to be held in  Mexico City. I wrote to the conference committee and asked if I could share the story of Booster and invite world-famous Dr. Bergin to lecture. I promptly received an invitation for the two of us to attend. Though the conference had already been scheduled, the organizers went back and took fifteen minutes away from other presenters so that they could accommodate us in their schedule.

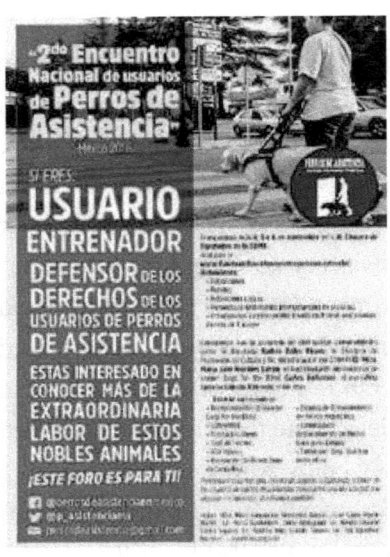

I was stoked, to say the least! I looked at Boosted and Busted and said, "Now it's up to you to continue your father's legacy." My eyes got misty. I missed my Booster so much. It'd been two tumultuous years since he passed away. I don't know that I could have made it without "Boo and Bus" by my side. Soon, it would be their chance to shine. I knew they could do it, as they were cut from the same cloth.

I called Bonnie, and she graciously accepted the invitation to lecture at the conference. I also called my good friend Sharon, who'd accompanied me to the Bahamas, and she was interested in attending. We wanted to surprise Bonnie. It'd been years since the two had seen each other. I knew Bonnie would be delighted to catch up on old times. I also invited my older brother and was surprised when he expressed an interest in going. Sitting on the couch with Boosted on one side and Busted on the other, I squeezed and hugged them, looked into their eyes, and smiled. Their mouths were open and their tongues hanging out, as if they, too, were smiling. Alas, anthropomorphism or not, I knew damn well they were smiling!

Enriqueta followed up a few days later and sent me a copy of the poster announcing, "The Second National Meeting of Assistance Dog Users." I was impressed and excited when I read that attendees from many other countries would be there. It was going to be so cool for BUCS to have a presence in Mexico. I was proud that Bonnie was willing to attend, especially since she was no fan of flying! I immediately began working on a new PowerPoint lecture. This time I'd be lecturing to professionals in the assistance dog field. I wanted to impart what I'd learned in the BUCS classroom, coupled with knowledge gained through real-world experiences. I also wanted my brother to know a little more about my personal life and what I'd been doing with the education he'd deemed a "waste of money."

MY BOOSTER!

As time went by, I spoke more with the SAR dog director and the team member about starting a service dog training facility at UNAM utilizing their training facility. The director was skeptical about having student volunteers, whereas I valued volunteerism highly. Anyone might work to get a check but wanting to work for free shows dedication. I think the director had been wronged by a volunteer in the past, but that shouldn't have preempted volunteerism in the future. Training service dogs is exhausting, physically and economically. The emphasis is on helping the disabled, not making a profit. Most assistance dog training facilities are nonprofits. Some trainers work for free and donate their time. Some trainers, many with college degrees, earn an average of $40,000 a year. Some guide dog trainers earn more than $100,000 annually. With that in mind, it still costs upwards of $50,000 to train a service dog and 100,000 to train a guide dog. Having a college composed of bright, aspiring students next door was a valuable resource indeed.

My conversations with the team member were often difficult but not because of a language barrier. He was keenly devoted to SAR work but expressed a *willingness* to learn to train dogs to help the disabled. It'd been a long time since the famous earthquake in Mexico City and the SAR dog team members still faithfully showed up day after day to work with their dogs in the most devoted manner. It was quite inspiring. I thought, *If I can tap into that same dedication to train service dogs, the team members will get instant gratification that'll inspire them, and others, to continue working with the dogs.* For me it was a no-brainer.

Time flew by, and before long I found myself seated adjacent to my brother in the bulkhead section of a plane headed to Mexico City. Boosted and Busted lay dormant at our feet, earning the admiration of the flight attendants. I remarked, "You can tell a fake service dog from a real one within seconds, can't you?"

"Absolutely," came the response.

Within an hour, we entered the airport in Mexico City. We were directed to the Office of Animal Health Inspection (OISA). Once again, Boosted and Busted wowed an audience, this time the animal inspectors!

An hour later, my brother and I checked into our rooms at the Hotel del Principado, a quaint, reasonably priced hotel I'd found upon a previous trip to the city. The manager was a dog lover, and the hotel staff was equally accepting. It had a nice little bar and restaurant and exuded charm. Later in the day, I met Sharon in the lobby and explained that Bonnie would be arriving soon. Sharon hadn't seen Bonnie since her graduation nearly a decade before. Sharon had put her degree into action by working in a Florida State prison, teaching inmates to train service dogs. I couldn't wait to surprise Bonnie, who had no clue that one of her graduates had also come to participate.

I had Sharon wait in the wings when Bonnie arrived. In good stead, I introduced my brother, Boosted, and Busted to Bonnie and then explained that I had a VIP I wanted her to meet. With that said, Sharon strolled in, and two radiant smiles collided in unfathomable exuberance. It was global warming at its finest as we all came together in the moment. We soon agreed to meet later for dinner in the hotel's little restaurant rather than go out and celebrate. We had a big day ahead of us, and we needed our sleep.

The following morning, we ate a quick breakfast. The hotel manager arranged for a taxi to pick us up and take us to the conference venue. When we arrived, Enriqueta was patiently waiting in front. After introductions, we all sauntered in together and took our seats. A projectionist came to meet us and collected our flash drives that would be used to project our presentations on the large screen. Bonnie presented first, addressing the history of the service dog and the evolution of the service dog concept since its inception. The translator was a sweet young lady from Venezuela whom I'd met at the last conference. She'd married a Mexican man and moved to Mexico to start a family. I hired her to translate for us; she did a great job!

When my turn came to speak, Boosted and I walked up to the podium. I was crying inside as I thought about Booster, who rightfully should have been alongside me. But I didn't let my thoughts overwhelm me as I resolutely petted Boosted, who proffered support by his mere presence. I spoke of my history and how Booster changed my life and the lives of others worldwide. Then, I explained service dogs are an extension of one's body and a means of independence for those with physical deficits. I further explained that it's imperative that the disabled, accompanied by all types of assistance dogs, be granted public access with their dogs. "Why

MY BOOSTER!

must a blind man sleep in the street because his eyes are, by proxy, the eyes of a guide dog?"

I talked about my travels to foreign countries with my service dog Booster and the need to enlighten other societies regarding assistance dogs. In addition, I shared that I'd been granted public access with my service dogs in Mexico City, even though no law guaranteed such. I expressed my heartfelt appreciation and hinted that I would strive to help the disabled community get an access law passed. Then, I demonstrated how Boosted performs tasks like opening the fridge and bringing water, taking off my socks, barking to summon help, and all the usual things. Boosted never missed a lick . . . so to speak. He exuded confidence, just like Booster always had. Once again, I teetered on an emotional teeter-totter, but pride and amazement saved me. I was so proud of Boosted and Busted . . . from whom I derived my emotional fortitude.

As I walked off the stage, I looked out into the audience. Bonnie was seated beside my brother, and both smiled as if to say job well done. At that moment, I was struck by gratitude that Bonnie had taken time out of her busy schedule to be so supportive. My brother, who'd once considered my educational pursuit a frivolous expenditure, was equally supportive. When Boosted and I got to our seat, Sharon leaned over and said, "Good job, Davis." I'd won the trifecta of support! I then turned to Boosted and Busted and hugged them tightly.

After a quick lunch, Enriqueta and I attended conference meetings together. I sat in a row with other presenters, and we shared ideas and concepts. I couldn't help but notice that many of the presenters who were accompanied by their assistance dogs had choke collars and pinch collars imprisoning their dogs. Elsewhere in the world, such control by pain is frowned upon.

A famous Mexican dog trainer universally extolled the merits of being dominant and forcing dogs into submission. That mentality is passé. His techniques purportedly included physical domination over dogs gained through pinches, kicks to the stomach, punches, electric shocks, prong collars, pinch collars, and other aversive actions. We no longer kick dogs into submission, alpha-roll them onto their backs to show them who's boss or stick torturous collar spikes into their necks. Frankly, I was appalled. I attended the conference to help the disabled and bring awareness to the value of dogs in society. I had no chance of changing the mindsets of dog trainers who subscribed to the old methodologies. Forcing a dog into submission creates fear and panic; it's detrimental to the dog. Instilling fear into a dog being trained for public access, utilized to help an individual with limited physical capabilities, is wrong. Parents (hopefully) don't slam their children to the ground or use choke chains to elicit proper behavior. I think the same holds true for pet parents and their dogs. It was hard to watch what I perceived to be unscrupulous behavior. Getting an individual to *unlearn* what they've been taught, often over decades of time, is damn near impossible. It reminded me of my older veterinarian who gave Booster the vaccination in the hip, giving rise to a lump, simply because he refused to adopt more modern, accepted practices of administering vaccinations below the neck on the dog's shoulder. I consciously chose my battle right then and there.

At BUCS, I'd read studies that showed dogs who were trained with shock collars would perform the task but rarely offered anything more because they risked being shocked. They might bring one shoe but not automatically bring the other one for fear of retribution. Most trainers today employ positive reinforcement, often in the form of food treats. I *treat* my canine kids to treats in the form of hugs and high-pitched emotional praise. I often supplement emotion with food treats, but emotional inspiration is my number one methodology of choice. As a child, my mother praised me, often in the accompaniment of others, when I built something or did something creative. I never forgot how motivated I felt as a direct result. I was spanked a few times, but never anything excessive. Even now, I'm still amazed by parents who extoll their methodology of beating the hell out of their children when they've done something perceived as wrong. Worse yet, I ask myself how the sickest of humans endorse electric shock, gay conversion therapy, to "cure" homosexuality. SHOCKING!

The following afternoon my entourage (Boosted, Busted, Sharon, and my brother) accompanied Enriqueta and me to UNAM to meet with a few department heads. Enriqueta had arranged the meeting far in advance. I wanted to discuss the opportunity for students, especially psychology and sociology students, to participate in training service dogs. I thought it would be a great opportunity for the students to learn canine motivation coupled with volunteerism. The students could train dogs on campus at the SAR dog facility. It would be an altruistic act benefiting the Mexican disabled community. I couldn't envision any downside to the proposition. The department heads and professors in attendance seemed keenly interested. At the end of the meeting, the room was well-lit with warm smiles.

That night, I'd arranged a dinner party at *my* Mexican restaurant. My brother and I were seated with Boosted and Busted at our feet. Dr. Edwards and her other half, Paco, were the first guests to arrive and brought a small dog. Interestingly, the restaurant staff interjected and said that they understood about my trained service dogs but dogs in general were not permitted in the restaurant. I was a little embarrassed that Dr. Edwards was challenged, but the staff was 100% correct in their assessment. They acquiesced in their decision and allowed Dr. Edward's dog to remain *this time*. I remember thinking that I wish more establishments in the US would challenge those with fake service dogs.

Before long, Enriqueta and her husband Antonio arrived and joined in the merriment that had already commenced. Within minutes, the SAR dog director and team member walked in. I shared what had occurred at UNAM earlier that day and mentioned that I would love to help start a training facility. I further stated that the university staff seemed interested and there was great potential. Then I mentioned I would like to help get an assistance dog public access law passed in Mexico because, without public access, the dogs and their human partners are handicapped. This mirrored my sentiments expressed in the Bahamas when I wrote a letter to the prime minister explaining that the lack of an access law for the disabled is a handicap.

I will never forget what happened next. The team member leaned forward and resolutely blurted out loud, "Nothing happens quickly in Mexico." The connotation was extremely negative, but perhaps reality in Mexico.

I hadn't lived in that country, so I didn't know. Instinctually and instantly, I retorted, "Well, if you *think* nothing can happen, then nothing *will* happen!" I then shared that I'd heard his exact thesis before in Cuba and yet things happened almost too quickly for me in that country. I then related my experience in the Bahamas helping to get an access law passed there.

The team member had a look upon his face as if to say, "You will see, you don't understand my country."

I thought, *He's absolutely right. Ignorance is bliss.* **I didn't understand what I couldn't accomplish.** I loved a good challenge. When I was a kid, my parents left town on a trip, so I stayed with one of their closest friends. I was diligently working on a go-kart at the time and needed an engine for it. I located a used engine and asked the lady if she would drive me to get it. I explained I had the money to buy it. She didn't want to be an accomplice in case my parents wouldn't approve of me spending money in such a manner. The following day, the lady came home and saw me washing the engine I'd bought earlier that day. She asked me how I got it, and I explained that I'd taken a city bus and lugged it across town. She said she'd told me to wait, and that it was a stinky thing I'd done. Thus, she nicknamed me Stinky, which stuck with me for years to come. I called it determination. I made it happen.

There were many occasions when I was hell-bent on doing something when I was told it couldn't be done. Telling me something was impossible motivated me all the more. Against all odds, I'd gotten into Cuba as an American, with a dog, and appeared on live television. I'd been instrumental in getting a disability/access law passed in the Bahamas. I'd returned to university at an advanced age, earned a master's degree, and utilized it beyond my wildest imagination. I'd also managed to clone Booster when the price tag was prohibitive. My onceconquered soul had considered speaking in public the bane of my existence. My Booster changed all that exponentially as time progressed. In my heart, I knew I was up to the *team member challenge!* I was willing to do whatever it took to perfect change in Mexico . . . and rapidly! That I so loved the Mexican people boded well for my potential success.

MY BOOSTER!

On the last day of the conference, I met all the conference attendees at the Plaza de la República Monument to the Revolution. There was a large public turnout as well. I was scheduled to give a live service dog demonstration in a public venue in the center of the city. I'd made many wonderful Mexican, dog-loving friends. Several of them showed up to help me arrange the public demonstration of service dog skills. One friend bought a small refrigerator, brought it in a truck and subsequently returned it for a credit immediately afterwards.

Another arranged for a taxi to be standing by with the understanding that a dog would be opening the door and jumping inside to locate a water bottle. Another friend brought a chair and table. Having such quality people coming together to promote assistance dogs was heartwarming.

Busted was my dog-of-the-day simply because Boosted had performed at the conference days before. When the time came for the demonstration, I turned to Busted and asked, "*Are you ready?*" It was a dumb question as Boosted and Busted were always ready to show off their talents, just like Booster had done the decade before. Whereas my dog training skills might be questionable, the clones' skills were not. I had 100% faith in them, just like I had in Booster.

I requested, "Busted, sit please," and he politely sat. I casually walked across the concrete and kicked my shoes off. Then I returned and sat in the chair and calmly requested, "Shoe please." Without hesitation, Busted ran and brought me my left shoe. I then asked him matter-of-factly, "Where's my other shoe?" I raised both palms to the sky, shoulders  hunched, in comedic fashion, and added, "Dondes?" (*where*). Again, the confident canine ran, fetched my right shoe, and handed it to me. I then calmly sat in a chair and said, "Sock please," and Busted grasped my sock in his mouth and tugged it off my foot. I then followed up with, "Other sock please," and Busted removed my other sock and gave it to me. His tail wagged, extolling his accomplishment. I started to tear up as I remembered when Booster had done the exact same thing in Cuba years before. My Mexican audience responded with smiles and instantly became even more attentive.

MY BOOSTER!

After praising Busted, I followed up with "Estoy sediento" (I'm thirsty). "Bring me some water please! *FRIDGE!!!*" Busted ran to the mini fridge, pulled the door open, and got the water bottle. Without hesitation, he ran and put it in my hand. I then asked the audience, which had swelled exponentially, to please wait one second as I needed a medicine bag from my car *over there*. I pointed to the taxi and told Busted, "I need my bag please . . . *TUG*." Like a knight in shining armor, he pranced to the taxi, opened the door, jumped in, found my medicine bag, and brought it to me.

At this point, the audience's energy level was equal to Busted's! Remember, dogs respond to energy levels and intensity of sounds. Busted was stoked and would have shown off all day, given the opportunity to do so. I issued one last request, "*HUG* please," and the persistently panting Busted jumped up and gave me the hug of a lifetime. I was like a father with his accomplished son. A synthesis of pride and love encapsulated in a canine–human hug.

We also met many disabled Mexicans who keenly watched our demonstration. It was such a warm and friendly experience. Many expressed their desire to have such trained dogs in their lives. I introduced everyone to Busted, and I'm sure I saw his head swelling more and more as the day progressed. I was silently thinking about how my life had progressed into such a blessing with Booster's help, along with that of my BUCS education and the magnanimous help of Korean professor Hwang. Without the professor's gift of cloning, this day and many others wouldn't have been possible. When the day came to a close, I was exhausted. I looked at Busted, and he looked at me, raring to go! How I longed for the energy level he possessed! We hailed a taxi, and off to the hotel we went. After a couple of drinks with my brother and Sharon, we returned to our room to retire for the night.

In the morning, we hastily ate breakfast and took a taxi to the airport I was getting to know so well. Mexico and its people were now ingrained into my soul, like the Bahamians, Thais, Cubans, and Koreans. Booster had changed the essence of my very being, and his high-tech offspring, Boosted and Busted, were doing the same. That night, I reflected upon that thought for hours. As exhausted as I was, the mainspring of my analytical mind was tightly wound. It took hours for me to unwind while my canine kids snored with the satisfaction of an accomplished day.

The following morning, I joined my brother and my canine kids for breakfast. Before long, we said goodbye to Bonnie and Sharon and off to the airport we went. The trip home was uneventful and Boosted, Busted, and I were given a royal greeting by the canine pack when we arrived home. I spent the following days sending out thank you emails. I also sent the SAR dog team member an offer to attend the BUCS service dog training seminar the following summer. That was the first of many email exchanges I had with the SAR dog team member and his supervisor.

As the months progressed, I received many emails and texts from Dr. Edwards and Enriqueta. They were both such divine, gifted educators. It was as though God put them on earth to teach and generate smiles and understanding. I considered myself so fortunate to have met them and incorporated them into my close-knit canine-loving clan. Enriqueta sent me many photographs and videos of me whenever I presented in various venues in Mexico. It was so heartwarming. My memory may fade but the photos and videos so caringly orchestrated will live on. In fact, I have used many in this very book. I wish I could include the videos because they are a montage of performances accompanied by wonderful music and subscripts. The good news is that they can be found on my author's webpage. You can watch Booster and the clone's evolution in videos, television clips, newspaper stories and more I encourage you to check them out! Please visit www.boostertheservicedog.com to learn more!

MY BOOSTER!

One morning, I awoke to yet another email from Enriqueta. She asked me if I would like to participate in the Mexican Canophila Federation meeting being held in Mexico City months down the line. I immediately answered, *por supuesto*! (of course). She subsequently arranged everything, and I received a formal invitation the following week. I relished the opportunity to help advance canine understanding in the country I was visiting so often. I was determined to help gain public access for assistance dogs. This was yet another opportunity to do so. We also had another presentation lined up at UNAM.

When the date for the conference drew near, I called my buddy Rocky and asked him if he'd like to go to Mexico. After securing permission from his wife, he agreed to go with me. I needed an extra pair of hands since I was determined to bring both Boosted and Busted. I'd also been in contact with a Mexican dog trainer and breeder who was enrolled in the BUCS associate degree program. Isaac was a decade younger than I, but equally devoted to the advancement of canines in society. He offered to help translate for me and coordinate things in Mexico.

I arranged for Rocky and Isaac to fly to meet me in nearby New Orleans. As a group, the humans and two service dogs boarded the flight to Mexico City. I befriended the cabin crew and introduced them to the "world-famous cloned service dogs." While in flight, as usual, I handed the flight attendant my dossier of canine accomplishments for them to read. It always helps to have friends in high places! Boosted and Busted behaved as always, earning compliments from the cabin crew and passengers seated nearby. It was heartwarming to have them both with me, behaving so professionally. I remembered back to the months I'd spent training them as pups in Korea, commencing when they were just weeks old.

When the plane landed, we arranged for transport to the hotel. I got into the back of the taxi with Boosted and Busted along with Rocky. Isaac sat in the front. I had Boosted, Busted, Rocky, and Isaac with me this time. The five of us were a winning poker hand if ever there was! We arrived at Hotel Principado, exuberantly jumped out of the taxi, and checked into our rooms. Shortly thereafter, we all took a walk down the wide boulevard adjacent to the hotel. We stopped at a corner cantina and celebrated our arrival. Boosted and Busted relished tacos as much as we did. We downed muchas margaritas (many margaritas). Since Boosted and Busted weren't old enough to drink, they quenched their thirst with bottled water. I wasn't about to give them tap water and have them get the Hershey squirts and not be able to attend the conference!

Enriqueta had arranged for us to tour the Mexican guide dog school, Escuela para Entrenamiento de Perros Guía para Ciegos IAP. I instantly recalled a BUCS field trip to visit the Guide Dogs for the Blind campus in San Rafael, California. One thing that left a lasting impression was the way different types of music were employed around the campus so the blind would know exactly where they were. They were training their last string of German Shepherds while I was there. Our guide explained people weren't going blind at an early age as much these days due to modern medicine. War veterans of yesteryear were often blinded in battle. Today's veterans are more likely to experience a traumatic brain injury (TBI). The blind population is older due to the advent of modern medicine and science. Often, a senior citizen can't handle the muscularity of the German Shepherd. Our guide explained the current canine of choice was the Labrador or Golden Retriever. That night was uneventful. We all went out to dinner and enjoyed the ambiance of Mexicans and tourists walking up and down the nearby boulevard. Many street vendors, young and old, were hawking their goods to the delight of passersby. I was happy that my friends were happy. I was also happy that Boosted and Busted were happy.

The next morning, we were off to visit the guide dog school. Boosted and Busted readily jumped into the taxi, ready to embark upon a new journey. When we arrived at the school we were met by the director and the head trainer. The director was a blind lady with a glorious smile with a personality to match. The trainer took Boosted and Busted to their *hotel rooms*. Instead of being center stage, they were confined to quarters, imprisoned in a foreign jail cell. I felt a little guilty, but the facility was exceptionally clean and hospitable.

We were escorted inside and beckoned to join others at the breakfast table. Once we were seated, our gracious hostess handed us blindfolds and asked us politely to put them on. Once donned, we, too, were blind. I was instantly helpless and very claustrophobic. We were then welcomed and told to chow

MY BOOSTER!

down. I was mesmerized, to say the least. *How in the hell can I eat a meal when I can't see the damn meal? Where is my fork, my plate, my glass?* I reached out to grab the glass of orange juice and knocked it over. Perhaps I can soak it up in a napkin and squeeze it into my mouth ... if I could find the napkin! This really sucks. I'm not prepared for this." My mind was on sensory overload. Instantly, I became entrenched in deep thought. Most people aren't prepared to be blind, yet it often happens.

For the record, that experience was like throwing someone who can't swim into a turbulent river. It was horrifying yet educational beyond compare. Rather than a look of reproach, I garnered an aura of satisfaction from the unique educational experience. I've never forgotten it, nor will I ever. I later reflected that I have Booster, Boosted, and Busted, to thank for yet another life-enriching experience. My brother, who'd once asked, "What are you gonna do with that dog?" The pertinent question in retrospect should have been, "What's that dog gonna do with *you*?'

When I was finally instructed to remove my blindfold, I instantly looked across the table to gauge Rocky and Isaac's reactions. Their facial expressions were as one, expressing an undeniable "wow." We learned a life lesson in an hour's time ... an invaluable "insight", even if just a glimpse, into the challenges faced by the blind. Simply eating a meal was a task to be reckoned with. I suddenly remembered my friend Ed Eames who had trouble hailing a taxi in New York City simply because he used a guide dog to *see* his way through the dangerous labyrinth of city streets. My experience at the school that day strengthened my resolve to further help the disabled employ canines to enhance their lives.

The next morning, Rocky and Isaac joined me, along with Boosted and Busted, for breakfast in the hotel restaurant. We discussed the previous day's visit to the school, and I looked forward to my lecture later that day. While I was a bit nervous, public speaking became easier over the years as I always found acceptance and never suffered rejection. Whether in a country whose citizens were a different color, spoke a different language, or had a different form of government. I'd always derived strength from Booster and his progeny, Boosted and Busted. We decided to take a long walk together that morning to stretch our legs and those of our canine compadres. We walked down the streets of Mexico City admiring the culture. It felt warm and friendly—an ambiance all its own. I felt safer there than I did walking in many cities back home in the US. Interestingly, the Mexicans didn't seem afraid of the two big dogs. I reflected on how I always saw a wide spectrum of dogs being walked on Sundays on the nearby main thoroughfare.

Before long, it was time to head out. We hailed a taxi, and the dogs were not an issue. I always made sure to say "gracias por ayudar" (thanks for helping) to the taxi drivers and often explained that I help train "los perros de asistencia para las personas discapacitadas." (I train dog service dogs to help the disabled.) Enriqueta met us at the venue's front door, and we walked in together and took our seats. We watched demonstrations and listened to insightful lectures. Before long, it was my turn to present, and I walked up on stage, accompanied by Isaac, who did a great job translating. I was totally in sync with the audience and felt totally comfortable. I was where I was meant to be.

When I finished my PowerPoint presentation, I brought Boosted onto the stage. He performed flawlessly, just as Booster did over the previous years, just like Busted had recently. It's so rewarding to see the hard work that goes into training a dog to perform service dog skills exhibited flawlessly time and time again.

When the conference came to a close, I was given a certificate of appreciation. For me, it was more than a certificate. It was an affirmation of years of study in conjunction with my Booster instilled cultural assimilation. I was accepted and appreciated, and it resonated deep within me. I was then introduced to a reporter that wanted to do a story. We went outside, talked, and I further demonstrated service dog tasks like opening a car door to bring a bottle of water or a medical kit. A nice gentleman saw me demonstrating Boosted and Busted and offered his car for the demonstration. I befriended him and invited him to join us at a large dinner I sponsored the following night. The reporter's sidekick took pictures all the while.

Within days, the large newspaper story appeared for all to read. It was also on the internet. I oozed with pride and was grateful that the newspaper covered the story. I was even prouder of Boosted and Busted, who again earned their wings. I remembered Stephen Huneck's dog art with Labradors posed as winged angels.

The next day, we strolled through the streets of Mexico City, befriending all kinds of people espousing the common denominator of friendship and love. Boosted and Busted attracted people from all walks of life who longed to greet them. It was reassuring to see humanity exhibit such an uncanny amount of love.

I concluded my visit the following night by sponsoring a formal dinner for all those who had helped me join in the struggle for assistance dog recognition and rights in Mexico. It was a wonderful dinner, and excitement filled the air. My Mexican friends came from all walks of life, from college professors to business executives, to journalists to dog lovers. One man's daughter accompanied him, and later attended BUCS. How cool is that?

Though the Mexican SAR dog team member assured me that nothing would happen in Mexico, I knew in my heart that it was going to happen. I had witnessed so much love, devotion, and dedication among Mexican citizens. The associations for the blind had been fighting for access for years. I was proud to have been supportive of their efforts.

One morning, while perusing my emails, I read the following:

> *Hello, a very good news! today the new Law of Rights of the Usuaries of Guide Dogs and Service Animals was approved. It will be just the beginning of a hard struggle. Bonita and you contributed with your participation to make visible the problems that people with disabilities have when trying to access their services to which we are all entitled. I send you the video of this historical fact.*

MY BOOSTER!

April 12, 2018

A day full of emotions, I thank the deputies of the LXIII legislature for their trust in unanimously passing the Law of the Rights of the Users of Guide Dogs and Service Animals. # EstamosContigo (We are with you)

They successfully passed a guide dog public access law in 2016 for Mexico City. That was about the time I first visited and promoted service dog advocacy. In 2018 the access law was amended to include service dogs. Regardless, I hoped that my advocacy had helped in some way. Even more exciting was a proposal in 2019 for a guide dog and service dog access law for the entire Mexican Republic. The bill was under review in the Senate in 2020. Damn It, there was H_2O in my eyes yet again!

Suffice to say I had more faith in the Mexican citizens than the SAR dog team member. Unfortunately, things never progressed further in Mexico. I was upset over the SAR dog team member's attitude upon his return to his beautiful country. He decided he didn't want to train service dogs and had asked how much I would pay him to do it. Truthfully, I should have expected that, given his mindset. I blamed myself, as usual. I also got no *push* from my friends south of the border. The SAR dog director seemed reluctant to take the bull(dog) by the horns and make things happen. I'll never know whether he was too busy or just reluctant to undertake another dog training venture.

Shortly thereafter, my health went downhill suddenly, and COVID-19 reared its ugly head. My world, and the world itself, was suddenly transformed. I couldn't travel, and public access was no longer an option. The quality of my life and the lives of others worldwide was abysmal. People adopted shelter dogs like never before. Humans needed the solace provided by the unique canine–human bond. Millions of people died due to the pandemic, and many families were comforted by their adoring pets. I have little doubt that many humans experienced canine companionship for the first time and would hold it in high esteem for the remainder of their lives, never again ignorant as to its value in society. It's like virginity; once lost, it never returns.

Though I couldn't travel, I was interviewed by a journalist associated with *Perros*, a Mexican dog fancier's magazine. The story appeared in the magazine months later. I was astounded at the content found within the magazine, from medical issues like lipoma tumors, to reproduction, to assistance dogs. The stories were extremely well written and comprehensive. I'd provided photos and spoke about myriad topics. The author miraculously synthesized the material I'd provided.

Months later, I was asked to do a video interview for a presentation to be placed on a video monitor in a museum in Mexico City. The interviewer posed wonderful questions based upon information I'd previously provided. I responded to myriad questions and hoped it was enlightening and canine-positive. Due to COVID-19, the interview was posted on Facebook instead of a video monitor in the museum. Whereas I'd once worried about my health, grateful to be alive, I watched the video embarrassed by the bags under my eyes. Such is life! All my answers were in the canine–human context. They may appear to be obvious to many, but they are not. This bodes especially true in foreign countries whose citizens may have never thought about entering public buildings with a dog . . . unless maybe an amphitheater with fighting dogs?

CHAPTER 20
THE LOVE RETURNED

After a couple of devastating years, my health improved, and COVID-19 became less problematic. I missed traveling and was ecstatic when I received an invitation to lecture at an assistance dog conference in Guadalajara, Mexico in December 2022. Dogs don't give up on the humans they love, and I don't either! My Booster taught me what love IS, to respect it, and to share it as often as possible. *He* certainly did! Those same qualities were manifested in his clones, Boosted and Busted; they were deeply ingrained. I was confident they would demonstrate their abilities as always, untarnished by the passage of time.

I, on the other hand, was a little older and a tad feebler. So, I asked my neighbor, my dear friend Ilene, to go with me and help out. She graciously accepted my invitation and, in turn, invited her friend Becky to join us. As a pack of five, we flew into Guadalajara. My Mexican friend Isaac joined us, and we grew into a pack of six. We toured the terrain and took the canine kids with us wherever we went. It was joyous. On the day of the conference, I gave my heart, soul, and PowerPoint presentation. There were tears on the faces in the audience when I concluded sharing. It was an absolute affirmation of my life's journey in the accompaniment of canine spirituality that had spawned the emotional reaction. It reassured me that I could successfully use words to convey unfathomable emotion emanating from deep within my psyche.

During a lunch break, two sweet ladies approached me and explained that they worked for Sistema Nacional para el Desarrollo Integral de la Familia (SNDIF), often simply referred to as DIF. It's a government agency that promotes the social welfare of Mexican families. They were from a small town named Tepic. They asked if I would be willing to attend their disability lecture two weeks in the future. Of course, I said yes, and plans were made. I was so grateful to be healthy enough to continue helping others.

We flew home a couple of days later, filled with fond memories. It was a learning curve for Ilene and Becky, who had never before left the country. Isaac had made sure the ladies were comfortable and accompanied them wherever they went, translating as need be. The pack members also learned skills regarding traveling with canine family members, from proper airplane etiquette to public access. Once home, I had about ten days before I was due to participate in the next conference.

Before flying to the conference in Tepic, Busted was urinating a lot because he was on a strong antibiotic due to an infected paw. I necessarily elected to take Boosted to join me at the conference. The United Airlines flight to Mexico City was uneventful, but trepidation arose when United once again put me on an Aeromar Airlines flight from Mexico City to Tepic. It was the only option. I would have to go to the Aeromar ticket counter two hours in advance because I was flying with a service dog. Had Aeromar indeed learned the lesson not to deny boarding to a service dog? I didn't have the supportive US law to fall back on in Mexico.

I spent the night in Mexico City and arrived at the counter at 4 a.m., ready to do battle. Fortunately, there was a gentleman there who knew about service dogs. It took a while, but the airline issued the ticket while Boosted chilled out in front of the counter for all to see. Boosted and I owed gratitude to Savior, who blazed the path years before!

MY BOOSTER!

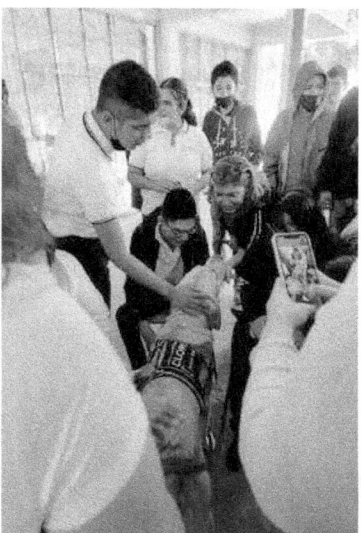

When I arrived at the airport in Tepic, I was met by the DIF ladies who'd originally invited me. We were all smiles. They took me to my Airbnb. The host's wife greeted me at the door of the unit and told me that her daughter was ***coincidentally*** in veterinary school. It was an exceedingly warm, emotional exchange. Shortly thereafter, the ladies whisked me off to a school for disabled children. The school was quite impressive, and the staff obviously enjoyed their vocation. My heart exploded, and my soul expanded.

Boosted performed like the magician he was. At the conclusion of the visit, I spontaneously pointed my finger at Boosted and uttered, "Bang!" I was shocked by his proficiency. He rolled over immediately and remained in the position until I said, "OK, all better." My tears that day were dual in nature. I was happy that the children were happy, and I was happy Boosted was happy demonstrating his canine abilities. I was simultaneously sad, because I was thinking about Booster the entire time, every passing second, minute, and hour. I remembered how my Booster had done the same trick for disabled Mexican children years before.

Later that day, we conducted two radio interviews. One host was a man, the other a lady. They both became emotional, their eyes shiny and moist as I shared my life's journey, made possible due to unconditional canine love. The following day, the mayor of Tepic was having a small press conference dedicating a road re-paving project. The DIF employees took Boosted and me to the press conference in hopes of meeting the first female mayor ever elected in that state. She greeted us enthusiastically; turns out she had five dogs.

The next day, the mayor held a large indoor press conference. She invited me, in advance, to speak to the locals as members of the press listened attentively. I'd asked the DIF employees to take me to a flower shop earlier in the day. I bought a wicker basket of flowers and put a small dog statue in it. At the press conference, I put the basket of flowers in the corner of the stage, behind the curtain.

As the news cameras rolled, I explained that "A person who loves animals has a big heart, is trustworthy, and likely helps others." I've learned that you've elected the first lady mayor in your State. I also learned that she has five dogs! You've likely elected the finest, most empathetic mayor in the city's history ... and I wasn't paid a peso to say that!"

As usual, I injected humor as a defense mechanism as I was bit nervous. I then had Boosted pick up the basket of flowers, walk across the stage, and hand it to the mayor. (You can view it on my author's webpage). After the conference, we returned to the DIF building where Boosted and I were interviewed by a reporter and film crew sent out by the largest television station in that state.

It aired a few days later. The film crew and editor did an amazing job. The interview lasted for over four minutes on the nightly news cast. People who saw it called the station and asked them to replay it on the following night's broadcast. They indeed aired the story the following evening. It

MY BOOSTER!

was explained to me that the station rarely reruns a news story as it's very expensive to do so. I was so proud of Boosted and my entire canine connection.

Later in the day, I took two of the employees to lunch. I explained I wanted to go to an upscale restaurant. The more upscale a restaurant is, the more likely there will be an access issue when entering with an assistance dog. I wanted the employees who work with the disabled to witness first hand what would happen. Sure enough, when we went to enter the restaurant, I wasn't permitted inside because *mascotas* (pets) weren't allowed. I looked at the manager, agreed, and stated matter-of-factly, "Good, because this isn't a pet. It's a service dog." I then marched in and took a seat at a table in the center of the restaurant. It happened so quickly that the staff didn't know how to handle the situation. It was conquered territory; the battle was over before it began!

After we finished eating, I summoned the chef to our table. I explained we enjoyed the meal very much and thanked him for sharing his talents with us. I also explained to the manager overseeing the discourse that the young man who set the dinnerware on the table had grabbed the

end of each fork with his thumb and forefinger . . . the end with the tines . . . that goes into your mouth. I stood, scratched my butt, then said, "Dog hair is a lot cleaner than the hand that wipes the butt and grabs the fork!" Before we left, the manager explained that they'd never had an assistance dog or guide dog in the restaurant. It was cordial, and he and the DIF employees received an education that day.

The following day, we went to a television studio and joined a talk show in progress. The host posed questions, and I did my best to answer. I shared how emotional I felt visiting the children that DIF helps. At one point, I broke down in tears as I explained how canines can help children who have suffered from abuse; abused children will sometimes talk to an animal but not a human. After all, it was a human that had hurt them. My *booster pump* of emotion was in high gear!

I'd gone to Tepic to lecture about disabilities, my forte being assistance dogs. I was to have been one of the two presenters; however, the other person canceled. The State President of DIF introduced me and Boosted. The conference was held in a Romanlike museum building with a huge, two-story amphitheater, which was packed, above and below. Though a bit overwhelmed, I delivered my presentation that'd been completely reworked by my DIF hosts. It boasted swirls, GIFs, caricatures, photos, etc. When Boosted and I finished, we experienced an earthquake. The entire audience stood and blessed us with a standing ovation.

Once again, emotional floodgates opened, *lagrimas* (tears) of appreciation were ever-present. Just as suddenly, a long line formed. People shyly asked if they could take a picture of me and Boosted. My Airbnb host and her veterinary student daughter popped up out of nowhere and gave me a big hug. They'd arranged their schedules so they could attend the conference. I just knew my Booster was looking down from heaven above, saying, "See, I told you humans aren't all bad!"

That night, I was determined to celebrate and thank the DIF employees for their excellent work. I invited a half a dozen dedicated employees out to eat dinner at a nice seafood restaurant. As an ensemble, we approached the restaurant's open double-door entrance. There was a bright yellow chain across the entranceway to ensure that diners waited to be seated. As if on cue, the manager flatly stated, "No dogs, sir!" My service dog explanation fell on DIF and deaf ears. I turned to my DIF guests and told them to go on in and enjoy

their meal. I then sat on the dirty sidewalk, dressed to the nines, and told the restaurant manager to please bring my sushi to me where I was seated. "If this is where you serve the blind or disabled, then so be it!" Within a few minutes, I was beckoned inside and Boosted and I joined my guests at the table.

The next afternoon, the DIF ladies took me to the hop-on/hop-off city tour bus. Boosted and I found it to be fun and very relaxing. On the last day, one of the DIF employees and her husband insisted on taking me to the beach about 35 miles away. It was a beautiful day, and we all got to relax.

As though that wasn't special enough, I got a call from my Airbnb host the following night. She said that she and her daughter had a gift they'd like to give to me in the morning. I explained my taxi was leaving promptly at 6 a.m., so I wasn't sure it was possible. She said she'd be there before I left. Sure enough, the following morning at 5:45 a.m., there was a knock at the door. They greeted me with "good morning." The daughter took my hand and gingerly raised it. She then attached a beautiful bracelet to my wrist. OMG it was a beautiful shade of dark blue with BOOSTER written in bright yellow.

Once again, my emotions overcame any sense of normality I might have had at the time. "We had this bracelet made for you. The glass beads were sewn together by the native Mexican peoples," she explained. I had needlepointed once in my life, so I had an idea of the talent required to make such a bracelet. Each bead had to line up, just like the loving Mexican people who'd honored me by requesting to take pictures the day before. I had a LOT to think about once I got home.

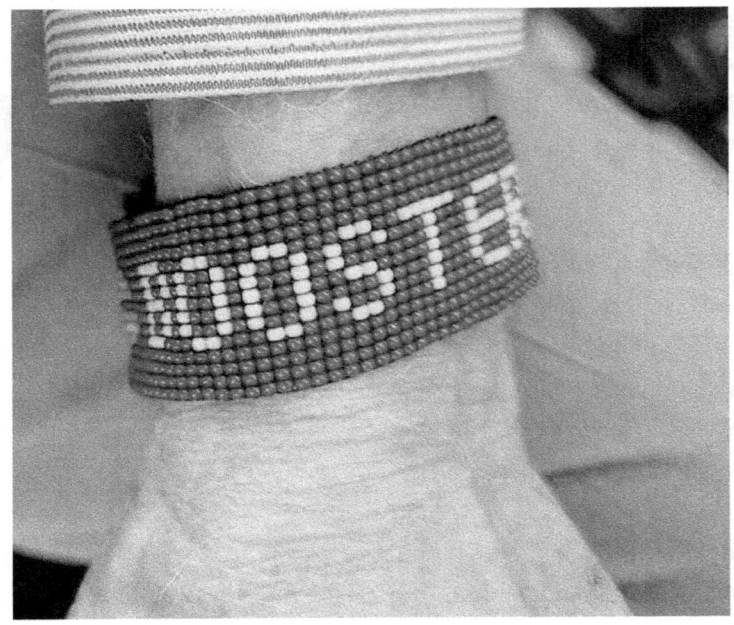

CONCLUSION

"What are you going to do with that dog? You know you can't take care of a dog," my brother extolled over a decade ago. Truth be known, that dog took care of *me!* He was indeed the greatest teacher I've ever known (sorry, Bonnie . . . but I know you'd approve). My Booster gave me my life back, the one I almost squandered. He reached into a soul I didn't know I had and motivated me to return to university in my latter years and earn my master's degree in Canine Life Sciences, with an emphasis on service dog education, at the miraculous, one-of-a-kind BUCS. That truly unique education propelled my life forward at such a pace as to have made up for all the living I'd missed out on. With my Booster by my side, I learned what genuine love truly is. I grew to love people, not resent them.

When Warren Buffet gave a lecture at the University of Florida's School of Business, he spoke about living a happy life and stated,

> *The way to do it is to play out the game and do something you enjoy all your life. Be associated with people you like. I only work with people I like. If I could make $100 million with a guy who causes my stomach to churn, I'd say no. Your overall happiness in life really comes down to four simple words . . . do what you love.*[6]

This truly resonates deeply within my psyche. I spent over two decades of my existence doing what I was programmed to do: rescue the wounded bird. Only later, in the sere and yellow leaf of life, did I discover that to which Buffet alluded. I surrounded myself with dogs and canine-loving people I like. I invested in myself by getting an education at BUCS so I

---

[6] Warren Buffett, "Warren Buffett Says Your Overall Happiness in Life Really Comes Down to 4 Simple Words," *Inc.* (Sept 16, 2022). https://www.inc.com/ marcel-schwantes/warren-buffett-says-your-overall-happiness-in-life-really-comesdown-to-4-simple-words.html

could do what I love. As the interest rate went up, so did my well-being. The more I invested, the more ROI I received . . . canine ROI.

CUBAN MISSILE CRISIS: The atomic bomb exploded in the US Cubans are comforted by their dogs. They have moments to live before retaliation. Learn about the Fat Man and Little Boy from a Manhattan Project who visited Hiroshima and Nagasaki. (left)

CAMBODIA: Famous European comic book character Tin Tin visited Cambodia with his dog and stepped on a land mine left behind from war. His dog teaches us that humans can't go on picnics with their dogs without fear of stepping on leftover ordnance. (right)

I traveled the world, often with Booster by my side, and shared the love. Whether my fellow humans were Black, white, yellow, gay, straight, male, female, communist, capitalist, Christian, or Muslim, I found universal acceptance worldwide, emulating my Booster. With few exceptions, he embraced all who met him. I followed his teachings and learned to trust and love unconditionally. My life changed direction as a direct result of miraculous canine intervention. What had once been a dead-end street became a superhighway of enriched enlightenment. My life became the Eighth Wonder of the World as I began to travel the world with Booster by my side. The three-story log home I'd built in Pyatt, Arkansas, on 120 acres near Branson, Missouri, became the Canine Retreat. I adorned the walls with canine art collected from around the world: Cuba, Nepal, Thailand, Colombia, Argentina, Vietnam, the Bahamas, and various other countries. Carved Labradors sit on the stairs as newel posts. The tops of the log furniture feature carved dog heads, and the upholstery features a collage of Labradors. Every floor has automatic water bowls for thirsty canine guests.

I decided to share the unique home with other dog lovers, so I listed it on Airbnb and VRBO. It was a tribute to Booster; it wasn't about the money. The result was a cascade of canine-loving families vying to rent it. All the reviews mentioned how their dogs loved the property. The Canine Retreat offers dogs an opportunity to invite their humans to hike the trails, swim the creeks, and watch the ever-present deer. For dogs, the Rainbow Bridge begins at the Canine Retreat in Arkansas and ends at Dog Mountain in Vermont. I connected with new canine and human souls espousing a kindred spirit. It was an uncanny affirmation of years of learning predicated upon my Booster and BUCS education.

To my chagrin, I rue the fact that I bestowed my trust in some who were undeserving. There's a saying: "Better to have loved and lost than to never have loved at all." In my case, it's "Better to have trusted and gotten screwed than to never have trusted at all." I was truly disappointed by the actions of some of the humans I'd trusted. The Cuban man I sponsored and spent my savings on simply used me to get into the United States. The SAR dog team member took the expensive education and stipend, returned home to Mexico, and never looked back. Both individuals let not only me down but also their fellow countrymen.

I often reflected on the fact that they both said nothing happens quickly in their respective countries. They were both wrong, victims of their negativity. Perhaps such conviction was a precursor to their failure to live up to their potential. I postulate they are only human and haven't ascended to canine status, espousing overwhelming positivity, an uncompromised thirst for learning, and unconditional love. Perhaps they, too, needed a *booster* in their lives.

My Booster cheated death on myriad occasions. I think both he and his Higher Power knew he had a destiny to fulfill. Though he passed away, he remains very much a part of me. I have his progeny, my Boosted and my Busted, to continue in his paw prints. I don't know if there was ever a more symbiotic relationship between a canine and his human. With that thought in mind, I share one last story.

In January 2020, I went to visit friends Booster had introduced me to in Thailand. I was there for about a month and got rather ill. I was going to go to a Bangkok hospital but decided to stick it out and return home ASAP. Upon returning home, I self-isolated to make sure I hadn't brought the coronavirus (covid) home with me. After enduring excruciating pain, I went to the hospital in my hometown of Gulfport, Mississippi. I had *E. coli* bacteria in my system (food poisoning), giardia (waterborne illness), and some form of a Mexican virus. I remained in the hospital for a week, receiving bags of high-powered antibiotics.

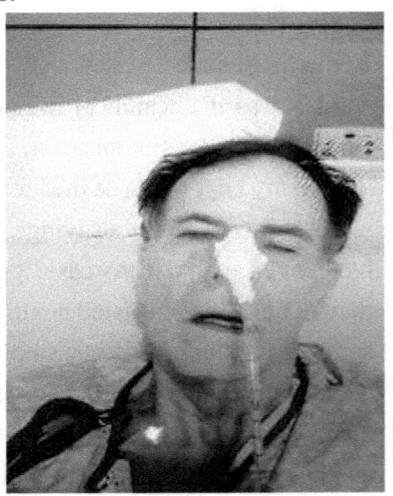

Before releasing me, the doctors ran upper and lower GI series tests on me and determined that I had several tumors in my body, including a 5-cm tumor partially obstructing my colon. The presumption was that I had colon and stomach cancer. It took five days to get the pathology report.

Turns out I had non-Hodgkin's lymphoma. I was within 48 hours of death. I was whisked onto a table and given a lumbar puncture, whereby chemo was injected into my spinal column in case the cancerous cells had penetrated the brain barrier. It was a preemptive move made by my brilliant oncologist, Dr. Tuli. A sample of my cerebral spinal fluid was taken.

MY BOOSTER!

Pathology revealed that the cancer cells had indeed invaded my brain. A few days later, a brain surgeon drilled a hole into my skull, pushed a tube through my brain, and implanted a port into my skull. Shortly thereafter, I was given five bags of chemo a day, five days a week, every other week for six weeks through a port implanted in my chest. I received two chemo shots a week into my head every week for three months, and once a month for three months thereafter. I was told there was a 75% chance that I might succumb to sepsis the first week when the chemo shrank the tumor in my stomach/intestines. If I survived the first week, the odds were 25% that it would happen the second week. I had a camera pushed down my nose into my heart, looking for tumors. My chest port got infected. The saga wore on.

My cancer was attributed to a herbicide used on my property. Its sale is prohibited in many countries around the world. I sent a letter to every US Congressperson and Senator detailing my plight. I felt it was incumbent upon on me to try to do something to keep others from being subjected to … a likely carcinogen sold for the sake of profit at human expense. I think I got one or two responses. When I thought about giving up, I instantly thought about Booster. He never gave up! He fought each and every time when confronted by near death experiences. I reconciled myself to the idea that "What's good for the Booster is good for the Davis!" I resolutely determined I'd fight for my life and told my oncologist, Dr. Tuli, that I wanted to live long enough to finish writing my book. She obviously managed to pull me from the abyss, but I likewise give credit to my Booster and My Higher Power.

Booster gave me the strength to elect to go through the rigors of extensive chemotherapy and have a hole drilled into my skull to implant a chemo port. He'd had no choice when I put him through the same treatment regimen. If I'd elected not to undergo treatment, I would have been an absolute hypocrite. In other words, he saved my life a second time. How can I not cry as I write these words?

My lifelong friend Robert Bodenheimer supported me in my darkest hours. He insisted on driving a great distance to take me to undergo the brain surgery for the port implantation. He subsequently interviewed the surgeon afterwards and reassured me all went well, then he looked into my eyes and said, "Dave, I *L* . . . *O* . . . *V* . . . *E* you!" Tears cascaded down our cheeks, a testimony to the purest love that ever existed. He was in perfect health when my life balanced precariously on the precipice. He and his son often visited me when I was undergoing treatment. A year later, my friend, my rock, was diagnosed with a brain tumor. Though I encouraged him to undergo treatment, he elected not to do so. He died, along with a piece of me, months later. I might also have elected to give up, had it not been for MY BOOSTER.

About the time I completed treatment, Booster's girlfriend Puffy passed away. I felt such pain and remorse. I was bombarded by a plethora of emotions. After considerable soul-searching, I decided to clone her. The company who'd shipped my Booster's cells to Korea for cloning, was now cloning dogs in the US. I rode an emotional roller coaster. Would I live to support the pup I decided to bring into the world? Was adding a sixth dog to my canine clan rational? I could hear my Booster barking, "Just go for it . . . trust me!"

When Puffy was cloned, two puppies were born. They had a significant overbite which made sucking milk from the surrogate's teat difficult, if not impossible. One passed away as a result, yet one survived. The company graciously offered to re-clone Puffy. I asked if I could have the defective puppy and the company graciously said "sure." The cloning was done for a second time, and as sometimes happens, the surrogate didn't get pregnant. The company agreed to try again, and one puppy was born with the same overbite issue. It didn't survive. At that point we mutually agreed to call it quits and not fight what seemed to be a dominant, defective gene. I was glad I'd asked to keep the one defective puppy. The benevolent company arranged to have oral corrective surgery done on the puppy, and subsequently delivered it to the Canine Retreat in Pyatt.

Once again, I used humor to navigate life's emotional minefields. Months later, I sent Dr. Tuli a card explaining, "You gave me my life back; it began anew as a result of your intervention." She knew about my history with Booster. I further explained, "Booster had a girlfriend named Puffy who recently passed away. Her life also began anew, as I had her cloned. She was so loving, caring, smart, and special ... just like YOU Dr. Tuli ... so, I named her in your honor ... Puffers Tuli Hawn! The only thing is, she's a real bitch, and that's where the similarity ends!" I would have loved to have seen the expression on her face as she read it, but alas!

MY BOOSTER!

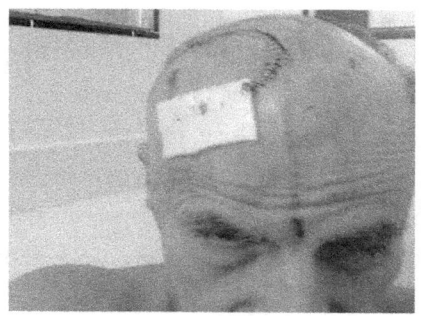

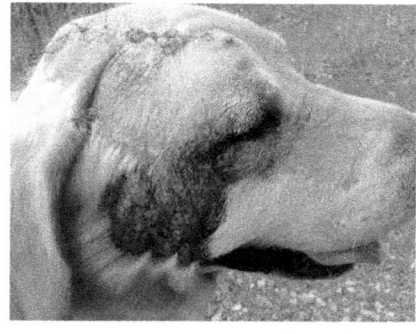

I had a wonderful rapport with all my doctors and staff. Many were from countries I'd visited, often with Booster in tow. That international comradery was a direct result of Booster's presence/presents in my life. It helped me survive when my survivability was questioned. Due to all my doctors at the little hospital in my hometown of Gulfport, Mississippi, I was able to finish my book and my life went forward with canine enrichment.

My relationship with Booster was a symbiotic relationship of uncanny proportions. We both had cancerous tumors, lost our hair, had holes cut in our skulls, and overcame seemingly insurmountable odds! They say a picture is worth a thousand words, but I will let you, the reader, decide for yourself. To this day, it's hard to fathom the enormity of the life-changing events that transpired in my life as the result of the powerful canine–human bond. There can be no doubt the profundity of events that have given meaning to my life were a capitulation of human frailty in favor of ubiquitous, unconditional canine love and unparalleled devotion.

I experience utmost remorse reflecting that I spent decades of my life in a cesspool of perceived purpose and love. The former, ill-conceived enmeshment of lives was supplanted by an all-encompassing life transformation brought about by my Booster. There's little room for doubt that he was the result of divine intervention, though I am not that devout. It's quite simple; there is no other explanation. Booster taught me that there's no such thing as **coincidence**. In my life's courtroom, it was obvious, based on an overwhelming preponderance of the evidence.

In retrospect, I'd once resented that I was cheated out of what life was meant to be. My self-imposed codependence almost cost me my worthless life. I'd watched television sitcoms and listened to songs extolling idyllic lives. That isn't reality. Every human on the planet faces adversity or strife, some more than others. I learned to live life on life's terms quite late in life. I learned to love Booster as he managed to learn to love me . . . unconditionally. I'm still not sure I was worthy of such love. I hereby make a new promise to my beloved Booster to strive to achieve self-acceptance, to continue to learn how to do so, and to help others achieve what my Booster helped me to achieve: independence granted through spiritually delivered canine assistance in the form of a service dog/assistance dog.

In closing, I ask you to pat your dog on the head, look into his eyes, and tell him you love him. Then give him an extended, all-encompassing hug. You will likely hear the melodic, simultaneous beating of his heart and tail, followed by a wet kiss on the face. Such is the pure expression of love beyond reproach.

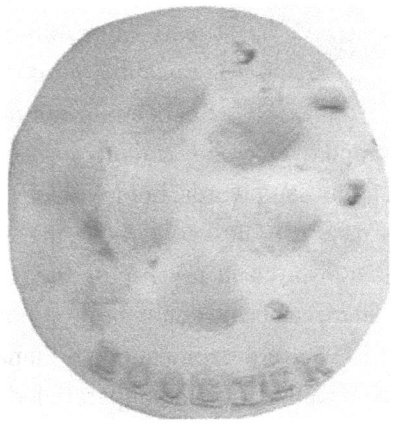

MY BOOSTER DIVINELY LEFT HIS INDELIBLE PAWPRINT ON THE WORLD

AFTERWORD

My Booster is the culmination of ten years of writing that often took place in an airplane at 30,000 feet, traveling the world with my best friend Booster in a supportive role, with his head resting on my feet. My burning desire to fulfill my promise, to share him with the world, motivated me to call myriad newspapers and television stations to immortalize his canine accomplishments. That promise resulted in an unintended internet presence that proved useful when I eventually decided to write his book. Another **coincidence?**

I reached out to the well-established self-publishing firm FriesenPress to help bring my promise to my beloved Booster to fruition. I presented my manuscript for review and wasn't prepared for what came next . . . tears and **coincidence** in the form of a response:

> *I'm going to start by saying that I'm a dog lover, a firm believer of the value service dogs provide, and mom to an autistic son (now 16) who has his second service dog now. I am incredibly thankful for all of the work that you and Booster, along with many others, have done to open doors (quite literally) to provide access for these integral companions in (dis)abled people's lives. I honestly don't know where my family would be today if it weren't for our service dogs, so being able to read your story and have the opportunity to assist with seeing it through to publication is a tremendous honor!*

Though I had once given up on myself, My Higher Power never did, never has. My Booster taught me what spirituality is, how to recognize it, and how to incorporate it into my life. I share with you this affirmation of My Higher Power's devotion to better my life in conjunction with my Booster's proffered teachings. I resolutely state once again, there is no such thing as **coincidence!**

My beloved clone Puffers just presented me with further proof that there's no such thing as **coincidence**. She's so loving yet rejects Boosted and Busted' amorous advances. I had her artificially inseminated with all that Busted *seemened* to offer. (For the record, I still infuse humor into my dialogue, but no longer cuss.) It was a clone-to-clone breeding. She was later x-rayed, and it was determined she likely had 7 puppies that were due on September 12th. She went into labor the night before and delivered 6 beautiful puppies. The clone-to-clone pups were born on 9/11 just like Boosted and Busted. Yep, another 9/11 event in my life! *How in the heck is that even possible,* I asked myself

Miraculously, the following day I went to clean the whelping box and counted 7 puppies! I thought I was dreaming! I looked at the photos I'd taken the day before and indeed there'd been only 6 puppies. It was as though My Higher Power reached out and said, "The pups were due on 9/12 but I moved the delivery up to 9/11 as I knew it was another 9/11 event in your life. However, I arranged for one to be born on 9/12 just to remind you of what should have been if not for divine intervention!" **Coincidence?**

There were two male puppies. One was white, and the other dark yellow just like my Booster. He will be my successor service dog. I got *Busted* in Korea, and it took 8 years, but I finally made *Bail*. My new puppy's name is Bail! The lawyer who got a large, white, male puppy years before, when his children were grieving, stayed in touch throughout the years and kept asking me if I had any puppies. He was elated when he heard about the white puppy and later received the puppy with open arms and open heart! Talk about a custom order delivered from heaven above! **Coincidence?**

I strived to find special homes for the other 5 very special puppies. I absolutely found the best of homes, but perhaps you might judge for yourself? One day, parents brought their 3 children to see the pups. The children loved the puppies but maybe a bit too much? Dad wanted the runt, yet some of the children wanted a different pup. Mom suggested taking 2, yet dad was hesitant. I agreed to hold onto the pups until they arrived at a decision. A couple of days later, the father called and informed me that

MY BOOSTER!

they wanted both pups. They came to pick them up after the Thanksgiving holidays . . . *how appropriate, right?*

I reached for one pup and placed it into the adoring and adorable girl's hands. The children went wild. I then picked up the second pup and the children looked bewildered. Dad then turned to the children and said, "Hey guys, you're getting them both!" Turns out, the parents hadn't told the children, preferring to surprise them! The kids were awash with excitement. I then asked the children, 'So who has the best parents in the world?" In unison they screamed joyfully, "WE DO!" "WE DO!" The following day, a proud grandfather, accompanied by his daughter and grandson, came to look at the puppies. It was a Christmas present in the making! The young boy was shy and a bit reluctant to bond with puppy when they first met. The following morning, I received two beautiful photographs of the boy loving his new puppy, Riley! When asked why the puppy was named Riley, grandpa said, "No idea, grandson came up with it!"

The boy's younger brother is autistic, and they share Riley's unconditional canine love.

Love begets love. My Booster's genetics, as sponsored by my Higher Power, were at it again! No ***coincidence!***

OMHP, Oh My God, oh . . . I resolutely state once again, there's no such thing as ***coincidence!*** There just isn't. My Booster taught me that over and over and over again.

**MY BOOSTER CHANGED THE WORLD
IN A PAWSITIVE WAY.
HIS CLONES, BOOSTED AND BUSTED ARE
DOING THE SAME.**

Be sure to visit Booster's webpage filled with photos and videos evidencing his devotion to bettering the lives of all those he met around the world!

www.boostertheservicedog.com

ABOUT THE AUTHOR

DAvIs HAWN promised Booster he'd share him with the world. In so doing, Davis became an advocate, sharing the enormity of the impact of dogs, in general, and service dogs, in particular, on society. He believes there is substantial future potential for our canine companions to do even more and will tell anyone and everyone that canines' unconditional love can and does change and save lives.

Davis has a master's degree in Canine Life Sciences: Emphasis on Service Dog Education from the acclaimed Bergin University of Canine Studies and trained under the tutelage of Dr. Bonita Bergin, EdD, founder of the service dog concept. He traveled internationally for over a decade, sharing his knowledge, lecturing, doing newspaper stories and television appearances, and occasionally starting "trouble" by standing up for the rights of service dogs and their humans. Together, Davis and Booster helped get disability laws passed around the world. A member of Al-Anon and the International Association of Assistance Dog Partners, Davis lives in Mississippi and Arkansas on rural land with his family of trained Labradors.

www.ingramcontent.com/pod-product-compliance
Lightning Source LLC
Chambersburg PA
CBHW070718160426
43192CB00009B/1237